Galileo's Early Notebooks:
The Physical Questions

Galileo's Early Notebooks: The Physical Questions

A Translation from the Latin, with Historical
and Paleographical Commentary

WILLIAM A. WALLACE

UNIVERSITY OF NOTRE DAME PRESS

NOTRE DAME   LONDON

Library of Congress Cataloging in Publication Data

Galilei, Galileo, 1564-1642.
   Galileo's early notebooks.

   Includes index.
   1. Astronomy--Early works to 1800. I. Wallace,
William A.   II.   Title.
QB41.G164 1977   520   77-89766
ISBN 0-268-00993-8

Manufactured in the United States of America

Preface

Galileo's first major work, the *Sidereus Nuncius*, was published on March 12, 1610, and gained for him almost instant fame. At the time of its writing he was already in his forty-sixth year, an accomplished mathematician and astronomer, who also claimed for himself considerable ability as a philosopher. Most students of Galileo have concentrated on his tumultuous career following the publication of the *Sidereus Nuncius*, and have not delved into the long period of preparation that led to that work. This is readily understandable, for the documents available for study are somewhat enigmatic, and it is no simple matter to extract from them the philosophy that Galileo was taught in his youth, or the way in which he elaborated on this to well beyond middle age.

The present work aims to fill this void by translating the major part of a manuscript, written in Latin in Galileo's hand, now preserved in the National Library of Florence as No. 46 of the Galileo Collection.[1] The composition is essentially a commentary, or better, a questionary, on the natural philosophy of Aristotle, treating special questions raised by the text of the *De caelo et mundo* and the *De generatione et corruptione*, and concluding with some memoranda on motion that were seminal for other early compositions of Galileo known generically as the *De motu antiquiora*.[2] The sources from which Galileo compiled these questions have eluded scholars for a long time, but now, owing to the researches of the translator and others, it is known that almost all the materials contained in

MS Gal. 46 derive from Jesuit professors at the
Collegio Romano. The date of composition of the
manuscript is disputed among scholars: the curator
who first collected and bound the folios identified
them as "the examination of Aristotle's work *De
caelo* made by Galileo around the year 1590,"[3] and
Stillman Drake has also assigned this date to the
concluding folios containing the memoranda on motion.[4] In 1590, of course, Galileo was already
teaching at the University of Pisa, and thus this
dating would make these the notes of a young professor. However, Antonio Favaro, the editor of the
National Edition of Galileo's works, was led by
internal evidence to date their composition in 1584,
while Galileo was yet a student at Pisa, and so
entitled them *Juvenilia* when transcribing and publishing them, for the first time, in the National
Edition.[5] The fact of their being called *Juvenilia,*
or youthful writings, in the National Edition has
induced most writers to accept the earlier dating,
and so to see them as a student composition.

The discovery of the dependence of this manuscript on the Collegio Romano now provides new information for dating its composition, and this generally favors the later date, though the evidence
is by no means conclusive. It is possible, to be
sure, that the various folios making up the present
codex were written at different times, even over
six or more years, and yet the manuscript has a
certain unity and style of composition that argues
for its being written approximately at one period.
The materials on which the manuscript appears to be
based, moreover, can themselves be dated, and it is
this circumstance that requires fuller explanation.

Some ten years ago the translator suspected a
connection between this manuscript and the published writings of two Spanish Jesuits, Franciscus
Toletus and Benedictus Pererius, both professors
at the Collegio Romano.[6] Working independently of
him, in 1969 Adriano Carugo identified works by
both these authors as possible sources of Galileo's
citations of ancient and medieval authors in the
manuscript, and in 1971 Alistair Crombie detected
that two of the questions from the treatise *De caelo* contained therein were based on a textbook by
Christopher Clavius, a third Jesuit also teaching

at the Collegio Romano.[7] In 1972 the translator
made a detailed comparison of MS Gal. 46 with all
of these publications, and found that they could
account for about fifteen percent of the manuscript's
contents. He then investigated *reportationes* of
Pererius's lectures on natural philosophy given at
the Collegio, and found that these contained materials not included in Pererius's book but which nonetheless had found their way into Galileo's manuscript.[8] This led him to search systematically for
reportationes of other lectures given at the Collegio and to check the content of those he could locate
against Galileo's composition. Working in this way
he has succeeded in uncovering possible sources of
another seventy-five percent of the manuscript's
content.[9] Most of this material can be located in
lectures given between 1577 and 1591, although there
are some parallels in *reportationes* dated as early
as 1566 and as late as 1597.

The principal lecturers whose notes he has
studied, together with the dates of their *reportationes*, are the following: Benedictus Pererius,
1565-1566; Hieronymus de Gregoriis, 1567-1568; Antonius Menu, 1577-1579; Paulus Valla, 1588-1589;
Mutius Vitelleschi, 1589-1590; Ludovicus Rugerius,
1590-1591; Robertus Jones, 1592-1593; and Stephanus
del Bufalo, 1596-1597. Details concerning these
sources and their relation to Galileo's composition
are given in the Introduction and at appropriate
places in the Commentary.

Because of the complexity of the dating problem, and in view of the obvious dependence of Galileo's composition on Jesuit sources, either directly or indirectly, the translator has preferred to
give Galileo's text in English translation and then,
in the accompanying commentary, simply to indicate
the likely sources of the various passages from a-
mong those presently available. It is possible,
even likely, that other *reportationes* will be discovered that have closer similarities to Galileo's
text and that will offer other clues for dating his
composition. The translator, however, has used all
available means to locate manuscripts, and feels
that he has now reached the point of diminishing
returns. Further discoveries, in his opinion, will
not alter the general character of the natural phil-

osophy embraced by Galileo, nor its essential dependence on the teaching at the Collegio Romano.

The translation here offered follows Favaro's
transcription of the Latin printed in Vol. 1 of
the National Edition[10]; this has been corrected only in the rare instances of a mis-reading. The
page numbers of Favaro's text are indicated in the
margins. Moreover, when necessary to identify a
word or expression, line numbers have been appended to page numbers after a decimal; thus 55.13
means line 13 of page 55 of the National Edition.
To facilitate reference to specific passages, the
translator has done his own paragraphing and has
inserted paragraph numbers in square brackets into
the text. Again, since MS Gal. 46 contains twenty
five questions, a single capital letter has been
assigned to each question; thus, the combination of
a capital letter and a number, e.g., B3, suffices
to indicate a particular paragraph and so is useful
for cross-reference.

With regard to the title, the translator has
chosen to include MS Gal. 46 under the rubric of
Galileo's Early Notebooks. Galileo himself provides no general title, but his manuscript is clearly on the model of the lecture notes discussed a-
bove. Most of these are proposed as commentaries
on Aristotle, to which are added questions and disputations. Galileo has no commentary and divides
his exposition first into treatises or tractates,
then into disputations or parts, and finally into
questions; in this he is closest to Valla's mode of
division. The earlier sets of Jesuit notes, up to
Menu, summarize Aristotle's text and generally give
a division into tractates and then into chapters,
some of which are equivalent to questions. After
Valla, Vitelleschi divides his work simply into
treatises and then into disputations; and Rugerius,
into disputations, then into tractates, again into
questions, and finally into queries. The diversity
of terminology argues against referring to these as
treatises or disputations, and in favor of designat-
ing them simply as notes, or collectively, as notebooks. The "early" in the title is deliberately
vague, meaning early with respect to Galileo's published works for which he is justly famous.

Preface

The further designation, *The Physical Questions*, has been added to distinguish these from another set of questions contained in MS Gal. 27, known as the logical questions.[11] Recently Adriano Carugo has transcribed this manuscript in its entirety and is readying it for publication. He has generously loaned the translator a copy of his transcription, and the latter, while working on the physical questions, has succeeded in locating sources for the logical questions similar to those described above. This additional material, however, is outside the scope of the present volume; occasional references are made to logical treatises, but this only when they pertain directly to the physical questions.

The commentary accompanying the text is both historical and paleographical, the first in that it identifies the major Renaissance works referenced by Galileo and the sources he likely used in composing the notes, the second in that it points out peculiarities of Galileo's handwriting such as corrections, insertions, and deletions in the manuscript that may provide clues to its manner of composition. The comments are generally brief and limited to points of significance for establishing Galileo's dependence on other authors. If a known author or source is not mentioned, in general this is an indication that he has nothing distinctive to offer on the matter under discussion.

The present work is intended as a first step in making the physical thought of the young Galileo available in English to a wide reading audience. It is expected to be followed by more detailed studies providing parallel texts and other technical aids for tracing the development of scientific thought from the late Middle Ages to the end of the sixteenth century. But until such studies become available, the essential content of Galileo's early natural philosophy is worthy of study in its own right, and it is hoped that this translation and commentary will facilitate such an undertaking.

The translator takes this opportunity to thank Stillman Drake for his continuous support and helpful criticism through many years of work, and also Alistair Crombie and Adriano Carugo for their inval-

Preface

uable cooperation in its early stages, including
the loan of a portion of the manuscript for their
forthcoming book on *Galileo and Mersenne*. He is
indebted to the director and personnel of the Biblioteca Nazionale Centrale in Florence for making
Galileo's manuscripts available to him and for providing microfilms of them that facilitated their
study; also to the many other curators of manuscript
collections mentioned in the Notes who rendered him
similar service. Special acknowledgment is owed to
Nancy McGeehan Spitler for several preparations of
a difficult typescript, and to Jean Dietz Moss for
her careful reading of the final draft of the manuscript. He is also grateful to the National Science
Foundation, whose grants have made possible the extensive research on which the book is based. Finally, it is a pleasure for him to thank Marshall
Clagett and the Institute for Advanced Study,
Princeton, which accorded him membership during
the academic year 1976-1977, thereby providing the
ambience and the stimulus to complete his research
and ready his results for publication.

William A. Wallace

Princeton, N.J.
April 15, 1977

x

Table of Contents

Contents

Contents

Galileo's Early Notebooks:
The Physical Questions

Introduction

The Physical Questions, as noted in the Preface, are Galileo's exposition of various difficulties raised by the texts of Aristotle's *De caelo et mundo* and *De generatione et corruptione*.
This exposition is quite detailed and difficult
for the modern reader to follow, even one well
trained in the natural science of the Schoolmen.
It gives evidence, moreover, of being composed in
somewhat complex dependence on various books and
lecture notes by Jesuit professors at the Collegio
Romano in the decade or so preceding its composition. The purpose of the Introduction is to facilitate comprehension of these questions and the
source materials on which they seem to be based.
To this end it is divided into three parts, the
first a synopsis of contents explaining the structure of the questions and the conclusions to which
they come, the second a description of the source
materials and their authors, and the third an account of the chronology of the various source materials and the bearing these may have on the dating of Galileo's exposition.

SYNOPSIS

Galileo's twenty five questions are summarized in the succeeding paragraphs, which are keyed
by a capital letter to the titles of the questions
as listed in the Table of Contents. A quick reading should suffice to grasp the type of problem
Galileo addresses and the solution he presents;
the reader may then wish to return to them later
as a guide for understanding the translated text.

1

In addition, the summaries should prove useful to
one who wishes to analyze the structure of Galileo's thought, for they include the paragraph numbers (in parentheses) and effectively outline each
question in detail.

Introductory Treatise

    A. This question begins Galileo's introduc-
tory treatise, wherein he sets out the subject matter of Aristotle's *De caelo* and discusses the order and connection of its books. He starts by enu-
merating six opinions (pars. 1-6), then gives four
conclusions (7-11), three of which reject adversary
positions and the fourth (11) states Galileo's own:
the subject matter is the simple body, and this includes both the heavens and the elements in its am-
bit. He then gives an argument to the contrary
and responds (12), raises five more objections (13-
17), and ends by replying to each of these in turn
(18-22).

    B. Three opinions (1-3) preface Galileo's
single conclusion (3): the books of the *De caelo*
come after the *Physics* and make up the second part
of natural philosophy. Two proofs are given in
support of this (4-5), followed by replies to the
arguments in support of the adversary opinions (6-
7). The question concludes by explaining the title
of the books (8) and how this is related to their
subject matter and to that of the *De generatione*
(9), viz: simple bodies include the heavens, treated in the first two books of *De caelo*, and the elements, considered either in themselves, in the last
two books of *De caelo*, or as they are principles
of compounds, in the two books of *De generatione*.

Treatise on the Universe

    C. With this question Galileo starts a new
treatise, that on the universe, made up of four
questions. The opening question considers what
the ancients taught about the universe, enumerat-
ing five opinions (1-5) and adding an objection
with its reply (6). Galileo's evaluation is presented in two conclusions: the first points out
the errors of early philosophers relating to the
universe's material cause (7) and its corruptibility (8), the second rejects Aristotle's thesis
on its eternity (9).

D. Here the doctrinal position concerning the origin of the universe is set out by Galileo in six conclusions, the first five asserting that there must exist a first uncaused cause (1), which is the final and efficient cause of the world (2), which exists by its essence and is infinite in perfection (3), which operates *ad extra* freely (4), and which created the universe in time (5). There follow an objection and its reply (6), and then a final conclusion stating that the universe was created 5748 years ago and accounting for this figure in terms of various Biblical epochs (7).

E. This question differs structurally from the preceding in that it investigates the unity and perfection of the universe by raising six questions and then replying to each, sometimes with multiple conclusions and with objections and their replies. The first query is whether the unity of the universe is demonstrable (1), and to this the reply is that there is only one universe (2), but that its unity is not demonstrable (3); defects are then shown to exist in three purported demonstrations found in Aristotle (4-6). Five additional queries relate to the universe's multiplication and perfection: first, could God make many universes completely the same -- by his ordinary power, no, but by his infinite power, yes (7); second, could God add new species to the universe -- yes, by his infinite power (8); third, could God make the universe more perfect (9) -- accidentally, yes (10), essentially, no (11), with the reply to an objection (12); fourth, is the universe perfect (13) -- including God in it, absolutely so (14), without God, only in a qualified way (15), with objections and replies (16-18); and fifth, is God together with the universe more perfect than by himself alone (19) -- various answers (20), but an affirmative reply seems indicated (21), provided it is for the proper reason (22-23).

F. The last question in this treatise concerns possibility: although the universe *de facto* was created in time, could it have existed from eternity? Four opinions are adduced: the first, that of the nominalists, with proofs and clarifications of difficulties (1-10); the second, that of Durandus and the moderns, with proofs (11-14); the third, that of Philoponus, some scholastics, and the Church Fathers, with proofs and confirma-

tions (15-17); and the fourth, that of St. Thomas,
the *Parisienses*, and Pererius (18). Galileo replies under three conclusions: first, the universe
has not existed from eternity, with supporting arguments (19-22); second, on God's part the universe
could have existed from eternity, with proof (23);
third, on the part of creatures, corruptible or incorruptible, it could not have, with proof and
confirmations (24-27).

Treatise on the Heavens

        G. This question begins another treatise,
that on the heavens, which is made up of six questions in all and is the lengthiest in the entire
manuscript. The first inquiry is whether there is
only one heaven, and the reply lists five opinions:
first, yes, only one (1); second, eight as a minimum (2-3); third, adding a ninth (4); fourth, adding a tenth (5-7); and fifth, adding beyond the
ten movable heavens an eleventh immovable one (8-
10). Galileo's single conclusion adopts the fifth
opinion (11) and gives proofs in its support (12-
20). He then adds three notations or clarifications (21-23), answers three somewhat technical
queries (24-32), and replies to arguments endors-
ing the first and second opinions (33-34).

        H. Having established the number of heavenly
orbs, Galileo turns in this question to the order
among them. The first opinion he lists is that of
Aristarchus and Copernicus, locating the sun in
the middle of the universe (1). This opinion he
rejects (2) and gives five arguments against it
(3-13), the last being most detailed and drawn
from the *Sphaera* of Sacrobosco (9-13). The second position is that proposed by the Egyptians,
and this too is rejected (14). The rest of the
question explains the order assigned by Ptolemaic
astronomers (15) and various proofs that can be
adduced to establish it (16-21). As an elabora-
tion on this Galileo gives four more proofs showing that the sun is located in the middle of the
planets (22-29), and concludes by raising two objections against this ordering and showing how
they can be answered (30-32).

        I. The next question investigates whether the
heavens are one of the simple bodies or composed
of them -- taking simple in the sense of elemental.

Galileo prefaces his exposition by three arguments
in support of an affirmative reply (1-6), and then
lists two opinions: first, that the heavens do not
differ in nature from the elements, the position
of philosophers before Aristotle (7-10); and second, that they do so differ, which he identifies
as Aristotle's teaching (11). Galileo's own conclusions are two: the heavens are a simple body
different from the elements, with six proofs and
one observation (12-18); and they are not composed
of the elements, with proof (19). A goodly number
of arguments are raised against the second conclusion, and these are all refuted (20-34). The final section is devoted to an extensive refutation
of the three arguments proposed at the outset (35-
47).

    J. This question addresses the corruptibility
of the universe and begins with two opinions, the
first taking the affirmative position (1) with
proofs and confirmations (2-7), the second the
negative (8) with arguments showing that this is
Aristotle's position (9-11). Then a distinction
is noted relating to God's natural and absolute
power (12), and in its light two conclusions are
presented: first, in a natural sense the heavens
are probably corruptible by the proper active power, with proofs (13-14) and objections and replies
(15-17); second, more probably they are incorruptible by nature (18), with various arguments and
corollaries (19-30). The concluding paragraphs
are devoted to a refutation of arguments in support of the first opinion (31-36).

    K. Having already shown that the heavens are
not composed of the elements (I), Galileo turns in
this question to the possibility of their being
composed of matter and form, and this becomes the
longest and most complex question in the entire
treatise. Its overall breakdown may be indicated
as follows: two general opinions (1-56), two conclusions (57-158), a subsidiary query and its reply (159-170), and a final query and its reply
(171-183). The first opinion is the Averroist
thesis that the heavens are completely simple (1),
for which Averroës's four proofs are given (2-5),
then some clarifications (7-9), and finally eight
more proofs, some with confirmations and replies
to objections (10-36). The second opinion is that
the heavens are elementary in nature and yet com-

posed (37-38), which is open to different interpretations (39-40): one is that the matter of the
heavens differs from that of sublunary bodies, with
one proof (41); the other that it is the same, with
seven proofs (42-56). Galileo's first conclusion
is the common peripatetic teaching that the heavens
are composed of matter and form, whatever the matter may be (57). For this he gives four main
proofs, three from Aristotle, with confirmations,
objections, and replies (58-81), the fourth from
nine other indications of composition in the heavens (82-92). Following this Galileo explains how
and why this conclusion is merely probable (93-
100), and then gives his replies to the arguments
of Averroës (101-121) as well as to other reasoning in Averroës's support (122-129). The second
conclusion is that the matter of the heavens differs from the matter of sublunary bodies, with
proof (130). This is followed by a presentation
of the arguments to the contrary from Giles of Rome
(131-151), with an indication of the ways in which
these can be answered (152-158). Thereupon a subsidiary query is introduced, viz, what is the basis for differentiating between these two matters
(159). Galileo explains the various proposals of
Capreolus and Cajetan to answer this, and his own
reflections on different principles of distinction
(160-170). The final query is related to the previous one: seeing that there are many heavenly orbs,
is the matter of which they are made one or many
(171). Galileo's reply explains various options
proposed by Thomists on whether or not the heavenly orbs differ specifically among themselves (172-
177), which last question he thinks is answered
affirmatively by Aristotle and involves corollaries
that are defensible against objection (178-183).

L. The final question of the treatise relates
to the animation of the heavens. Galileo prefaces
this with four opinions (1-5), then lists three
preliminary conclusions: first, there is no vegetative soul in the heavens (6); second, no sensitive soul either (7-9); and third, the basic problem is whether an intellective soul is there (10).
On the last point he further notes that there are
three positions: first, that the heavens have not
only intelligences but their own proper souls (11-
12); second, that the intelligences serve as souls
by being forms informing the heavens (13), with
ten proofs (14-23); and third, that the intelli-

gences are merely assisting forms, i.e., not informing the heavens but only assisting their motions (24). Galileo's own resolution is expressed
in two propositions: first, there are no proper
souls in the heavens apart from intelligences, with
four proofs (25-28); and second, though it is not
completely improbable that the intelligences are
informing forms, it is more probable that they are
only assisting, with proofs (29-31). He concludes
by proposing and answering objections against this
solution (32-41).

Tractate on Alteration

M. Here begins Galileo's exposition of questions relating to Aristotle's *De generatione et
corruptione*, the previous question having concluded his treatment of problems raised in the *De caelo
et mundo*. The initial tractate deals with alteration and is made up of three questions, the first
of which is incomplete at the beginning and discusses the nature of alteration. Presumably after
first giving various definitions and distinctions
relating to alteration (0), Galileo discusses their
different termini (1) and concludes that the terminus of any alteration that takes place between
primary qualities is a quality perceptible to the
sense of touch (2).

N. This question expands the notion of alteration to include intension and remission (1), and
then lists the various authorities who have treated the latter subject (2). Three notations follow
relating to the nature (3), existence (4-6), and
kinds (7-8) of intension, and after these four
conclusions that formulate Galileo's teaching. The
first conclusion states that intension does not
take place through a change intrinsic to the quality being intensified (9), and for this five general proofs are offered (10-14), together with two
particular proofs directed against Giles of Rome
(15-17). The second conclusion is missing from
the manuscript, but probably maintains that intension comes about through the addition of a new
part to the quality intensified. The third conclusion, consistent with this, is that the prior
part of the quality does not perish when it intensifies (18), and for this four proofs are given
(19-27). At this point the conclusion is restated
and two possibilities are noted for the manner of

intension, viz, either continuously or discretely
(28). The fourth conclusion, directed against the
Thomists, holds that intension comes about continuously (29); two proofs are then adduced in support
of this (29-30), and finally two objections are
raised and responses given to them (31-32).

O. The last question is brief and consists of
a series of six notations plus a concluding query.
The first notation distinguishes the kinds of degree found in quality (1-2), the second, how lati-
tudes occur in both quantity and quality (3), and
the third, how quality can be said to have both
qualitative and quantitative parts (4). The fourth
notation then explains how intension comes about
through a simple, continuous eduction (5), the fifth, how it does not come about by addition alone
(6), and the sixth, why intension is not, properly
speaking, that of the pre-existing degree (7-8).
The query relates to whether, in intension, the
first degree is produced in an instant and the
others then successively, but its answer is referred to treatments elsewhere (9).

Tractate on the Elements

P. With this question begins the last of Galileo's tractates, that on the elements. Unlike
previous treatises this has a separate introductory question to treat preliminary details, after
which it is divided into two parts or disputations,
one on the nature of the elements, the other on
their qualities. With regard to preliminaries,
Galileo first mentions the authors who have treated of the elements in general (1). He then makes
four notations, which constitute the body of the
question: the first discusses nominal definitions
of the elements (2), including four erroneous definitions (3-6) and four deriving from Galen (7-10);
the second notes various distinctions based on composition and alteration (11-12); the third explains
how the elements are referred to (13); and the
fourth, why element is a relative term (14). The
question concludes with a division of the entire
projected treatise (15).

Q. The first part of the treatise, that on
the quiddity and substance of the elements, begins
with this question on the definitions of an element. Its prologue explains that definitions are

given through causes (1), after which there are
two notations that go to make up the rest of the
question. The first explains the various kinds of
definition (2) and how each of these can be applied
to the elements, viz, the metaphysical definition
(3), the physical (4), and the absolute and the
relative, for which seven different examples are
given (5-11). The second notation focuses on Aristotle's definition (5) and explicates all of its
component parts (12-17).

R. Galileo here turns to a causal analysis of
the elements, explaining first their efficient
cause (1-3), then their final cause (4), and finally their matter, or material cause, giving seven
brief opinions (5) and concluding that the common
matter of all the elements is primary matter as affected by primary qualities (6). The formal cause
of the elements is left for the following question.

S. The focus of interest here is identifying
the forms of the elements, presupposing that these
forms are substantial and not accidental (1). Galileo notes four opinions, viz, those of Nobili (2);
Achillini (3); Alexander and the Greeks, with
three arguments supporting it (4-7); and St. Thomas, the Latins, and others (8). He then presents
three conclusions: the forms are not alterative
qualities (9-10); nor are they motive qualities,
answering Achillini's arguments to the effect that
they are (11-13); rather each element has a substantial form that is complete and different from
its alterative and motive qualities (14). Galileo
concludes with replies to the three arguments given
in support of the Alexandrian and Greek positions
(15-17).

T. The forms of the elements being what they
are, the next inquiry is whether they undergo intension and remission (1). This question is pa-
tently incomplete, for Galileo merely enumerates
two opinions and has no resolution of the difficulty. The first opinion is that of Averroës and
his followers, answering in the affirmative (2-3),
the second that of Avicenna, Aquinas, and others,
answering in the negative (4). Then follow various proofs of the second opinion, which Galileo
says is true, together with objections, replies,
and confirmations (5-13); after these come further
objections raised by followers of the first opin-

ion against the second, to which there are no answers, since here the text ends abruptly (14-21).

   U. The title of this question is missing, as
are its introductory paragraphs explaining the
first query. From the material covered, however,
one can reconstruct that the question treats the
number and the quantity of the elements, and that
it is made up of three queries, concerned respectively with the number of the elements (0-6), their
size and shape (7-8), and whether they and other
natural things have termini of largeness and smallness (9-80). With regard to the first query only
the third and fourth arguments, together with
their objections and replies, survive; these establish that the elements are four in number (1-6).
The answer to the second query is brief: the elements do not require any particular shape (7-8).
The third query, on the other hand, leads to a
lengthy disquisition on maxima and minima involv-
ing eight notations, four opinions, ten conclusions, and replies to arguments in support of the
first opinion. The notations make preliminary distinctions (9-23) so as to state the basic question,
viz, whether each subsistent natural thing of a
particular species has a simple and absolute terminus of largeness and smallness (24). Four different opinions are listed, viz, those of St. Thomas and the Thomists, with five proofs (25-29);
Averroës and the Averroists (30); Paul of Venice
(31); and Scotus, Ockham, and Pererius (32). Galileo's own teaching is summarized in ten conclusions: the first states that no things have maxima
and minima in relation to God, followed by various
objections and replies (33-46); the second, third,
and fourth maintain that living things and heterogeneous compounds have termini of largeness and
smallness (47-48), and that these are intrinsic
and *per se* by way of generation (49-51), extrinsic
and *per accidens* by way of corruption (52-56); the
fifth through the seventh, that elements have termini of largeness and smallness with respect to
rarity and density (57-58), but they have no termini *per se* (59-64); the eighth and ninth, that
qualities naturally have a maximum but no minimum
(65-70); and the tenth, that powers have an intrinsic *maximum quod sic* but no minimum (71-75).
The question concludes with replies to the five
arguments in support of the Thomistic position
(76-80).

V. Here begins the second disputation of the
tractate on the elements, dealing with their qualities. The first question treats the number of
primary qualities and is brief, containing only
three notations, each with objections and replies.
The first describes the method used by Aristotle
to show how this number is four (1-3), the second
states what is required for a quality to be primary (4-6), and the third explains why no qualities
other than hotness, coldness, wetness, and dryness
can fulfill the requirements for primacy (7-10).

W. The problem discussed here is whether all
four primary qualities are positive, or whether
some are privative. Galileo begins by listing four
opinions: first, that of Cardanus and the ancients,
to the effect that some qualities, coldness and
dryness, are privative, with appropriate proofs
(1-4); the second, that of some physicians, holding for two kinds of coldness, one positive and
the other privative (5); the third, maintaining
that wetness and dryness are not qualities but substances (6-7); and the fourth, the true position
and that of Aristotle and Scaliger, stating that
all four qualities are true, real, and positive
(8). Following the opinions are three conclusions,
viz: coldness is a real and positive quality (9);
dryness is likewise positive (10); and neither wetness nor dryness are substances, with various
proofs (11-14). Galileo concludes by replying to
the arguments in support of the first opinion (15-
17).

X. Having shown that all four qualities are
real and positive, Galileo turns here to the question whether all are active, and replies merely
with six notations, some of which include objections and replies. The first explains the source
of the difficulty, viz, Aristotle says that all
four qualities are active and yet he refers to two
as passive (1); the second notes what needs to be
done to make Aristotle consistent (2). The third
and fourth notations describe how hotness and coldness produce some effects of wetness and dryness,
but show how they do so *per accidens* and not *per
se* (3-9). The fifth notation explains how wetness
and dryness have a kind of proper action and so
are not purely passive (10-13). The sixth notation, finally, offers various interpretations of
Aristotle's statements that solve the initial dif-

ficulty (14-15), with three animadversions (16-20),
and an objection and reply (21).

Y. The final question aims to explain how
primary qualities are involved in activity and resistance; the question is incomplete, but what survives of it comprises two problems, one on the nature of resistance, the other on the activity and
resistance of primary qualities. The first problem is posed by Vallesius's definition of resistance as action (1). Galileo solves this under
three conclusions stating respectively that resistance is not action formally (2), that it is not
reception (3), and that it is permanence in a proper state against a contrary action (4). From the
last follow three corollaries explaining what resistance is (5-6) and the factors it involves (7)
-- contrary to the positions of Nobili (8) and
Vallesius (9). The second problem is how primary
qualities are related in activity and resistance,
a matter that has been discussed by many authorities (10). To this Galileo does not give a solution, for all that remains are four notations and
the beginning of a fifth. The first notation explains various ways of making comparisons (11-12),
and the second, how intension and remission mean
different things when applied to quality, to activity, and to resistance (13-15). The remaining
three notations attempt to apply these distinctions to various orderings of the primary qualities as more active and more resistive, depending
on how the specific comparison is made (16-25).

SOURCES

As noted in the Preface, all of these questions are similar to those treated by Jesuit professors at the Collegio Romano in the years between 1566 and 1597. Some of the teachings are
contained in the published works of these professors, but the majority are preserved only in manuscript, as reports or summaries of lectures given
at the Collegio. The following is an enumeration
of the books and lecture notes that have been
studied by the translator and identified as sources
on which Galileo's composition could have been based.

Books:

> Franciscus Toletus, *Commentaria una cum quaes-*
> *tionibus in octo libros Aristotelis de*
> *physica auscultatione,* Venice 1573
> _____, *Commentaria in librum de genera-*
> *tione et corruptione Aristotelis,* Venice
> 1575
> Benedictus Pererius, *De communibus omnium re-*
> *rum naturalium principiis et affectionibus,*
> Rome 1576
> Christophorus Clavius, *In sphaeram Ioannis de*
> *Sacrobosco,* Rome 1581

Lectures on Natural Philosophy:

> Benedictus Pererius, 1565-1566, *Physics, De*
> *caelo,* and *De generatione*[12]
> Hieronymus de Gregoriis, 1567-1568, *Physics,*
> *De caelo,* and *De generatione*[13]
> Antonius Menu, 1577-1579, *Physics, De caelo,*
> *De generatione* and *Meteorology*[14]
> Paulus Valla, 1588-1589, *De generatione* (por-
> tions) and *Meteorology*[15]
> Mutius Vitelleschi, 1589-1590, *Physics, De*
> *caelo, De generatione,* and *Meteorology*[16]
> Ludovicus Rugerius, 1590-1591, *Physics, De*
> *caelo, De generatione,* and *Meteorology*[17]
> Robertus Jones, 1592-1593, *Physics, De caelo,*
> and *Meteorology*[18]
> Stephanus del Bufalo, 1596-1597, *De caelo,*
> *De generatione,* and *Meteorology*[19]

In what follows, a brief biographical account
of each professor will be given, to the extent that
such information is available, and then a description of his work as this relates to the contents of
Galileo's notebooks. The details are somewhat com-
pendious, but when studied in conjunction with the
comments on the various paragraphs of the notebooks,
they should provide the reader with the essential
elements of comparison between Galileo's presentation and that found in the individual Jesuit authors.

Toletus

Franciscus Toletus (1533-1596) studied under
Domingo de Soto at Salamanca, later taught there
himself, and, on becoming a Jesuit, was sent to

the Collegio Romano as a professor.[20] Here he
taught logic in 1559-1560, natural philosophy in
1560-1561, and metaphysics in 1561-1562; after
this he taught theology. His printed commentaries and questionaries on Aristotle include various works on logic, the *Physics*, the *De generatione
et corruptione*, and the *De anima*, all of which
went through many editions. For purposes here
only the commentaries on the *Physics* and the *De
generatione* are of interest; the first was published at Venice in 1573, and a second edition in
1580; the second was published at Venice in 1575,
and again in 1579. Brief portions of Toletus's
commentary on the *Physics* are similar to Galileo's
exposition of questions F, N, O, and U, and parts
of the commentary on the *De generatione* are likewise related to Galileo's S, V, and X; these correspondences are indicated at appropriate places
in the commentary by page references to the 1580
and 1579 editions respectively. Some of Toletus's
manuscripts still survive, but these show no resemblances to Galileo's notebooks.

Pererius

Benedictus Pererius (1535-1610) taught logic
at the Collegio Romano in 1561-1562 and 1564-1565,
natural philosophy in 1558-1559, 1562-1563, and
1565-1566, and metaphysics in 1559-1561, 1563-
1564, and 1566-1567; he also taught Sacred Scripture and theology at various times.[21] His course
on Aristotle's *Physics* is summarized in his *De communibus omnium rerum naturalium principiis et af-
fectionibus*, published at Rome in 1576, with many
later printings; an earlier version, with a different title, was published at Rome in 1562. Portions of Galileo's questions C, F, and U show correspondences with the edition of 1576, as indicated by page references in the commentary.

Apart from this, *reportationes* of Pererius's
lectures on the *Physics*, the *De caelo*, and the *De
generatione* are extant. Those on the *Physics* are
undated, but some of the material they contain relating to Galileo's questions C, F, and U was printed, apparently later, in the *De communibus*. The
notes on the *De caelo* are also undated, and portions of their material likewise reappear in the
De communibus. They have a brief *Praefatio*, and
then the remaining exposition is organized under

the title *Tractatus de caelo*, which is made up of
four parts respectively entitled *De substantia caeli, De partibus caeli, De accidentibus caeli*, and
De actione caeli. The first part has five questions, with correspondences to Galileo's questions
as follows: 1 = K, 2 = L (the equal sign is used
throughout to denote similarity only, not complete
equivalence); the second part has seven sections,
with the similarities 1 = G, 2 = H; none of the
remainder has a counterpart in Galileo's treatment.

Two sets of *reportationes* of Pererius's course
on the *De generatione* survive; one of these is undated, the other was taught in 1566. The first
contains a *Tractatus de alteratione*, made up of six
chapters corresponding to Galileo's questions as
follows: 2 = M, 3 = N, 4 = N & O. The second is
more complete, being made up of seven disputations
entitled respectively *De generatione, De alteratione, De augmentatione, De rarefactione, De actione,
De reactione*, and *De elementis*. Of these the second shows some similarities with Galileo's questions N and U, and the sixth with Y; the seventh
begins with a *Praemissa seu Prolegomena* corresponding to Galileo's P, and then is divided into four
books with the following counterparts in Galileo:
1 = Q, S, & R; 2 = U & W.

Clavius

Christopher Clavius (1538-1612) taught mathe-
matics, including astronomy, at the Collegio Romano from 1564 to 1571, again from 1576 to 1584, and
yet again beginning in 1587 but with no terminal
date.[22] Known as the Euclid of the sixteenth century, he corresponded with Galileo, and the latter
visited him in Rome in 1587; he is the most likely
contact through whom Galileo could have obtained
access to the *reportationes* here described. Clavius composed many mathematical works and an im-
portant commentary on the *Sphaera* of John of Sacrobosco; the latter was first published at Rome in
1570, with a second edition in 1581, reprinted in
1585 from the same type, and with many other editions. All of the material contained in Galileo's
questions G and H has counterparts in the 1581
edition (page numbers are given in the commentary),
strongly suggesting that Galileo copied from this
work or from a source that derived from it in almost verbatim fashion.

De Gregoriis

Hieronymus de Gregoriis taught natural philosophy at the Collegio Romano in 1567-1568 and metaphysics in 1568-1569.[23] *Reportationes* are available for his course on natural philosophy, which
covered the *Physics*, the *De caelo*, and the *De generatione*. Most of the manuscript in which these
are contained is written in a very small hand and
is difficult to read. The contents, however, are
similar to the notes of Pererius and to those of
Menu, described below. Because of the difficulty
of reading the manuscript, only portions of it were
analyzed for comparison with Galileo's work. The
structure of the exposition, however, is revealed
by the list of questions at the beginning of the
codex: the number of questions is extremely large,
and they are grouped according to the various
books of the *Physics*, the *De caelo*, and the *De generatione*. Some questions on the eighth book of
the *Physics* correspond to Galileo's D and F. For
the questions on the books of the *De caelo* there
are counterparts in Galileo as follows: 1 = A-E
& I-L, 2 = E, G, H, & L; for those of *De generatione:* 1 = M & N; 2 = P, U, S, T, & V.

Menu

Antonius Menu taught logic at the Collegio
Romano in 1579-1580, natural philosophy in 1577-
1578 and 1580-1581, and metaphysics from 1578 to
1582; he later served as prefect of studies from
1606 to 1608.[24] *Reportationes* of his lectures on
the *Physics*, the *De caelo*, the *De generatione*, and
the *Metaphysics* are extant. None of the matter of
Menu's *Physics* or *Metaphysics* relates directly to
Galileo's physical questions. The content of his
notes on the *De caelo* and the *De generatione*, however, bears considerable resemblance to Galileo's
exposition, and so deserves examination in some
detail.

Menu's *De caelo* is made up of two treatises,
the first *De mundo*, the second unnamed but obviously *De caelo*. The first treatise consists of
seven chapters, whose contents agree with Galileo's
questions as follows: 1 & 2 = C, 3 = D, 5 = F,
6 & 7 = E. The second treatise is divided into
three sections or disputations, the first of which
is entitled *De natura et essentia coeli* and is made

up of six chapters, corresponding to Galileo's
questions as follows: 1 = I, 2 = K, 3 = J, 4 & 5
= L. The remaining two disputations, *De accidentibus coeli* and *De actione coeli*, have no counterparts in Galileo's notes.

   None of Menu's treatises dealing with the matter of the *De generatione* is identified or named,
but space has been left in the manuscript for the
insertion of such titles, and from the contents one
can see that there is material for four treatises,
viz, *De generatione*, *De alteratione*, *De actione et
passione*, and *De elementis*. The treatise *De alteratione* comprises four chapters, with counterparts in Galileo's questions as follows: 2 = M,
3 = N, 4 = N & O. The final treatise, *De elementis*, has an extensive division, but the matter of
interest here is contained in its first section,
De elementis in genere, whose introductory part
contains matter relating to Galileo's question P.
The first section is then subdivided into five disputations, the first three of which are unnamed
and unnumbered, but probably should be entitled
De definitione elementorum, *De distinctione elementorum*, and *De quantitate elementorum*. Of these
the first has six chapters, with counterparts in
Galileo's material as follows: 2 & 3 = R, 4 = S,
5 = T, 6 = Q; the second disputation has no counterparts; and the third, only Galileo's question U.
The fourth disputation, *De qualitatibus alterativ-
is*, comprises eight chapters whose contents are related to Galileo's questions as follows: 1 = V,
2 = W, 3 = X, 4 = Y. The last disputation, *De
qualitatibus motivis*, contains no matter duplicated
in the physical questions, though it is obviously
related to the subject of Galileo's *De motu antiquiora*.

Valla

   Paulus Valla (1561-1622) was a Roman by birth,
entered the Society of Jesus in 1582, and taught
philosophy and theology at the Collegio for thirty
eight years.[25] He gave the logic course in 1587-
1588, natural philosophy in 1588-1589, and metaphysics in 1585-1587 and 1589-1590. In the preface
to his two-volume *Logica* (Lyons 1622) he indicates
that he has commented on all the philosophical
works of Aristotle and has his commentaries ready
for publication. All that survives of these, how-

ever, apart from the published logic course, is his
commentary on the *Meteorology*, to which is appended a single tractate, *Tractatus quintus: De elementis*, which in all likelihood originally pertained
to his course on the *De generatione*. This tractate is made up of two disputations, *De elementis
in genere* and *De elementis in particulari*, the
first of which alone is of interest and is divided
into five parts. Its first part, *De essentia elementorum*, comprises six questions, related to Galileo's questions in the following manner: 1 = P,
2 = R, 3 = S, 4 = T, 5 = Q, 6 = P & U. The second
part is entitled *De qualitatibus activis elementorum*, and its seven questions are also related to
Galileo's as follows: 1 = V, 2 = W & X, 3 = Y.
The fourth part, finally, is concerned with *De
quantitate elementorum*, and contains material relating only to Galileo's question U.

Vitelleschi

Mutius Vitelleschi (1563-1645) was also born
in Rome and entered the Society in 1583. He
taught logic in 1588-1589, natural philosophy in
1589-1590, and metaphysics in 1590-1591; later he
was professor of theology, then prefect of studies, and finally he was elected General of the
Society in 1615.[26] *Reportationes* of all of Vitelleschi's course in natural philosophy are still
extant; of these, those on the *Physics* and the *Meteorology* do not relate directly to Galileo's
notes. His *De caelo* begins with a single disputation entitled *De obiecto horum librorum* that contains material similar to Galileo's A and B; it is
then divided into three treatises, *De mundo, De
caelo*, and *De elementis* respectively. The first
comprises five disputations, with matter similar
to Galileo's as follows: 1 & 2 = C & D, 4 = F,
5 = E. The second is made up of thirteen disputations, related to Galileo's material as follows:
1 = I, 2 = K, 3 = L, 6 = J. The third treatise
has six disputations, but none of these is related
to Galileo's composition.

Vitelleschi's *De generatione* has some introductory material and then is made up of unnumbered
treatises on *De alteratione, De augmentatione, De
actione et passione, De mixtione*, and *De elementis
ut sunt materia mixtionum*. The first four of the
twelve disputations of *De alteratione* are related

to Galileo's questions as follows: 1 = M, 2-4 = N
& O. Only one of the twelve disputations of *De
augmentatione* is similar to Galileo's work, viz,
5 = U. Likewise only the sixth disputation of the
treatise *De actione et passione* is related to one
of Galileo's questions, viz, Y. The final treatise
is made up of fifteen disputations (all unnumbered
in the manuscript except the first), with the following relationship to Galileo's composition: 1 = T
& U, 2 = P & Q, 3 = S, 4 = W, 5 = V, 6 = X, 7 = Y.

Rugerius

    Ludovicus Rugerius, a Florentine, followed
Vitelleschi in teaching the philosophy cycle at
the Collegio, giving the logic course in 1589-1590,
natural philosophy in 1590-1591, and metaphysics
in 1591-1592.[27] His entire philosophy course survives in the form of *reportationes*. Of these, only
the *De caelo* and the *De generatione* are of immediate interest for their relevance to Galileo's
thought.

    The *De caelo* is divided into three disputa-
tions, entitled respectively *De universo, De corpore caelesti*, and *De gravi et levi*. The first of
these is prefaced by an *Exordium* and then is made
up of four questions, related to Galileo's questions as follows: 1 = A & B, 2 = C, 4 = F. The
second disputation comprises four tractates, but
only the first and third are of interest here.
The first, *De natura caeli*, has three questions,
corresponding to Galileo's as follows: 1 = E, 2 =
K, 3 = L. The third, *De motibus et aliis accidentibus manentibus caeli*, has three questions, the
first of which alone corresponds to one of Galileo's, viz, J.

    Rugerius's *De generatione* begins with an in-
troductory question and then is divided into four
disputations, viz, *De generatione et corruptione,
De mixtione, De elementis*, and *De forma et effici-
ente mixtionis*. The second tractate of the first
disputation is entitled *De alteratione*, and its
three questions contain materials relating to Galileo's questions as follows: 1 = M, 2 & 3 = N & O.
The third tractate of the second disputation de-
votes its third question to matters relating to
Galileo's question Y. The third disputation comprises four tractates; the first is entitled *De*

substantia elementorum and is divided into four
questions containing matters relating to Galileo's
as follows: 1 = P, 2 = Q, 3 = S, 4 = T. The second tractate, entitled *De numero et quantitate
elementorum*, has four questions containing materials related to Galileo's question U. Finally, the
third tractate, *De qualitatibus activis et passivis
elementorum*, has nine questions, related to Galileo's as follows: 1 = W, 2 = V, 3 & 4 = X.

Jones

Robertus Jones (1564-1615), an English Jesuit
who also used the names of Holland, Draper, and
perhaps Northe, entered the Society in Rome in
1583 and taught logic at the Collegio Romano in
1591-1592, natural philosophy in 1592-1593, and
metaphysics in 1593-1594; after this he returned
to England, later to be head of the mission there.[28]
A *reportatio* of his course on natural philosophy
is extant, but this covers only the *Physics*, the
De caelo, and the *Meteorology*. The portion treating of the *De caelo* is quite brief, being appended
to the *Physics* commentary with the title *Disputatio
quinta physicae: De universo, vel de coelo et mundo*. It consists of ten questions, corresponding
to those of Galileo as follows: 1 = D, 2 = F, 3 =
I, 4 & 5 = K, 6 = J, 7 = L. There is no explicit
treatment of alteration or of the elements in
Jones's notes.

Del Bufalo

Stephanus del Bufalo taught logic at the Collegio Romano in 1595-1596, natural philosophy in
1596-1597 and 1598-1599, and metaphysics in 1597-
1598 and 1599-1600; he also taught ethics in 1595-
1596 and theology from 1605 to 1609 and from 1612
to 1618, and was prefect of studies from 1617 to
1623 and again from 1632 to 1634.[29] Two sets of
reportationes survive from his course on natural
philosophy, one from 1596 and another (anonymous)
from 1597; these do not comment on the *Physics*,
but they do contain commentaries on the *De caelo*,
the *De generatione*, and the *Meteorology*.

In the first *reportatio* the commentary on the
De caelo is divided into two disputations, entitled
De mundi origine and *De caelo*. The first of these
comprises three questions, related to Galileo's as

follows: 1 = D & E, 2 = C, 3 = F; the second also
contains three questions, similarly related: 1 =
I-L, 2 = L. The commentary on the first book of
De generatione follows this and is made up of three
disputations, entitled respectively *De essentia ge-
nerationis eiusque causis, De iis quae praerequirun-
tur ad mixtionem,* and *De mixtione et miscibili.* The
first of these has two parts; the second, treating
of alteration, is composed of three questions related to Galileo's as follows: 1 = M, 2 = N & O,
3 = O. Likewise the second disputation has two
parts, the first of which contains matter relating
to Galileo's V and Y. After this comes the commentary on the second book of *De generatione,* made
up of three disputations, the first of which treats
of the substance of the elements and contains a
question similar to Galileo's Q.

The second *reportatio* has a similar content
to the first, though with different titles and a
different mode of division. Thus the *De caelo* has
a preliminary disputation, *De universo seu de mundo* (paralleling Galileo's C-F), then three disputations on, respectively, *De natura coeli* (Galileo's
I-L), *De accidentibus coeli,* and *De actione coeli.*
Relating to the first book of *De generatione* there
are four disputations, viz, *De generatione, De alteratione* (Galileo's M-O), *De actione* (Galileo's Y),
and *De mixtione,* and relating to the second book,
four more: *De numero et formis elementorum* (Galileo's U & S), *De qualitatibus activis elementorum*
(Galileo's V-Y), *De mutu [sic] generatione et corruptione elementorum,* and *De qualitatibus motivis
elementorum.*

Eudemon & Spinola

In addition to the above, the translator has
also studied *reportationes* of the courses on natural philosophy given at the Collegio Romano by
Andreas Eudemon-Ioannes in 1597-1598[30] and by Fab-
ius Ambrosius Spinola in 1625-1626.[31] These bear
fewer marked resemblances to Galileo's questions,
and are not described here on that account.

DATING

The foregoing account of the similarities between Galileo's notes and those of the Jesuits at
the Collegio Romano offers some clues to dating

Galileo's composition, but the correspondences are
so abundant and extend over such a long period of
time that it is difficult to draw convincing evidence from them to establish a particular date.
As noted in the Preface, external evidence favors
"around 1590" as the time of composition, whereas
internal evidence, as analyzed by Favaro, favors
1584. However, Favaro's analysis, as noted *infra*
in the comment on D8, is not beyond question, for
the text he uses more clearly indicates 1580 as
the date of its writing than it does 1584. Now it
could well be that Galileo copied this portion of
the notes from a source written in 1580, but he
himself could not have done the copying then, in
view of the obvious dependence of his questions G
and H on the 1581 edition of Clavius's *Sphaera*.
Moreover, there are so many similarities between
Galileo's composition and lectures given at later
times, all the way down to 1591, that the later
dating, "around 1590," seems more likely.

     It is possible, to be sure, that the later
notes of the Jesuits were themselves culled from
an earlier source thus far undiscovered, which
could also have been used by Galileo at an earlier
time. The *rotulus* of professors of natural philosophy at the Collegio during the years of interest
is not particularly helpful in this regard, however, because of gaps in the list, which is shown
on the facing page.[32] Of the names that survive,
Mutius de Angelis is the most likely prospect,
particularly since Sommervogel records that he
composed commentaries "on almost all the philosophical works of Aristotle."[33] Unfortunately these
commentaries have not been discovered to date.
After De Angelis, Caribdi lectured in 1587-1588,
but no *reportationes* are known to survive from his
work either. With regard to the possibility of
repeated copying year after year, the translator
would merely observe that he has made many comparisons of *reportationes* covering the same subject
matter in successive years, and has yet to discov-
er any case of one Jesuit making a verbatim copy
of another's lectures. Frequently, though not in-
variably, the thought remains the same over a period of years, but it is always organized differently and expressed in different terms in the successive *reportationes*.

Academic Year	Professor
1577-1578	Antonius Menu
1578-1579	Antonius Menu
1579-1580	?
1580-1581	Antonius Menu
1581-1582	?
1582-1583	?
1583-1584	?
1584-1585	Mutius de Angelis
1585-1586	Mutius de Angelis
1586-1587	Mutius de Angelis
1587-1588	Iacobus Caribdi
1588-1589	Paulus Valla
1589-1590	Mutius Vitelleschi
1590-1591	Ludovicus Rugerius
1591-1592	Alexander de Angelis
1592-1593	Robertus Jones

As the paleographical comments should make abundantly clear, Galileo's composition is derivative from one or more sources, probably handwritten like his own, and possibly incomplete in the form in which he used them. Perhaps some intermediate author had already made his own redaction of a variety of source materials, and Galileo obtained this and adapted it to his own purposes. Alternatively, Galileo himself may have had access to several sets of *reportationes*, and from these culled the notes on his own initiative. The fact remains, however, that the only materials thus far available for study are those described above under sources (pp. 12-22), and substantive portions of these were not composed until around 1590. Thus, in the absence of other evidences, and considering the inconclusiveness of Favaro's argument for 1584 based on D8, the 1590 dating alone has more than conjectural support.

Additional arguments for the later dating are given in the translator's "Galileo Galilei and the *Doctores Parisienses*."[34] To these may be added the fact that there are a number of similarities between the later *reportationes* discussed above and Galileo's memoranda and early treatises on motion, which have consistently been dated "around 1590." Thus these early compositions of Galileo would all seem to be of one piece, and on this account should not be regarded merely as student exercises, but

rather as serious note-taking by Galileo in conjunction with his early teaching career. The soph-
istication and internal consistency of the notes,
which, as the reader can verify for himself, cover
some very difficult subject matter, argue against
any immaturity on the part of their redactor.
Either Galileo was already proficient at the time
of their writing, or, less likely, he was extremely precocious in his grasp of the Aristotelian corpus. In any event these notebooks give a remark-
able indication of the natural philosophy that
formed the initial background against which this
"Father of Modern Science" made his revolutionary
discoveries.

Translation

[Introductory Treatise]

[A] First Question. What is Aristotle's Subject
Matter in His Books *De Caelo*?

[1] Those who make the generable and corruptible body the subject of the whole of the *Physics*
think that the heavens and the elements are considered by Aristotle as they are principles of generable and corruptible things; for the heavens,
according to them, is the efficient cause of generation and corruption, the elements the material
cause. We have refuted their opinion in the question "On the subject of the whole of the *Physics*."

[2] Alexander, as referenced by Simplicius in
the introduction to these books, thinks that the
subject is the universe as it is made up of the
heavens and the four elements, which are simple
bodies; for this reason he thinks that the word
"heavens" in the title of these books is to be understood as "universe," following Aristotle, who
in the first book, text 96, lists this among the
other meanings of the word "heavens." In his *Table*
Zimara attributes this opinion to Averroës, and St.
Thomas clearly follows it, teaching that the subject is the universe with all its integral parts.
And if you argue counter to this that plants and
animals are integral parts of the universe, he replies that the reasoning is not the same for simple bodies, plants, and animals: for plants and
animals have no determinate place except by reason
of their predominant elements, nor are they proper-

ly speaking integral parts of the universe.

16   [3] Iamblichus and Syrianus Magnus make the
subject of these books the heavens, concerning
which they would have Aristotle treat first and
per se, and following this, the elements; for he
does not treat of the elements except insofar as
they lead to a knowledge of the heavens or depend
on the heavens.

[4] Albertus Magnus makes the subject bodies
that are capable of movement to place. His reason
is this: the subject of the whole of the *Physics*
is bodies that are movable in general; therefore
the subject of these four books, which are a part
of the *Physics*, should be the first species of
movable bodies, i.e., bodies movable to place.

[5] Simplicius, in the introduction to these
books, thinks that the subject is simple bodies,
including the heavens and the four elements. His
basis is: because Aristotle in the eight books of
the *Physics* treats of the principles and properties of natural things; therefore in these books,
which follow those immediately, he ought to treat
of the first species of natural bodies, i.e., simple bodies.

[6] Nifo, seeking to find agreement among
these four opinions, holds with Alexander that the
subject of aggregation is the universe; with Albert, that the subject of predication is bodies
movable to place; with Simplicius, that the subject
of attribution is simple bodies; and with Iamblichus and Syrianus, that the subject of principali-
ty is the heavens.

[7] But I say, first: the universe is not the
subject of these books. The conclusion is Aristotle's, in the third *De caelo* at the beginning,
and in the first *Meteors*, first chapter; in these
places, explaining what had been said previously,
he makes no mention of the universe. And this
stands to reason. For "universe" means either [a]
being in its most common understanding, embracing
both corporeal things and those that exist apart
from bodies, and in this way the universe is not
the consideration of physics -- it pertains to the
wise man or to the metaphysician in some way, insofar as he contemplates being in general. Confir-

mation: for otherwise, if the universe were the
subject, it would follow that these books would
have no connection with those previous, because
the universe, as such, is neither a species nor a
part of the subject of physics. Or, [b] "universe"
means a type of whole containing various natures
that are warring amongst themselves; and understood in this way, since it cannot be the subject
of any science (for it is an aggregate *per accidens*), a fortiori it could not be the subject of
a part [of a science]. Or, [c] "universe" means
a type of whole integrated from several parts; and   17
in this way it is indeed the consideration of physics, not however as its subject but as a property
of its subject, since its subject is some type of
natural body.

[8] I say, second: the heavens *per se* are not
the only things considered in these books. The
conclusion, which is Aristotle's as cited above,
is proved by argument. First, from Simplicius:
the greatest portion of this work is concerned
with the elements; for in the third and fourth
books Aristotle treats of the nature and qualities
of the elements; in the second book, from text 77
to the end, he treats of the earth; and in the
first, where he treats of eternity and of unity,
he considers the elements also; therefore the elements are not considered consequentially and *per
accidens* but rather *per se*. Second: the elements
are knowable *per se* and this only by the physicist;
therefore [the elements are considered here].
This also is apparent from the fact that Aristotle
employs an introduction in the second book which
indicates that the elements are being treated *per
se*.

[9] I say, third: the subject is not a body
capable of movement to place. Proof of the conclusion: because the subject of any part must correspond to the subject of the whole; but the subject of the whole of the *Physics* is the natural
body precisely as natural; therefore the subject
of a part of the *Physics* cannot be a body capable
of movement to place. The conclusion is Aristotle's, not indeed in so many words, but in effect;
for he himself treats of the elements *per se*, as
we have said, in two of the books.

[10] I say, fourth: the opinion of Simplicius
seems to me most probable. For a better under-

standing of this I suppose two things: one is that
the subject of the whole of the *Physics* is natural
bodies precisely as natural; the other is that the
total subject of any science is that to which the
other things treated in the science are reduced,
whereas the partial subject is that which contains
any part or species of the total subject. Proof
of the conclusion: in the eight books of the *Physics* Aristotle treats of the principles and properties of natural bodies; therefore, since these four
books are a part of the whole of the *Physics*, in
these Aristotle must have treated of some part or
species of the total subject; but there are only
two species and parts of the total subject of physics, the simple body and the compound body, and
he treats of the compound in the book of the *Meteors*; therefore, of the simple in these books.
It is obvious that the subject is simple bodies,
from Aristotle, who calls the heavens an element
-- not that it is an element in the strict sense,
but because it is a simple body like the elements.
But here he treats of the heavens and the elements,
therefore of simple bodies, in which respect the
heavens are similar to the elements.

18

[11] You say: the principles of simple bodies
have not been explained by Aristotle in these
books; therefore simple bodies are not their subject. I reply: the principles of physical bodies
were explained in the eight books of the *Physics*,
and this is sufficient; for simple bodies are contained under natural bodies as a species, and the
principles of natural bodies have been explained
in the books of the *Physics*.

[12] First objection: there are demonstrations
concerning simple bodies, i.e., the heavens and
the elements, as is apparent from text 5 to 10,
where it is proved that a substance exists distinct
from the elements, which is the heavens, and from
the third *De caelo* from text 31 to 37, where it is
proved that elements exist; but the subject of a
science is supposed to be known and not demonstrated; therefore [the elements are not being considered here].

[13] Second objection: there cannot be a science of singulars, as we have shown elsewhere,
since, from the first *Posterior Analytics*, chapter
11, singulars can be neither defined nor demonstra-

ted; and this is also apparent from the seventh
Metaphysics, texts 54 and 55. But the heavens and
the elements, considered in their entirety, are so
singular that they cannot be multiplied and made
other; therefore [they are not the subject of these
books].

[14] Third objection: the subject of a science
should be one, according to Aristotle in the first
Posterior Analytics, chapter 43. But simple bodies,
i.e., the heavens and the elements, are not one,
since the former is incorruptible and the latter
are corruptible, though not in their entirety. But
corruptibles and incorruptibles differ primarily
and *per se*, from Aristotle in the tenth *Metaphysics*, chapter 26; therefore [they cannot be the
subject of the same science]. Nor can you say that
the heavens and the elements, precisely as simple
bodies, have only one definition. For this definition is not analogous, according to those of us who
locate the heavens in the same category as the elements; nor is it univocal, for then Aristotle
should have treated simple bodies in this work, and
he does not even mention them or their species.
And this is confirmed from Themistius, in the second *De anima*, text 30, where he teaches, following   19
Aristotle, that the analogous differs from the univocal in that the univocal must first be treated
in general, since it implies "one nature distinct
from its inferiors," but not the analogous, which
implies "its inferiors" directly.

[15] Fourth objection: in these books simple
bodies are considered not merely in themselves and
with their motive qualities, but also with their
active qualities and as they are principles of compounds; for in the second book the heavens are considered not simply in terms of motive force but
also as they are principles acting along with elemental bodies, and in the third and fourth *De caelo*
the elements are treated not with their motive
qualities alone but with their alterative qualities
also. Nor is this to be wondered at, since elements by their very nature are ordered to the generation of compounds; therefore, when being considered in themselves, they should also be considered
as related to compounds.

[16] Fifth objection: from the authority of
Aristotle in the first *De caelo*, text 4, promising

that he will treat of the universe, and in the
third *De caelo*, text 1, calling the heavens an element (though not of alteration but of composition),
and then admitting that he is treating of the heavens insofar as they, along with the other elements,
compose the universe. Add to this, since the adequate subject of a science is the thing whose parts
and properties are considered in it, and in these
books the parts and the properties of the universe
are considered, the universe is the subject. That
the parts and properties of the universe are considered in these books is obvious: for in them is
shown first that the world is perfect, in the first
De caelo at the beginning; that it is finite, from
text 38 to 77; that it is one and cannot be many,
from 76 to 101; and from 101 to the end that it is
eternal.

[17] To the first objection [12], some reply
that the subject of an entire science cannot be
demonstrated; but that a partial subject, if it is
unknown, can be, provided that a middle term is
available that is taken solely from the science itself, especially if the formal definition of the
total subject does not depend on that middle.
Therefore, since the heavens and the elements
might be unknown and a physical middle term would
be available to demonstrate them, [the partial subject could be demonstrated]. But it would be better to say that Aristotle did not demonstrate in
the first *De caelo* that the heavens exist, because
this was known *per se* but in a qualified way, i.e.,
their nature was known to be different from that
of the elements. So also in the third *De caelo*,
from text 31 to 37, he does not demonstrate simply
the existence of elements but also their kind,
i.e., that they are resolvable into compounds and
20   not divisible into other kinds.

[18] To the second [13], some deny that there
cannot be a science of singular incorruptible
things. A better reply is that the natures of the
elements and of the heavenly spheres can be abs-
tracted from individuating conditions and made universals; nor for this is there required a physical
aptitude to exist in many -- a logical aptitude
through non-repugnance is sufficient.

[19] To the third [14], I reply that the simple body that is the subject of this work is one

with a unity of univocation, as we have shown [when treating] the category of substance. Nor was it necessary for Aristotle to dispute first in these books of simple bodies in general, so long as the principles and properties of natural bodies in general, as we said [11], were explained previously in the eight books of the *Physics*. From this, together with those few things that pertain to the introduction to these books, can easily be gathered everything the physicist need know about simple bodies in general.

[20] To the fourth [15], I reply by conceding the argument: for we think it quite probable that the four books *De caelo* and the two *De generatione* go to make up one work, and that in it simple bodies are considered both in themselves and as they are the principles of compounds. In the first and second *De caelo* are treated the substance and accidents of the heavens, in the third and fourth, the elements in themselves and with their motive qualities, and in the first and second *De generatione*, the elements with their active qualities and as they are principles of compounds.

[21] To the fifth [16], I reply that the argument proves only that the universe is somehow treated in these books, as is apparent from the first conclusion [7], but not as the adequate subject; unless perhaps it is understood that the universe is the subject by reason of its parts, which is to say that simple bodies are considered in this work, and this is what we hold.

[B] Second Question. On the Order, Connection, and
Title of These Books

[1] With regard to the order and connection,
Mirandulanus, in book 15 of *Singularis certaminis*,
in the first section, thinks that these books are
the first part of natural philosophy: [a] because
in the beginning of the first *De caelo* there is a
very general introduction to natural philosophy,
21 and [b] because the eight books of the *Physics*,
treating as they do the principles of both corruptible and incorruptible things, can only be ordered
to metaphysics. Therefore [these books should come
first].

[2] Certain moderns think that this work is
to be inserted into the books *De animalibus*, [a]
because Aristotle, in the second *De caelo*, text 7,
treating of the position of the heavens, says that
he has already disputed extensively on those matters in his treatment of the motion of animals,
and [b] because a little later on he teaches that
the heavens are animated.

[3] Simplicius and Albertus Magnus, whom we
and everyone else follow, hold that these books
come after the eight books of the *Physics* and make
up the second part of natural philosophy.

[4] This is true, first: because in the books
of the *Physics* Aristotle has treated of the principles and properties of natural bodies in general;
therefore, immediately afterwards, he should treat
of the first species of natural body, which is the
simple body. For the prior according to nature
ought to precede the subsequent; but compounds,
concerning which he treats in the book of the *Meteors*, are subsequent to the elements, since they
are composed of them; therefore in this work he
rightly has treated of simple bodies. This is

32

likewise proved from Aristotle, who wrote in the
introduction to the *Meteors:* "We have already discussed the first causes of nature, and all natural
motion, including even the stars arranged according to their higher movement, and the corporeal
elements, how many and what kinds they are, and how
they change into one another, and the generation
and corruption of bodies."

[5] Second: because Aristotle in the eighth
Physics treated of the first mover; therefore, immediately after that, he should treat of the *primum
mobile* and the first revolution, which are explained in these books. This argument proves not only
that these books follow the eight books of the *Physics*, but also that the first two precede the two
that follow. But this can also be confirmed with
another argument: the heavens are simpler and nobler than the elements; therefore [they should be
treated first].

[6] To the first argument in support of the
first opinion [1a], I reply, with Simplicius, that
Aristotle wrote an introduction of this type in
order to connect these books with the eight books
of the *Physics*, and because he was preparing to explain the first species of natural body. To the
second [1b], this is obvious from the *Physics*.

[7] To the first argument in support of the
second opinion [2a], I reply that for the same reason it would follow that the books of the *Perihermenias* should come after the books *De anima*, for
in the former Aristotle says that he has treated
extensively of terms, as they are symbols of things,
in the books *De anima*. To the second [2b], this
will be apparent from what is to be said later [Ll-
41].

[8] Concerning the title, according to Alexander, Simplicius, and the Greeks, these books are
entitled *De caelo* from the more noble portion; according to Albertus Magnus, St. Thomas, and the
Latins, they are entitled *De caelo et mundo*. By   22
the term *mundo* they understand the four elements,
and this meaning was known also to Aristotle, in
the first *Meteors*, chapter 1, saying that the lower
world, i.e., the elements, should be contiguous
with the movement of the higher.

[9] The division of this work is apparent
from the solution of the fourth argument of the
preceding question [A20], and will be more obvious from the explanation of the context that follows.

Treatise on the Universe

[C] First Question. On the Opinion of Ancient
    Philosophers Concerning the Universe

[1] Although, as Plato taught, there are three
universes, one ideal or intelligible, another sensible and large, and a third sensible but small,
for the present the discussion here is of the large
sensible universe. The latter is nothing more
than the universe of things, so named originally
by Pythagoras because of the ornamentation it contains or because in itself it is cleansed (*mundus*)
of all dirt. Similarly Aristotle called it a "universe," for it contains everything within itself;
a "whole," for it has integral parts; and a "heav-
en," naming it from the nobler part, or also because he sometimes takes "heaven" to mean the universe, as seen in text 96 of this first book.

[2] That this universe began at a certain time
and was made in time has been the opinion of practically all the naturalists of antiquity, as Aristotle testifies in the first *De caelo*, text 102,
and the eighth *Physics*, text 10; though Galen, in
the book *De claris physicis*, asserts that Xenophon
thought it existed from eternity. But while they
agreed on that, they yet disagreed on the following. [a] First, on its matter, as can be seen in
the question on the opinions of philosophers near
the beginning of the *Physics*. Second, on its efficient cause, for some of them were unaware of
this or made no mention of it; others posited such
a cause, the first of whom was Anaxagoras, who pro-

posed a kind of mind bringing all things together,
and then Empedocles, who thought of strife and
love, as Aristotle attests in the eighth *Physics*,
texts 2 and 77. [c] Third, on the mode of its production: for, as Aristotle teaches in the place noted above, some, such as Empedocles and Anaxagoras,
thought that it was generated by aggregation and
desegregation; others, by condensation and rarefaction; yet others, such as Democritus and Leucippus, from a concourse of atoms and an interstitial
void; and finally others made the soul, by its own
motion, the principle of all movement. [d] Fourth,
on this, that some thought it was so constituted
that it must cease to be after the fashion of other things and never return to being; others, that
it might cease to be but still should return to
being -- read Simplicius on the eighth *Physics*,
text 3, and Aristotle in the first *De caelo*, 102.

[3] Concerning Plato, there is uncertainty
among philosophers as to what he did think. Taurus, in the *Timaeus* of Plato, Porphyry, Proclus,
Plotinus, Alcinous, and Simplicius, in the eighth
Physics, texts 3 and 10, thought that for Plato
the universe was sempiternal. And if one show
them Plato's text where he teaches in so many words
in the *Timaeus* that the universe was generated,
they reply that "generated" has different meanings
for Plato, and in that place it means that it is
made up of many component parts.

[4] Many learned men, on the other hand, hold
that Plato thought the universe was made in time
and from a matter that previously moved with a kind
of disordered motion; also, that it is corruptible
by nature, although by God's will it will never
corrupt. Aristotle teaches that this was Plato's
opinion in the eighth *Physics*, text 10 and elsewhere; also Alexander (as referenced by Philoponus
in the solution of the sixth argument of Proclus),
Theophrastus, Themistius, and practically all commentators on Aristotle; Plutarch, Cicero, Diogenes
Laërtius, Apicus, Seleucus, and Pleto the Platon-
ist; and these are followed by St. Basil in his
Hexämeron, Justin Martyr, Clement of Alexandria,
Eusebius of Caesaria, Theophilactus, St. Augustine,
and all the Schoolmen.

[5] With regard to Aristotle it is certain
that he defended tenaciously that the universe had

existed from all eternity and that it would never
end. This he thought he had proved in the eighth
Physics when he attempted to establish that motion
is sempiternal and, in the first *De caelo*, last
chapter, that everything that is generated has a
corruptible existence; as opposed to this, he frequently stated that the universe would never cease
to be. Add to this that if the universe was made,
it was made from something and not from nothing,
since for Aristotle there is no such thing as creation. Here also the authority of all philosophers
and theologians citing Aristotle agree on this
point.

[6] Yet some object that Aristotle, in the
first *Topics*, chapter 9, states that it is a "problem" that the universe existed from eternity. But
then one may reply, first, that Aristotle said this   24
by way of example, especially since in his time
there was doubt concerning this matter. Second, it
might be called a problem by Aristotle in the sense
that probable arguments could be adduced for both
sides; but from this it does not follow, as is apparent from the principles of the teaching he passed on, that Aristotle denied that the world existed from eternity.

[7] The opinion of the philosophers of antiquity concerning the creation of the world [2],
while favoring the truth in asserting that the universe had a beginning, nonetheless departs from it
in two respects. First, in that it says that the
universe was made of matter [2a], and thus is refuted by this argument: if the universe was made
from some kind of matter, either this was generated from another kind, or it existed from eternity;
if the first, then there would be a regress to infinity in matters, and so on; if the second, either
some efficient principle existed together with matter from the beginning, or not; if not, then everything was made from such matter by chance, which is
absurd; if so, then such matter existed to no purpose for all eternity; therefore [the universe was
not made from matter].

[8] Second, it is opposed to the truth in that
it asserts that the universe, while created in
time, is not going to corrupt, or that it will corrupt in such fashion as to return to being [2d].
Therefore it can likewise be refuted, by this argu-

ment: if the universe was generated, then either
it will corrupt at some time or not; if the first,
then it is not incorruptible; if it does not corrupt, to the contrary, everything that is generated in time is corruptible, as is obvious from experience and by induction; therefore [the universe
will corrupt]. Confirmation: because the universe
is said to be generated either from corruptibles
or from incorruptibles; not the second, as is obvious; if the first, then it will corrupt. You
say: it will cease to be, but in such a way that
it will come back into being. To the contrary:
because no cause can be assigned for such a return.

[9] The opinion of Aristotle [5] is opposed
to the truth. For his arguments and those of Proclus, Averroës, and others supporting the eternity
of the world, together with the solutions, read
Pererius, book 15.

[D] Second Question. The Truth Concerning the
       Origin of the Universe

[1] I say, first: there must exist some first
uncreated and eternal being, on whom all others depend, and to whom all others are directed as to an   25
ultimate end. Proof of the first part of the conclusion: because otherwise it would follow that a
thing would have produced itself, or that everything would have come into existence without an
agent, and either is absurd. Proof of the second
part: because there must be some first efficient
cause of everything; but this cannot be other than
a first and uncreated being; therefore all things
will depend on, and be referred to, that being.
Confirmation: because the correct order requires
that we proceed from inferiors to the heavens, and
from the heavens to the first mover, which is this
uncreated being; it requires, moreover, that there
be only one universal end of all things, which cannot be other than the said being.

[2] I say, second: this eternal and uncreated
being is not only the first final cause of all
things but also the efficient cause of all existence in an unqualified way. Proof of the conclusion: for a particular effect there must be a particular cause; therefore a universal effect must
have a universal cause; but this universal cause
must also be the first, and this is the aforemen-
tioned being; therefore [there must be a first final and efficient cause]. Second: wherever there
is more and less there must also be something absolute in that order; but in the genus of being
there is more or less; therefore there is also a
being in the absolute sense on whom all things depend efficiently. For, since all the finite beings of the universe are also imperfect, they cannot have existence from themselves in the order of
efficient causality; existence of itself can only

39

be said of the most perfect being, which is the uncreated being that is God. It is not to be wondered that this attribute should be said of God, moreover, insofar as he himself gave natural agents the
power to educe forms from the potency of matter.

[3] I say, third: this first and uncreated being has existence through its essence, and therefore is infinite, and has infinite virtue and power. Proof of the first part of the conclusion: because what has existence of itself has an unlimited
existence; but unlimited existence is infinite;
therefore, since the aforesaid being has existence
of itself and otherwise would not be first and uncreated, it must have infinite existence -- for
whatever is finite is "finished," [i.e., terminat-
ed] by something. Confirmation: because whatever
lacks all potency in the order of being is infinite being; but the first being lacks all potency
in the order of being, for otherwise it would not
have existence of itself nor would it be first;
therefore [it is infinite being]. Proof of the
second part of the conclusion: because virtue and
power follow on existence; therefore, infinite
existence implies infinite virtue and power. From
this it follows that the first being can create
things from nothing: for if an agent can produce
an effect from a more remote potency the more perfect it is in power, and the first being has infinite power, it is no wonder that it should produce an effect from the most remote potency, that
is, from nothing.

26
[4] I say, fourth: this being, first, uncreated, and infinite, operates freely and contingently
ad extra. Proof of the conclusion: because, since
it is infinite, if it were to operate *ad extra* necessarily, it would produce as much as it were able
and, as a consequence, an infinite effect; but
there is no such effect; therefore [it does not act
necessarily]. Add to this: a necessary cause is
uniquely determined; but this infinite being can
produce whatever it wills. Proof: because, since
it is first, it has nothing over it that can force
it to do anything; and, since it is completely sufficient unto itself, it can depend on no other.
Hence it happens that freedom in operating is a
perfection and so is not to be denied to the first
being as most perfect and as the creator of other
free beings.

[5] I say, fifth: this first being, uncreated, infinite, and free, could have created the universe *de novo*, and in fact did create it. Proof of the first part of the conclusion: because, if it could not, either it could not because from nothing nothing can be made, or because it was a necessary agent, or because it was unchanged. The first is no argument, because of the first being's infinite power, which can take away any defect; nor is the second, because of the freedom of the same being in acting; nor is the third, because relations that come to be between God and creatures are relations of reason -- therefore, just as a column does not change when my position changes, though it is now on my right and now on my left, so neither does God change; he is purest act and free of all potency whatever (even though he may be called creator, etc., which previously he would not have been), and so he remains always the same. Proof of the second part of the conclusion: first, because [creation in time] cannot be demonstrated, from the authority of Holy Scripture and from the determination of the Lateran Council; second, because it would follow that infinite numbers of arts and disciplines would have come down to us, and this is contrary to history -- read Aristotle, second *Metaphysics*, chapter 2; again, no one has been found among writers worthy of credence who affirms that the universe existed more than six thousand years ago.

[6] You say: fires and floods destroyed everything. But, to the contrary: how could it be that these fires and floods were never written about? Add to this: since, according to Aristotle, what is actually infinite cannot exist, the universe could not have existed from eternity and, as a consequence, it came to exist in time; otherwise, since rational souls are immortal, they would be actually infinite in number.

[7] I say, sixth: the universe must have been created by God in time -- so that it might be shown that it depends on God and that God is in need of no other thing, and so that we might know him to be most perfect, and having infinite power, and most free in his operations; also, so that the human mind, awakened by such goodness, liberality, and power, might be more readily moved to worship God.

27

[8] To anyone asking how much time has passed
from the beginning of the universe, I reply: though
Sixtus of Siena in his *Bibliotheca* enumerated various calculations of the years from the world's beginning, the figure we give is most probable and
accepted by almost all educated men. The universe
was created 5748 years ago, as is gathered from
Holy Scripture: for from Adam to the flood 1656
years intervened; from the flood to the birth of
Abraham, 322; from the birth of Abraham to the exodus of the Jews from Egypt, 505; from the exodus
of the Jews from Egypt to the building of the tem-
ple of Solomon, 621; from the building of the tem-
ple to the captivity of Sedechia, 430; from the
captivity to its dissolution by Cyrus, 70; from
Cyrus, who began to reign in the 54th Olympiad, to
the birth of Christ, who was born in the 191st
Olympiad, 560; the years from the birth of Christ
to the destruction of Jerusalem, 74; from then up
to the present time, 1510.

[E] Third Question.   On the Unity and Perfection
                of the Universe

    [1] We inquire, first, concerning this diffi-
culty, whether it is demonstrable that there is
only one universe, for Aristotle, in the first *De
caelo*, at text 77, thought he had demonstrated it.

    [2] I say, first: there is only one universe.
The proof: first, from Plato, there is only one
exemplar of the universe; therefore [the universe
is one].   Second, from Albertus, on the first *De
caelo*, tract 3, chapters 5 and 6: because this is
clearly gathered from the first mover, who is only
one and cannot be multiplied, not being material,
and from the places of the movable objects that
are in the universe.   Add to this: if there were
many universes, a reason could not be given why
these would be all and no more.   Third, from St.
Thomas in the First Part, question 47, article 3:
from the order existing in things created by God.   28
For the universe is said to be one by a unity of
order, according to which certain things are ordered to other things; but whatever things come from
God have an order to each other and to God himself;
therefore all things must pertain to one universe.
And this manner of arguing is also that of Aristotle, second *Metaphysics*, reasoning from the unity
of order in existing things to the unity of the
first mover governing them.   From this is seen the
error of Democritus and his followers, who held
that there were many worlds; for they thought this
because they made the cause of the universe not
Wisdom disposing everything in its place, but
chance, thinking that this world and also infinite
others resulted from the chance concurrence of a-
toms.   Fourth, the proof from reason: the world
was created to this end, that our minds might come
to the knowledge of God; but one universe is sufficient for acquiring this knowledge of God; there-

fore [there is only one universe]. Proof of the
minor: two things can be considered in God, the
unity of his essence and the infinity of his perfection; but the universe represents both of these
to us, since it is one and contains within itself
various and diverse species of things; therefore
[one universe is sufficient to give us knowledge
of God].

[3] I say, second: it cannot be demonstrated
that there is only one universe, although it is
certain that there are not more. The second part
of the conclusion is apparent both from Holy Scripture, for Moses describes the creation of only one
universe, and from the arguments given. Proof of
the first part: because if it could be demonstrated that there is only one universe, this would be
either through sense knowledge, or through experience, or through cogent reasoning. Not the first,
because no one sees that many universes do not exist; nor the second, because experience depends on
the senses; nor the third, because it is not impossible that many universes could have been created
by God.

[4] The arguments of Aristotle, given in this
book at text 77, by which he thinks he has demonstrated the unity of the universe [1], can easily
be answered. The first is: the universe has all
the matter possible; therefore it implies a contradiction that there be another. The answer:
this is based on a false supposition.

[5] The second argument: if there were many
universes, it would follow that the earth of one
would be naturally borne to the earth of the other,
and a like judgment applies to the other elements;
but this is absurd, because the earth would not
have a determinate place, and because it would both
rise and fall, which is contrary to reason. The
answer: if there were many universes, earth would
only move to the center of its universe; and the
reason for this is that earth would not have a determinate place except insofar as it was an integral part of the universe, and so it would not move
except to that place wherein it was a part; and the
same applies to the other elements.

[6] The third: if we accept that the earth of
another universe could be transferred to the center

of this universe, such a motion would be either
natural or violent; if the first, then it would
not rest naturally in the center of the other universe, which seems absurd; if the second, then it
would rest naturally in the center of this universe, which seems contrary to reason. The answer:
as long as the earth existed in that universe and
were translated from that center, it would move
violently; but as soon as it arrived in our universe, it would move naturally in this. Others
reply that if many universes had been created
there would be a determinate motion for each element in its universe.

[7] You inquire here: whether, since God could
make many universes, he could make them all completely the same; for St. Thomas seems to deny this
in the place cited above [2], teaching in the solution to the third objection that it is not possible
that there be an earth other than that of this universe, because, if it were possible, the earth
would move naturally to the center of this universe
from wherever it might be. To this it should be
said, however, that St. Thomas is to be understood
as speaking of natural or of ordinary power, as he
himself states elsewhere, and the common opinion
of theologians agrees, teaching that God could make
many universes exactly similar to this, because his
infinite power is not exhausted by one effect and
whatever he makes is made in the best way.

[8] One may ask, second: whether God could add
new species to this universe, or make other universes having more perfect species essentially different from those that exist in this universe.
Scotus, in the third [Sentences], distinction 13,
question 1, and Durandus, in the first [Sentences],
distinction 44, question 2, deny this, holding that
one must ultimately come to some finite creature
than which nothing more perfect can be made; in
fact Durandus asserts that it is most probable that
God created all possible species in this universe
and so, as a consequence, neither this universe nor
another could be made more perfect by God. Better,
however, St. Thomas, in the First Part, question
25, article 6, and practically all others, think
that God could make more perfect universes to infinity because of his infinite power; from this it
is likewise apparent, since God can make many universes to infinity, that he could also make them

more perfect to infinity.

[9] One may ask, third: whether God could have made creatures in this universe more perfect than he did. It seems not: because something cannot be made better than the best; but all things that God has made are the best; therefore [better could not be made].

30   [10] Note that there are two kinds of perfection: one essential, the other accidental. I say, first: everything in the universe could have been made better by God with an accidental perfection; for God could have made man wiser, and so on. The reason: since it is not incompatible on the part of God's having infinite power, nor of the thing, he could have [done so].

[11] I say, second: God could not make creatures essentially more perfect than they are. The proof: because the essences of things are indivisible; for this take the example of St. Thomas in the place cited above [8], concerning the number four, that it cannot be increased or decreased without changing it; this is taken from Aristotle in the *Metaphysics*, who said that essences are the same as numbers in this respect.

[12] To the argument [9], I reply: all created things are best when referred to the universe, not however when considered in themselves, because of the exceedingly beautiful order given them by God, in which the good of all things consists. Thus it follows that if any one of the things in the universe were better, it would destroy the proportion of the entire universe, just as if one string were made too loud, it would destroy the melody of the musical instrument.

[13] The fourth question is whether the universe is perfect. It seems not: for [a] monsters and defects are found in it; [b] it does not always have its species in actual existence; and [c] many species that are more perfect can be added to them, since all have some imperfection.

[14] Note, for an answer: a thing can be said to be perfect in two ways, absolutely, or in a qualified way. The absolutely perfect is that to which nothing can be added by way of perfection;

the perfect in a qualified way is that which, while
perfect in its kind, lacks all possible perfection.
Note, second: "universe" can be taken in four ways:
either for something made up of God, intelligences,
celestial spheres, and sublunary bodies; or for
something made up of the foregoing with the exception of God; or for something made up of the heavenly and sublunary bodies; or, finally, for something made up of sublunaries alone.

[15] I say, first: the universe taken in the
first sense is perfect absolutely, since God contains what is most perfect within himself; and
second: the universe in the three other meanings
is perfect in a qualified way, but not absolutely.
Proof of the first part: because, as Aristotle also
teaches in text 4 of this book, the universe is
perfect in its integrity because it contains all
beings, contingent and necessary, corruptible and
incorruptible, corporeal and incorporeal, and finally because the most wise God would have been imperfect in his work had he not made it perfect.
Proof of the second part: because something per-   31
fect, viz, God, can be added to the universe taken
in these three ways; and God could have created another universe that is more perfect, and many more
perfect species in this.

[16] To the first argument to the contrary
[13a], I reply: monsters and defects can be taken
in two ways, either in themselves alone, and in
this way they imply imperfection, or in relation
to the universe, and in this way they imply perfection; for the perfection of the universe consists
in the variety of things, just as the ornament and
perfection of a figure is found in the variety of
its colors, some of which are less perfect than
others.

[17] To the second [13b], Jandun replies that
species always exist actually, and, when they do
not exist in our hemisphere they are found in the
other. Others reply that it is sufficient that
species exist potentially in their causes. I would
say that for the perfection of the universe the
actual existence of imperfect species is not required, but that it is sufficient, for the perfection of the universe, that these exist at their
own time [and place].

[18] To the third [13c], the reply is obvious from the foregoing [14].

[19] One may inquire, finally, whether God together with the universe is more perfect than by himself alone. Some deny this: because God contains all perfections that are found spread out in creatures; and thus he is just as perfect alone as when taken with all his creatures.

[20] Others, on the indication of Durandus, think the same but for another reason: no wonder, because creatures are related to God just as a point is related to a line; indeed, there is much greater similarity between point and line than between creatures and God; but a point added to a line does not make it any longer; therefore neither do creatures added to God make him more perfect.

[21] Durandus, in the first [*Sentences*], distinction 44, question 3, thinks that creatures add some perfection, not intensively but extensively. The reason for this is that numerous goods are more perfect, extensively, than fewer; but God and the world are numerous goods; therefore [they are more perfect extensively]. Confirmation: because God does not contain the perfections of all things formally, but only eminently; the perfections of creatures, however, are formally in them; therefore [creatures together with God have more perfection formally]. Add to this that otherwise God, in creating this universe of things, would have made nothing good. This opinion I regard as proved.

[22] To the first argument to the contrary [19], the response is obvious from the foregoing [21].

[23] To the second [20], I reply that the example is not relevant: for a point is completely indivisible and so it is no wonder that, when added to the line, it produces no extension; but creatures are something good, and so when added to God they can make a greater good, extensively.

[1] The first opinion is that of Gregory of
Rimini, in the second [*Sentences*], distinction 1,
question 3, articles 1 and 2, and of Gabriel Biel
and Ockham in the same place; although Ockham does
not hold this opinion so tenaciously that he cannot
also assert its contrary as probable. Following
these are Ferrariensis, in the eighth *Physics*,
question 15, John Canonicus, in the eighth *Physics*,
question 1, and many of the moderns, thinking that
the universe could have existed from eternity with
respect to both successive and permanent entities
and to corruptibles and incorruptibles. St. Thomas
seems also to incline toward this opinion in question 3 of *De potentia Dei*, and in the First Part
of the *Summa theologiae*, where he has proved that
the creation of things cannot be demonstrated.

[2] Proof of this opinion: because whatever
does not imply a contradiction can be done by God;
but that the universe should have existed from all
eternity does not imply a contradiction; therefore
[it could have existed from eternity]. Proof of
the minor: if it were to imply a contradiction it
would do so either [a] on account of God as creator, or [b] on account of the creation itself, or
[c] on account of creatures; but none of these preclude the universe's having existed from eternity;
therefore [it could have].

[3] Proof of the minor: it does not imply a
contradiction on the part of God producing [2a],
because if it were to imply this it would do so
either [a] because no produced thing can coexist
temporally with its producer; or [b] because, since
God is a free agent, he must precede his effects
by some period of time; or [c] because, if a creature were coeternal with its creator, God would not

be superior to it in all things but would be its
equal in duration. But none of these rules out
the creature's eternity; therefore [the universe
could have existed from eternity].

[4] Proof of the minor: not the first [3a]:
because in the divinity the Father truly generates
the Son, who nonetheless is coeternal with the
Father; and because philosophers grant that in natural things some efficient causes coexist temporally .with their effects. Hence St. Augustine,
proving that it is not incompatible that the Son
be coeternal with the Father in the divinity, adduces the example of brightness coming forth from
fire, for this would be coeternal with its cause
if the latter existed from eternity.

[5] You say: Aristotle, in the twelfth *Metaphysics,* text 16, teaches that the form differs
from the efficient cause in that the form exists
at the same time as that of which it is the form,
whereas the efficient cause precedes its effect;
therefore [the universe cannot be coeternal with
its efficient cause]. I reply: there Aristotle
was only contending that the form exists simultaneously with the composite, that is, is produced at
the same time as it is, whereas this is not the
case with moving causes, for otherwise they would
produce themselves, and this cannot happen. It also could be said that the form as form always exists with the composite, but not the efficient
cause as such, since sometimes it precedes its effect, and indeed for the most part; or also, that
Aristotle is speaking of causes operating through
motion, and these, since they are presupposed to
motion and motion takes place in time, must precede their effects.

[6] Not the second [3b]: because even if God
acts freely, since he is still of infinite power
he has no less power in acting than if he were to
act necessarily; but if he were to act necessarily,
he would produce the world from eternity; therefore [he can freely produce the world from eter-
nity]. Confirmation: because a free agent precedes
its effect provided the act of its will is not
simple and all at once; but the act of the divine
will is all at once, simple, and coeternal with God
himself; therefore, since in God to will and to be
powerful are the same, it follows [that he need not

temporally precede the act of his will].

[7] Not the third [3c]: because even if the creature were to exist from eternity it would still be inferior to God in duration; for God's duration would be, as it is, completely necessary and independent, whereas the duration of creatures is contingent and dependent on the divine.

[8] Nor does it imply a contradiction on the part of creation [2b]: because if it were to imply this it would do so either first, [a] because creation signifies some action that must take place at some instant, since it does not take place in eternity; but in eternal duration a first instant cannot be assigned; therefore [creation cannot be from eternity]; or second, [b] because creation is a production from nothing, with the result that the creature must first be nothing and then receive existence through creation, and so it would not be eternal. But neither of these obviates [the conclusion]; therefore [the universe could have existed from eternity].

[9] Proof of the minor: not the first [8a], because when it is maintained that the universe was created from eternity, the term creation is not understood as some action going forth from God to creatures; rather it means only a relation of the universe to God similar to the way in which, when we say that being able to laugh proceeds from [the essence of] man, we merely indicate the dependence of risibility on him as an intrinsic principle: read St. Thomas, in the First Part, question 41, article 1, reply to the second objection. Nor the second [8b], because when we say that creation takes place from nothing (*ex nihilo*) we do not mean a transition from non-existence to existence, but only the negation of matter or of a subject, in the sense that being made from nothing means being made from no pre-existing subject; and this is compatible with any creature, even an eternal one.

[10] Nor does it imply a contradiction on the part of creatures [2c]: for, if it were to imply this, it would do so [a] because either a creature has non-existence of itself or it has non-existence after existence, and this cannot be said since there are many incorruptible creatures; or it has non-existence together with existence, and this

34   implies a contradiction, as is obvious; or it has
      non-existence before existence, and so it would be
      inconsistent that a creature could have existed
      from eternity. Or second, [b] it would imply a
      contradiction because a creature receives a parti-
      cipated existence from God; but if it existed from
      eternity, that would be false; therefore [it can-
      not exist from eternity]. Yet neither of these
      obviates [the conclusion]; therefore [the universe
      could have existed from eternity]. Proof of the
      minor: not the first [10a], because when it is
      said that a creature has non-existence of itself,
      this is said because it receives existence from
      God, so that if it were abandoned by him it would
      immediately return to nothing; nor the second
      [10b], because even if the creature existed from
      eternity it would still have an existence that is
      acquired, i.e., dependent on God.

          [11] The second opinion is that of Durandus,
      in the second *Sentences*, distinction 1, who is
      followed by very many moderns; and it seems also
      to be that of St. Thomas, in the First Part, ques-
      tion 46, article 2, holding that eternity is in-
      deed incompatible with corruptible things but not
      with incorruptibles such as the heavens and intel-
      ligences.

          [12] The proof of this opinion, with respect
      to the second part, is from the argument in sup-
      port of the first opinion [2]. Proof with respect
      to the first part: first, because, if corruptibles
      could exist from eternity, it would follow that an
      infinity would have been actually traversed, again-
      st Aristotle and reason. Proof of the inference:
      because infinite days, months, years, etc., and
      infinite individuals would have been traversed.
      Even more, since the souls of men are immortal, it
      would follow that an actual infinite would exist
      and that there would be addition to it continually.

          [13] Second: another greater absurdity would
      follow, i.e., something greater than infinity would
      exist, and this to infinity. Because if the uni-
      verse existed from eternity, an infinite number of
      years would have elapsed; but the year contains
      365 days; therefore more days than years would have
      transpired, to infinity.

          [14] Third: it would follow that a creature

would exist having infinite power. Proof of the
inference: because, since an intelligence knows
all the revolutions of its sphere, if the universe
existed from eternity the intelligence would com-
prehend infinite revolutions; and so, since the infinite can only be comprehended by an infinite, it
would follow that intelligences would have infinite power of understanding.

[15] The third opinion is that of Philoponus
in the book in which he replies to the arguments
of Proclus for the eternity of the world, of [Henry
of] Ghent in the first *Quodlibet*, St. Bonaventure
in the second [*Sentences*], distinction 1, question
2, and Burley in the eighth *Physics*, in the question concerning this matter on text 15. Also, of
the Church Fathers, such as Athanasius in the second prayer against the Arians, Ambrose in the first
of the *Hexämeron*, Augustine in the book against
Felician the Arian, Damescene in the first book of
De fide orthodoxa, chapter 8, Basil, and Hilary;
again, of Augustine and Athanasius using this argument against Arius, who held that the Son of God
is a creature: no creature can be coeternal with   35
its creator; but the Son of God is coeternal with
the Father; therefore [the Son of God is not a
creature].

[16] Proof of this opinion: because, just as
it is inconceivable for a creature to have an infinite essence and power, so also infinite duration, since this is proper to God. Confirmation:
because if any creature existed from eternity it
would have being necessarily and would be completely indefectible, even to God's absolute power. For
it could either be annihilated from eternity or
not: if it could be, since it was posited as existing from eternity, it would both exist and not exist at the same time; and this implies a contradiction; if it could not be, throughout eternity
it would possess necessary existence -- for everything eternal, from the ninth *Metaphysics*, text 17,
lacks the potency of contradiction to existence
and non-existence, and this is opposed to the omnipotent power of God, on which all created things
must depend for their existence. Add to this: if
a creature could exist from eternity, there would
be no difference between its creation and its conservation; but it is certain that there is a difference between creation and conservation, both

from their different definitions and from the fact
that a particular efficient cause is not conserving; and if an efficient cause should be conserving, it differs insofar as it is efficient and insofar as it is conserving.

[17] Second: because creation is production
from nothing, and from this it follows that non-
being must necessarily precede the thing created.
Confirmation: because it is true to say of whatever
is produced that it is produced; but a creature
that is produced cannot always be being produced,
for otherwise it would have its existence successively and not permanently; nor need it be produced in time, for there is no incompatibility on the
part of its production, and so it could be produced in an instant, with the result that it would
not exist from eternity. Further confirmation:
because a creature has existence acquired from God;
therefore it obtains this after non-existence,
since one acquires what he does not possess, not
what he already possesses.

[18] The fourth opinion is that of St. Thomas,
in the third question of *De potentia*, article 14,
in the opusculum *De aeternitate mundi*, in the second book of the *Contra gentiles*, chapter 38, and in
the First Part, question 46; of Scotus in the second [*Sentences*], distinction 1, question 3; of
Ockham in *Quodlibet* 2, article 5; of the *Doctores
Parisienses* on the eighth *Physics*, question 1; of
Pererius in his [book] 15; and of others. These
think that the universe could have been made from
eternity with respect to incorruptibles, for the
reasons given above, but that with respect to corruptibles there is a problem. For, if anything
should prevent corruptibles from having existed
from eternity, the absurdities Durandus adduces
would result; but these can easily be solved by admitting that an actual infinite can exist, that an
actual infinite can have been traversed, and that
one infinite can be greater than another; therefore [the universe could have existed from eterni-
ty].

[19] I say, first: the world has not existed
36   from eternity, since our faith instructs us on
this, teaching that it was made in time. All the
arguments that are brought against this position,
of Aristotle, of Averroës, and of Proclus, once the

following two fundamentals are posited -- and they
should be unquestionable for all -- come to no result whatever. The first: God has infinite power
and therefore he can produce all created things
from nothing; the second: God is free in all his
works *ad extra*, and he can do them or not, whenever
and however he wishes.

[20] This conclusion is proved by the following arguments, which also give support to the fact
that the universe could not have existed from eternity. The first: because, since Aristotle and all
physicians agree that food and drink do not properly restore the radical humidity required for human
life, if the universe existed from eternity such a
humidity would long ago have disappeared and, as a
consequence, nutritive and generative powers.

[21] Second argument: because men decrease in
size, as is apparent to us from the Holy Scriptures
and from history. Read Pliny in book 6, chapter 6;
St. Augustine in the fifteenth *City of God*, chapter
9, where he remarks that he and many others have
seen a human tooth, a molar, of such size that it
would be equivalent to a hundred teeth of the men
who were living in his time; Nicholas of Lyra, on
Genesis; the Conciliator in difference 9; Peter
Crinitus in book 6 of *De honesta disciplina*, chapter 2; and Averroës in the second *De generatione*,
chapter 2.

[22] The third: because an infinite number of
men would result, for if such a large number as
live in our time were procreated from an individual
6748 years ago, if the world had existed from eternity without doubt an infinite multitude of men
would exist.

[23] I say, second: there is no incompatibility on God's part that the universe could have existed from eternity. The foundation of this conclusion: because God has been omnipotent from eternity, and he knew and willed the universe; therefore, as far as things are on God's part, the universe could have existed from eternity. The antecedent is admitted by all, because otherwise God
would not be immutable. Proof of the consequence:
because it is just as easy for God to produce the
universe as it is for him to think and to will,
since God produces things by thought and by will

alone; therefore [he could have produced the universe from eternity]. Nor can you say that God
could not have communicated his duration, i.e.,
eternity, to any creature, because otherwise he
would also be able to communicate infinite wisdom,
etc.; for duration, as such, does not imply a perfection; and, if God had communicated eternal duration to a creature, such a duration would never-
theless have always been dependent on the divine
duration.

37   [24] I say, third: on the creature's part,
whether this is corruptible or incorruptible, permanent or successive, it is impossible that the
universe could have existed from eternity. Proof
of this conclusion: because what is produced by
God must be produced from nothing by some transient action; but what is produced in such fashion
cannot be coeternal with the producer, as is obvious; therefore [creatures as such are not coeternal
with their creator]. Proof of the minor: because
what is produced from nothing did not exist previously; and what is produced by a transient action
cannot be eternal, since it is measured by some instant and this instant must be preceded by the duration of the producer. Since there is eternity
in God, however, it implies [a contradiction to
make him coeternal with creatures].

[25] Confirmation: because it is contradict-
ory for a proper efficient cause to exist simultaneously with its effect in the same first instant. Nor can you object with the cases of fire
and heat and of the sun and light: because the ultimate disposition of fire, which is induced with
its form, is not an effect of that form but of
whatever generates such a form; just as the light
of the sun is not the effect of the sun itself but
of the sun's generator. Add to this: creatures
have no common specific measure with God, nor are
they the same as he is; from this it results that
they cannot coexist with him -- for in the Divine
Persons the Son coexists with the Father, and the
Holy Spirit with both, because, since they are one
in essence, the Father's eternity is the measure
of all.

[26] Second: for otherwise it would follow,
if the universe were posited as existing from
eternity, that the universe came forth from God

necessarily; for no instant could be indicated
wherein the universe did not exist simultaneously
with God, as is obvious from the above. Confirmation: because if the universe were produced through
emanation, whenever it emanated the sun came to exist either in the east or west or south or north,
or in all places at once, or in none. The second
and third cannot be said, as is obvious on considering them; therefore, the first. But if you say
that it was in any part, I counter: either it existed there immobile for an eternal time, and this
cannot be said, because it would have been at rest
there violently over an infinite time; or it immediately began to move toward another part from
eternity. And if it began to move immediately, I
counter: either it moved over an infinite time before it arrived at that part to which it was moving; or, in a finite time. Not the first: because
an infinite number of revolutions would have been
made in an infinite time; therefore the second:
but if so, it neither was made, nor could it be
made, from eternity; therefore [the universe was
not produced from eternity]. And this argument can
be applied to all mobile entities.

[27] To the objections [1-18], the reply is
apparent from the foregoing.

Treatise on the Heavens

[1] The first opinion was that of certain ancient philosophers, whom St. [John] Chrysostom and
some moderns follow, holding that there is only one
heaven. Proof of this opinion: all of our knowledge arises from the senses; yet, when we raise
our eyes to heaven we do not perceive several heavens, for the sun and the other stars appear to be
in one heaven; therefore [there is only one heav-
en]. Nor do the heavens fall under any sense other
than sight.

[2] The second opinion is that of the Egyptians, the Chaldeans, and other astronomers up to
the time of Plato and Aristotle, who admitted at
least eight heavens because of the eight motions
they observed in the stars. For they noted that
the sun, moon, and other stars move continuously
from east to west; but these bodies are not always
in conjunction and disjunction at the same distance, as is apparent with the moon and the sun,
which are in conjunction at new moon but in diamet-
rical opposition at full moon; therefore there must
be a variety of motions in the heavens, and, as a
consequence, as many heavens as there are distinct
motions, since each heavenly body should have only
a single motion.

[3] There are eight such motions, for, since
all the fixed stars always progress uniformly with
the same ordering, as is apparent from reading

Ptolemy, diction 7, and the *Epitome* of John Regiomontanus, diction 7, such stars may be assigned to
a single heaven as being carried along by its motion. For the stars that we call "errant," however, since these do not maintain the same distance
among themselves nor do they keep the same arrangement with the fixed stars, there must be seven
spheres whose movements account for their motions.
Thus they wish to have eight heavens in the universe.

[4] The third opinion was that of Arsatilis
and Timocharis, who lived 330 years before Christ,
and, observing the course of the stars at Alexandria, discovered that the stars of the firmament,
which antiquity thought to be the *primum mobile,*
were carried by an extremely slow motion from west
39   to east and not merely by the daily motion from
east to west, as the ancients thought. So they
posited a ninth heaven, though they left us nothing certain concerning its motion because of its
extreme slowness. Hipparchus followed them almost
two hundred years later, and then others, who, comparing their observations with those of their pre-
decessors, observed the aforesaid motion even more
closely. After 170 years had passed, Agrias in
Bithynia, Milaeus a geometer in Rome, and last of
all Ptolemy in A.D. 131 observed the same motion
much more precisely. And from the fact that a
simple body cannot move with two contrary motions,
i.e., a motion from rising to setting (which all
heavenly bodies have in common with the fixed
stars) and a motion from setting to rising, they
inferred that there must be another ninth heaven,
which moves within the space of twenty four hours
from rising to setting, and carries the eighth
heaven with it; with the result that the eighth
moves with its own motion but at the same time is
moved ever so slowly from setting to rising. John
of Sacrobosco follows this opinion in his *Sphaera.*

[5] The fourth opinion is that of Thebit, who
lived 1140 years after Ptolemy, of Alphonsus the
king of Spain, who lived in A.D. 1250, of George
Peurbach, John Regiomontanus, and others, who,
finding the fixed stars to have apart from the two
motions already explained an additional third one
that they called accession and recession, added to
the nine heavens yet a tenth. Their reason was
this: since a simple body can have only a single

motion, the ninth heaven cannot be the *primum mobile*; so beyond this there must be another heaven
that has a proper diurnal motion from east to west
and carries with it all of the lower spheres, including the firmament of the fixed stars, within a
space of twenty four hours; the ninth heaven then
has its proper motion from west to east, revolving
around the eighth heaven and all of the lower
spheres; and finally the eighth heaven, which carries the fixed stars, moves with its own proper
motion, the accession and recession which those
cited had discovered.

[6] The sacred writings and many theologians
are favorable to this opinion, since in the Holy
Scriptures one reads that God placed a firmament
dividing the waters from the waters, and in Psalm
148 it is said: "And all the waters that are above
the heavens." And these expressions, as many theo-   40
logians interpret them, refer to the ninth heaven;
or better, to a combination of the ninth and the
tenth, because of its transparency, since it has no
parts that are denser as do other spheres like
those of the stars, and so it is rightly referred
to as "waters"; on which account it is also called
"glacial" by some theologians and "crystalline" by
others.

[7] To one inquiring how the motion of the
eighth heaven was discovered -- and astronomers
call this the motion of trepidation -- they reply
in this fashion. Astronomers observed that the
fixed stars go from west to east at an unequal
rate; for at one time they were seen to move more
slowly in the zodiac, at another more rapidly, and
at another not at all; sometimes they even go back-
wards because of their diurnal motion, and nonetheless they keep the same distance from the center.
For this reason they maintained that the stars move
from north to south and back again; for the entire
inequality in the motion of the fixed stars is accounted for by this movement, as is easily confirmed with an instrument made to observe this. Astronomers also thought this to be the reason why
there are so many opinions of the motion of the
fixed stars and of the quantity or period of their
motion from west to east. Again they observed that
the sun had different maximum declinations at different times: and for this they could assign no
cause apart from the motion of trepidation; but

when this had been posited, it followed that the
eighth sphere would at one time go from north to
south, at another from south to north, and as a
consequence the two tropics in the solar orb would
be closer at one time to the equinox, farther away
at another. Finally they observed that the equinox had occurred before the sun arrived in Aries or
in Libra, and occasionally even after it had passed
the beginning of Aries or Libra; for the same reason the solstices had occurred even when the sun
had not been at the beginning of Cancer or of Capricorn. Since, therefore, the sun must be in the
equinoctial if an equinox is to occur, and again
in the tropics if there are to be solstices, no
other cause for this diversity can be adduced except the motion of trepidation, for this alone permits such an anticipation of the equinoxes and of
the solstices. Note here that all seven globes of
the planets move with the same motion also, such
that all of them accompany the zodiac exactly.

[8] The fifth opinion is that of Strabo, of
the Venerable Bede, and of all the theologians,
who beyond the ten movable heavens posited an elev-
41   enth immovable one also. They named this the "empyrean" heaven from fire, which is most lucid, and
they regarded it as the seat of the angels and of
the blessed; they acknowledged that it was not
known to astronomers, however, since it does not
move.

[9] Yet, others were not lacking who tried to
prove its existence from experiences of various
types. For, as Pliny testifies in book 8, chapter
16, in Europe between the Achelous and Nestus rivers lions are bred that are stronger by far than
those born in Africa and Syria. Now, since this
does not happen throughout the entire tract of land
from east to west where the aforesaid rivers are
situated, their birth can only be accounted for by
an influence from some immovable heaven; for if
they were born under the influence of the stars or
the planets, such lions would be bred throughout
the entire tract of land, because of the continuous movement of the stars and their influence.
Again, in Hungary, at a latitude of forty-seven degrees, horses are born that are extremely speedy
and strong, and these are not bred in other regions. Finally, in Mauritania large numbers of apes
are produced.

[10] Philosophers reply that this diversity
of effects in the same climate depends entirely on
different dispositions of the earth. But, to the
contrary: the earth is so disposed by the differing orientations of the stars; therefore [the conclusion still stands]. For sometimes all parts of
the same climate successively have the same orientations with respect to the movable heavens and
stars.

[11] We maintain that there are ten movable
heavens, and, beyond these, that there is an eleventh immovable heaven. The second part of the
conclusion is apparent from the common opinion of
theologians. Proof of the first part: the number
of celestial spheres is to be calculated from the
diversity of motions, since we have no other means
of investigating it; but there are ten proper and
diverse motions in the heavenly bodies; therefore
[there are ten movable heavens].

[12] Proof of the minor: the tenth heaven,
which also is called the *primum mobile*, progress-
ing with a uniform regular and extremely rapid motion about the poles of the world and through the
equinoctial circle, completes its revolution from
east to west in the space of one natural day, that
is, of twenty four equinoctial hours. Its impetus
is so great that it carries all the lower spheres
along with it, and without doubt causes them to
revolve with a velocity equal to that of its own
rotation, although they might retrogress a small
amount by their own proper motions, since they en-
counter no resistance. Indeed it carries along
with it the entire sphere of fire and a great part
of the air, and, according to the opinion of some,
a good part of the ocean.

[13] The ninth heaven, apart from the motion
of the *primum mobile* communicated to it, progresses   42
by its own motion, though much more slowly, from
setting to rising; and according to the Alfonsine
Tables it completes its entire course through the
zodiac in a space of 49000 years. This interval
of time is customarily called the Platonic Year,
for Plato thought that in this period of time all
the stars would return to the same position; according to others, whatever is now taking place in the
universe will reoccur in the same order as now observed. But this is said gratuitously: for, since

it is commonly agreed that the motions of the heavens are not commensurable, it can never happen that all of the stars will have the same arrangement and ordering as they now have or did have at one time. According to Ptolemy the ninth sphere completes its course through the zodiac in a space of 36000 years; according to Albatenius, in a space of 23760 years. Whatever the number may be, this much is certain, that the ninth heaven moves from west to east with a very slow motion and carries with it the eight inferior spheres, but not the *primum mobile;* for, as all astronomers agree, each superior sphere carries along with it the inferior sphere that is concentric and contiguous with it, but not the superior.

[14] The eighth heaven, the firmament, apart from the two motions impressed on it by its superior spheres, revolves with its own proper and peculiar motion, and this motion many call accession and recession, or trepidation. Such a motion takes place around the beginnings of Aries and Libra of the ninth sphere, as poles; for the beginnings of Aries and Libra of the eighth sphere describe rather small circles whose radii measure four degrees, and this is the amount by which the beginnings of Aries and Libra of the eighth sphere are distant from the beginnings of Aries and Libra of the ninth sphere, as Alfonsus teaches. From this motion of the beginnings of Aries and Libra of the eighth sphere around the beginnings of Aries and Libra of the ninth sphere it follows that no other point of the eighth heaven completes a perfect circle, but each wobbles a little -- it goes at one time toward the arctic pole, at another toward the antarctic. The period of the resulting motion, according to the mathematicians, occupies a space of 7000 years; and this motion carries along with it the spheres of all the planets, since they are concentric with the eighth sphere.

[15] The orb of Saturn has, apart from the three aforesaid motions that it shares with all of the inferior spheres, its own proper motion, which it completes from west to east in about thirty years.

[16] Jupiter also has its motion from west to east, which it completes in a space of twelve years; Mars likewise its motion from west to east,

43

which it completes in about two years.

[17] The sun completes its proper motion in 365 days, 5 hours, 49 minutes, and 15 seconds; and this interval is called a solar year. From this it is apparent that, as Clavius correctly notes in his *Sphaera*, "the year does not contain exactly 365 days and 6 hours," for it misses this by about 11 minutes. And this teaching is taken from Alfonsus, for Ptolemy found a greater quantity for the year, and Albatenius a lesser; Copernicus regards it as equal to the year of Ptolemy, but almost all astronomers think it unequal.

[18] Venus and Mercury complete their orbits in almost the same time as the sun. For while the sun on any day is traversing 59 minutes, 8 seconds, 19 thirds, 37 fourths, Venus also is traversing 59 minutes, 8 seconds, 19 thirds, approximately; Mercury does almost the same each day.

[19] The moon, finally, completes its circuit from west to east in 27 days and approximately 8 hours; thus it takes about two days to catch up with the sun. For, since the sun traverses almost 27 degrees in 27 days and 8 hours, and the moon covers the same degrees in about two days, 29 days and about 12 hours must elapse between conjunctions of the moon with the sun, and this interval is called the lunar month.

[20] From all of this, since there are ten proper motions in the heavens, there must also be ten spheres.

[21] But note here, first: what we say of the periods of the planetary motions is to be understood not of spheres or of entire heavens, but only of proper spheres that carry planets. I hold these for certain to be eccentric from the center of the heavens, since otherwise many appearances could not be saved, as the mathematicians abundantly demonstrate in their Theories of the Planets; for all the planetary spheres move from west to east with exactly the same speed as the ninth heaven.

[22] Note, second: although all inferior and total spheres also have a motion of trepidation, no inferior planet is carried along with the proper motion of a superior planet, because their proper

translations are not around the same center.

[23] Note, third: the nine spheres that are
below the *primum mobile* would complete their orbits
in exactly the same times as they now complete
them, and not faster, even if the *primum mobile* did
not move or were not to carry them along with it
from east to west. An example illustrating this
would be the shipmaster whose proper motion is con-
44   trary to the motion of the ship. Indeed they would
then be carried from west to east absolutely, for
there would be no instant after any other at which
they would not recede more from the west and approach the east; so also the sailor, if the ship
were to remain at rest, would reach the ship's
stern in the same time. And [the movement would
be] to the east absolutely, not merely in an eastern direction.

[24] You inquire here how it has been ascertained that the heavens move from east to west, and
again from west to east. I reply, first: the initial motion from rising to setting was discovered
in this way. Astronomers saw that the sun, the
moon, and all the other stars gradually rise in the
east and are elevated above the horizon until they
come to the meridian, and then they set to the
west, until they again are found in the east; from
this they concluded that the motion of the heavens
is from east to west.

[25] They gather that such a motion is made
from the east absolutely, first, from the shadows
of bodies: for from the rising of the sun up to the
meridian all shadows projected on the horizontal
decrease continually until they become smallest at
noon; then from noon to the sun's setting they increase again; and this could not happen if the sun
were not moving along from rising to setting. The
same conclusion is reached concerning the moon: for
its shadows decrease continually while it moves from
rising to the meridian, and they increase again
when it departs from the meridian toward setting.
Second: from the altitudes of the stars, which always increase from the stars' rising until they arrive at the meridian, where they attain maximum altitude; they then undergo a decrease of altitude
from the meridian to their setting. This certainly
indicates that they move absolutely away from the
east and toward the west.

[26] I reply, second: the relative motion from setting to rising was discovered in this way. Astronomers observing the seven planets, as is gathered from John Regiomontanus in the *Epitome* of Ptolemy's *Almagest*, noted that the sun, the moon, and the other planets do not always keep the same distance from each other and the same arrangement; this is obvious in the case of the moon, which at one time is in conjunction with the sun and at another goes into disjunction toward the eastern regions, and in the case of other planets, not only among themselves but also in relation to the fixed stars, for at one time they are in conjunction with a particular fixed star, at another they depart in disjunction toward the eastern regions. From this they gather that the seven spheres of the planets have, in addition to the motion from east to west, a motion from setting to rising, and thus undergo a kind of retrograde movement also.

[27] You wish to know what is to be said concerning the eighth heaven. I reply: although practically all the ancients before Aristotle believed that the starry heavens move only from east to west because the fixed stars maintain the same distance and arrangement, and although they thought that their places of rising and setting in the east were always the same because of the small period of time over which they observed these, nonetheless after Aristotle things were found to be different by the mathematicians. For as Ptolemy states in diction 7, chapter 2, and John Regiomontanus in the *Epitome* of the same diction, second proposition, the distance of the fixed stars from the solstices and the equinoctial points do not always remain the same, but following the succession of the signs [of the zodiac] increases gradually toward the eastern regions. Thus the fixed stars that in ancient times were located before the solsticial and equinoctial points, as is apparent from a comparison of the observations of the ancients and the moderns, are now found after the solsticial and equinoctial points -- read Ptolemy and Regiomontanus in the places cited above. From this one may gather that the eighth heaven also moves from east to west.

[28] To give an example of what we have said taken from the cited authors, note: Timocharis, observing the course of the stars, located the star Azimet, which the Latins refer to as Spica Virginis,

45

before the point of the autumnal equinox, that is,
before the beginning of Libra of the *primum mobile*
by almost 8 degrees, that is, in 23 degrees of
Virgo; then, when two hundred years had elapsed,
Hipparchus found the same star only 6 degrees before that point, namely in the first 25 degrees of
Virgo. After these, Ptolemy found that the same
star had moved further in proportion to the time
intervening, and the same was observed by Albatenius, Avenestra, and Zacut. Now the astronomers of
our own time find that this same star is already
past the beginning of Libra, indeed, practically
in 17 degrees of Libra.

[29] You inquire, second, whether all the inferior spheres, moving as they do from setting to
rising, rotate on poles different from the poles
of the world. I reply in the affirmative. For,
as astronomers observe, they move not only through
the equinoctial circle but also around the poles
of the zodiac and through the zodiacal circle,
since all the planets continually vary their points
of rising and setting on the same horizon. This
is apparent with the sun, which rises at one time
exactly on the equinoctial, at another time on the
far side of it, and at yet another on the near
side. Such a variation would not exist if it moved
46   from west to east on the poles of the world, as is
apparent, for then it would always arise at the
same point on the horizon, just as the parallels
of the equator, wherein the sun necessarily rises
and moves in its daily motion, always intersect the
horizon at the same points. And what has been observed of the sun is true also of the other planets.

[30] Second: astronomers observe that the
planets do not always keep the same distance from
the poles of the world, but at one time approach
the arctic, at another the antarctic. And this
arises from the fact that they do not always have
the same meridian altitude: for the sun has a maximum in the tropic of Cancer, a minimum in the tropic of Capricorn; this is apparent from the noontime
shadow of any sundial, which is shortest when the
sun is in Cancer, longest when it is in Capricorn.
And from the various altitudes of the sun and other
planets, astronomers gathered that the planets move
from setting to rising around the poles of the
world -- the more so when they saw that this varia-

tion in the motion of the planets always falls
within the same limits, and that they are carried
around in a circle whose maximum declination from
the equinoctial is twenty three and a half degrees. From this it necessarily follows that the
poles of this circle are distant from the poles of
the world by the same number of degrees, and consequently that the motion of the planets takes
place around the zodiacal poles and along the zodiacal circle. Thus much concerning the seven
planets.

[31] Concerning the eighth sphere, then, what
is to be said? Note that it tends from west to
east, and that this was discovered to take place
around poles different from those of the world by
the same astronomers for the same reasons; for,
since the stars did not always rise in the same
places as they now rise with respect to the same
horizon, nor are their meridian altitudes the same
as those that were observed in times past, it
plainly follows that they do not progress from setting to rising around the poles of the world.
Moreover, as Ptolemy correctly observes in diction
7, chapter 3, and Regiomontanus in the *Epitome* of
the same diction, and as they also prove, the fixed
stars do not always keep the same distance with
respect to the equinox; for the southern declinations of the fixed stars that are in the middle of
the sphere that extends from the beginning of Capricorn through Aries to the beginning of Cancer
are decreased, whereas the northern are increased;
on the other hand, for those stars that are in the
other half of the sphere contained between the beginning of Cancer through Libra up to the beginning of Capricorn, the southern declinations are
increased and the northern decreased. Note that
here by southern declination I mean the declination
a star has when it moves away from the equinox toward the antarctic poles, and by northern, the dec-   47
lination a star has when it moves from the equinox
toward the arctic.

[32] To one inquiring how the maximum difference of declination in the fixed stars is ascertained, I reply: from their greater propinquity to
the beginning of Aries and of Libra on the *primum
mobile;* just as, on the other hand, the minimal
difference is known from their greater propinquity
to the beginning of Cancer and to the beginning of

Capricorn. For a better understanding of what we
have said we provide an example. The star that is
called Oculus of Taurus at the time of Timocharis
departed from the equinoctial toward the north by
8 1/2 degrees; at the time of Hipparchus, by 9 degrees, 45 minutes; at the time of Ptolemy, by almost 11 degrees; in our own time, by about 16 degrees. From these data it is apparent that this
star has taken on a greater increment of northern
declination, since it is in the center of the
sphere that goes from the beginning of Capricorn
through Aries to the beginning of Cancer. The same
conclusion is drawn concerning the other stars, and
so on.

[33] To the argument of the first opinion [1],
one may reply: it is indeed true, while we are in
this mortal life, that our science arises from our
senses; but it is not true that a plurality of
heavens cannot be perceived by the senses. For,
although we perceive neither the number nor the
unity of the heavens by sight, we do perceive that
many stars move with opposing motions. From the
number of these we calculate the number of heavenly bodies; because the stars cannot move the way
birds move in the air, as some have poorly reason-
ed, since they move with the motion of their
spheres; and because no other reason can be assigned why they move with motions that are opposed
to each other.

[34] To Aristotle [2], on the other hand, we
reply with him in the twelfth *Metaphysics* that astronomers are to be consulted in astronomical matters. Nor can you say, with Aristotle in the same
book, chapter 8, that the celestial spheres exist
for the motion of the stars, and therefore that
there are only eight heavens, since [there are only
eight heavenly bodies]. For, although there are no
stars in the ninth and tenth heavens, the motion of
those heavens has an effect on some of the motions
of the stars. Apart from this, the assumption itself can be denied.

[H] Second Question.   On the Order of the Heavenly
                       Orbs

[1] Aristarchus, forty years before Ptolemy,
whom Nicholas Copernicus among the moderns has followed in his work *On the Revolution of the Heavenly*   48
Spheres, established this ordering: that the sun
is located in the middle of the universe; and
around this, the orb of Mercury; around that, the
orb of Venus; around this, a great orb containing
the earth with the elements and the moon; around
this, the orb of Mars; then the heaven of Jupiter;
after that the globe of Saturn; and finally the
firmament.

[2] This opinion is opposed to the common
teaching of philosophers and astronomers, and to
reasoning establishing that the earth is in the
center of the universe.

[3] First: because, from Averroës in the second *De caelo* and from Ptolemy, diction 1, chapter
5, if the earth were not situated in the middle of
the universe eclipses of the moon would occur not
only when the two luminous bodies were diametrically opposed but even when they were not located at
opposite positions on the zodiac.   This is contrary
to the experience of astronomers, who teach that
eclipses always occur when the moon is in opposition to the sun, and never when it is not.

[4] Confirmation: because, if the earth were
located in the middle of the universe, for an e-
clipse to occur the two luminaries would have to
be in opposition to permit the interposition of the
earth; similarly, if the earth were located off
from the center, an eclipse could not occur, since
there would be no interposition of the earth.   In
fact, an eclipse would happen generally when the
moon was at the greatest distance from the sun, for

then it would have a minimum of light.

[5] Second: because, from Regiomontanus in the *Epitome*, book 1, conclusion 3, and from Aristotle in the second *De caelo*, all heavy objects that fall freely along a diameter of the universe intersect the surface of the earth at equal angles no matter from what part of the sphere they descend; therefore they tend to the center of the earth, for otherwise they would not approach the surface of the earth at equal angles. As a result, since the diameters of the universe along which heavy objects fall pass through the center of the universe and intersect each other there, the center of the earth and that of the universe must be the same.

[6] Third: because, following Aristotle, earth is the heaviest body and so should tend to the lowest place; moreover, it should also be the most distant from the heavens and so can be located nowhere else than in the center of the universe.

[7] Confirmation: since earth is the least noble body of all, by right it should be located in the center, lest the remaining bodies suffer harm by reason of their closeness to it, and because in this way its imperfections can be supplemented better and more suitably through the influence of other bodies.

[8] Fourth: because, from Alfraganus in difference 4 and from John of Sacrobosco in his *Sphaera*, if all the vapors, clouds, and exhalations that can impede our vision were taken away, and if we were placed anywhere on the surface of the earth, the stars would always appear of the same size whether they were rising or setting or in the middle of the heavens. This could not happen unless the earth were in the middle of the universe, equally distant from all parts of the heavens.

[9] Fifth, from Sacrobosco in the same place: for a man situated any place on earth six signs of the zodiac are always rising and six are always setting, as Ptolemy correctly teaches, diction 1, chapters 5 and 6, and Alfraganus, difference 4, and other astronomers. This could not happen unless the earth were situated in the center of the universe.

[10] Sixth, from Ptolemy as cited above: if
the earth were not situated at the center of the
universe, either [a] it would be in the plane of
the equinoctial circle but not on the axis of the
universe (for if it were on the axis of the universe and in the plane of the equator, it would be
situated in the center); or [b] it would be on the
axis of the universe but not in the plane of the
equinoctial circle; or finally [c] it would be
neither in the equinoctial plane nor on the axis
of the universe. But none of these can be said.
[Therefore the earth must be at the center of the
universe.]

[11] Proof of the minor: not the first [10a],
for otherwise an equinox would never occur in the
right sphere, nor even in the oblique sphere; or
an equinox would never occur at all; or, it would
not take place at the midpoint between the summer
and winter solstices. Moreover, in the same right
sphere one would not see half of the heavens; nor
would stars of equal magnitude be observed; nor
would there be an horizon dividing the heavens into equal parts; nor, finally, would the excess of
the longest day over the equinoctial day be equal
to the corresponding defect of the shortest day.
All these consequences the mathematicians prove
are in conflict with daily experience.

[12] Not the second [10b], for otherwise no
horizon other than the right horizon would cut the
heavens into equal parts, and as a consquence neither would the zodiac; but this conflicts with experience, since half of the zodiac, i.e., six
signs, are always to be seen above and below the
horizon. Again: an equinox would occur in the
right sphere, for only the right horizon would divide the equator into equal parts. Third: because
the sequence and ratios of increase and decrease
of days and nights would be mixed up, and the days
would not be equal to the nights twice a year.
Fourth: because the shadows of gnomons that stand
perpendicular to the horizon would not be projected on one and the same straight line from east to
west at the time of the equinoxes. Fifth: because
two signs of the zodiac would never be seen through
a diopter to be diametrically opposed; and this is
contrary to experience, which teaches us that the
rising and setting of the sun in the equinoxes can
be seen through a diopter to lie along a single

50 straight line, just as do its rising in the summer solstice and its setting in the winter solstice; and again, its rising in the winter solstice and its setting in the summer, through a diopter along the straight line corresponding to it on the particular horizon.

[13] Nor the third [10c], because for a similar reason we would fall into all the foregoing absurdities: for there would never be an equinox in the right sphere, and in the oblique sphere there would be one only when an horizon passing through the center of the universe divided the sphere into equal parts; the entire sequence in the decreasing and increasing of days and nights would be mixed up, and so forth.

[14] The Egyptians, whom Plato followed in the *Timaeus*, and Aristotle in the second *De caelo*, chapter 12, and in the first *Meteors*, chapter 4, think that the following order is to be found in the heavenly spheres: that the moon should occupy the lowest place, that the sun follows this, that Mercury comes after the sun, then Venus, fifth Mars, sixth Jupiter, seventh Saturn, and last the eighth sphere. This opinion conflicts both with the astronomers and with reason: for Ptolemy, Regiomontanus, Sacrobosco, and others hold that the moon indeed occupies the lowest place, but above it they put Mercury, then Venus, then the sun, beyond this Mars, then Jupiter, then Saturn, then the eighth, ninth, and tenth spheres and the empyrean heaven. It is true, however, that Aristotle, in the little book *De mundo ad Alexandrum*, puts Venus immediately above the sun and below Mercury.

[15] Proof of the ordering that astronomers give for the heavenly spheres, from which will follow the refutation of the Egyptians' ordering, and also of that conjectured by Metrodorus and Crates, who regarded the sun and the moon as the highest planets; of Democritus, who put Mercury higher than the sun; and lastly of Alpetragius, who thought that Venus was higher than the sun.

[16] First: the first opinion, that the moon holds the lowest place among the planets and that the eighth sphere is the highest of all, is proved from the eclipses or occultations of the planets. For any star is lower if it hides another star from

us; but the moon, when in conjunction with other
planets, blocks out our view of them; therefore it
lies below them. By similar reasoning one can formulate arguments for Mercury in relation to Venus,
for Venus in relation to Mars, and so on.

[17] Confirmation: the more a luminous body
is remote from the earth, all other things being
equal, the smaller shadows it will cast on the
plane of the horizon; the closer it is, on the other hand, the longer the shadows. But the moon when
at the same angle from the horizon as the sun, but
at a different time, throws longer shadows, as is   51
apparent; therefore [the moon is closer than the
sun].

[18] What we have said concerning the moon
with respect to the sun, moreover, can be applied
to the other planets; for although these do not
shine with sufficient brightness to throw shadows,
one can measure the angle at which their rays are
projected through the vertex of the gnomon.

[19] Second proof that Mercury comes immediately after the moon, that Venus comes after Mercury, and that the sun comes after Venus: a star
is closest to the earth when, all other things being equal, it has a greater diversity of aspect.
(For me a diversity of aspect -- others refer to
it as an aspect of diversity -- is the difference
between the true and the apparent position of a
star. The true position of a star is defined as
the point on the great circle passing through the
vertex of the head and the star at which a straight
line drawn from the center of the earth through the
center of the star intersects that circle. The
apparent position of a star, on the other hand, is
the point on the same great circle at which a
straight line drawn from the eye through the center
of the star intersects the great circle.) But the
moon has the greatest diversity of aspect; after
the moon, then Mercury; after Mercury, Venus; and
after Venus, the sun, as the mathematicians clearly
prove; therefore [they are closer in this order].

[20] You say: what of the other planets? I
reply: nothing certain can be determined about them
by this method, since they have no diversity of aspect because of their very great distance from the
earth. In particular, however, it is apparent that

Mercury is above the moon and below Venus -- and
concerning this there used to be some doubt -- because its motion is more irregular than that of
Venus. This is why astronomers assign five orbs
and an epicycle to Mercury and only three orbs and
an epicycle to Venus.

[21] Third proof that the ordering of the
spheres given by us is correct: from the veloci-
ties of their motions. For the more a heaven is
removed from the nature and condition of the *primum
mobile* the lower the position at which it should be
put; but of all the planets the moon travels with
greatest velocity from setting to rising, as is apparent from the foregoing, and after the moon,
Mercury, and so on, following the order of the
spheres just given. It should be noted here, however, that from this method nothing certain can be
stated concerning the ordering of the sun, Venus,
and Mercury, although these are known to lie above
the orb of the moon, since they complete their motions from west to east in about the same time.
Hence Alpetragius, as Regiomontanus attests in book
9 of the *Epitome,* proposition 1, contends that the
heaven of Venus is placed under Mars, and under
this heaven the sun, then Mercury, and finally the
moon; for the reason that Venus, by reason of the
epicycle, is slower than Mercury, and the moon completes its course the most rapidly.

[22] That the sun, moreover, should be placed
in the middle of the planets, and that the assigned
ordering of the heavenly spheres is correct, is
52   proved from Regiomontanus, cited above, and from
Ptolemy, diction 5, chapter 15; Albatenius does not
differ from Ptolemy in chapter 50 of his work. [The
proof:] because the distance of the sun from the
center of the earth when at its minimum, that is,
when the sun is opposite apogee, is 1070 semi-diameters of the earth; but the distance of the moon
when at its maximum, that is, when it is in apogee,
is 64 semi-diameters. From this it is apparent
that the difference between the minimum distance
of the sun and the maximum distance of the moon is
1006 semi-diameters, as is obvious. But it cannot
be admitted that a vacuum, to which nature is generally abhorrent, exists between the heaven of the
sun and that of the moon; nor is it reasonable that
the deferents of the apogees of the sun and the
moon be so large in size, for such a size would be

vain and superfluous. Thus it is with good reason
that an intermediate space is attributed only to
the orbs of Mercury and of Venus, and therefore
that the sun must be in the middle of the planets.

[23] The same result is confirmed from the
fact that the motion of the sun is the rule and
measure of the motion of all the other planets,
for one or another reason. For Mars, Jupiter, and
Saturn have an epicycle in common with the motion
of the sun; Mercury and Venus, on the other hand,
share with the motion of the sun the deferents of
their spheres, as mathematicians explain fully in
their Theories of the Planets. From this it follows that the sun should be located in their midst, so that it separates the three superior planets
from the inferior, even though they do not have
motions common to it, for the same reason.

[24] Second proof of the same: from the fact
that the sun is the king and so to say the heart
of all the planets, and for this it is fitting that
it be placed in their midst. For the king lives
in the center of the kingdom and the heart is in
the center of animals, so that they can provide
equally therefrom for all the people and for the
members.

[25] Confirmation: because, according to astronomers and philosophers, all stars and planets
receive their light from the sun, at least in the
more perfect way. This is manifest in the eclipse
of the moon during which the moon, on entering the
shadow of the earth, loses its light, and is illuminated differently at different times. The same
judgment is made concerning the other stars that
are of the same nature as the moon.

[26] Confirmation from the planets: these,
when closest to the sun, are more brilliantly illuminated, as is apparent with Mars and Venus.

[27] From all these results it is apparent
that the sun should be situated in the center.
Writers allude to this when they make a republic
out of the seven planets: for they put the sun as
the king in the center, make Saturn a counsellor
for its old age, Jupiter a judge for its magnani-
mity, Mars a leader of the military, Venus the dis-
penser of good, Mercury his scribe, and finally

53 the moon filling the office of messenger, since it
moves most swiftly from setting to rising so that
it can carry the commands of the king to any one
in a single month.

[28] Third proof of the same: from Albumasar
in his *Magnum introductorium*, tract 3, difference
3, because the sun, being the most noble and most
active of the planets, should be located in the
center. Otherwise, if it were placed above, it
could not easily act on those below; if placed below, on the other hand, it could not readily communicate its power to those below, for not only
would it move too slowly because of its distance
from the *primum mobile*, but its heat would be lacking also; correctly, therefore, [is it said that
the sun is in the center]. To this Phoebus al-
ludes, from Ovid, second *Metamorphoses*, when he ad-
monishes his son Phaeton to mount the chariot of
the sun: "Higher going, the heavenly signs you will
burn."

[29] Fourth proof: from the ancient origina-
tors of the days of the week, who named the days
after the planets from the fact that each has do-
minion during the first hour of its day. For the
individual planets are said to take precedence
with a certain order at the various hours of the
day; therefore, since the day contains twenty four
hours, if on Saturday the first hour is dominated
by Saturn, for which it is named, on the next day
the first hour will be dominated by a planet in
the reverse order with two omitted, namely, the
sun, for which Sunday is named. For if the first
hour of Saturday is dominated by Saturn, the second will be dominated by Jupiter, the third by
Mars, the fourth by the sun, the fifth by Venus,
the sixth by Mercury, the seventh by the moon, the
eighth by Saturn, the ninth by Jupiter, the tenth
by Mars, the eleventh by the sun, the twelfth by
Venus, the thirteenth by Mercury, the fourteenth
by the moon, the fifteenth by Saturn, the sixteenth
by Jupiter, the seventeenth by Mars, the eighteenth
by the sun, the nineteenth by Venus, the twentieth
by Mercury, the twenty first by the moon, the twenty second by Saturn, the twenty third by Jupiter,
the twenty fourth by Mars; the first hour of the
second day by the sun, and so on. From this is apparent why the days are not named after the planets
according to their order directly, but always in

the reverse order with two omitted, because it is
in this order that they preside over the hours of
the days; nor would this order be such if the planets were not placed in the exact order we have
given. Concerning this matter there are two verses
that enable one to know at what hours of the day
each planet is dominant, and in this the ordering
they have among themselves is also apparent:

> Cynthia, Mercury, Venus, and the sun,
>   Mars, Jupiter, Saturn,
> In the reverse order will claim for
>   themselves each of the hours.

[30] You object: the sun cannot be in the
midst of the planets since it never suffers an e-
clipse from Mercury or from Venus, and therefore
it is not above them; for otherwise it would be
hidden by them as it is hidden by the moon.

[31] I reply, with Ptolemy, diction 9, chapter
1, and Regiomontanus, book 9, proposition 1: two
planets can be conjoined, that is, be at the same
degree of the zodiac, in such a way that a straight
line going from the eye and passing through the
center of one will not pass through the center of
the other, and this is required for an eclipse to
occur. Thus it happens that very frequently we see
the moon, when new, to be conjoined with the sun
and yet not eclipsing it. Add to this: according
to Albatenius, Thebit, and other astronomers, the
visual diameter of the sun has a tenfold ratio to
the visual diameter of Venus (these are the visual
diameters of the circles that the stars appear to
have for us). So it happens that the visual diameter of the sun, according to geometrical demonstrations, has a hundredfold ratio to the visual
circle of Venus. For since circles are in the same
ratios as the squares of their diameters, and the
ratios of squares described on the diameters of
circles are as squares of the ratios between the
diameters, the result is that the visual diameters
of the circles of the sun and Venus are in a tenfold ratio, and the squared diameters and therefore
the visual circles are in a hundredfold ratio --
since the latter is the square of the former, as is
apparent in the numbers 1-10-100, which have a tenfold ratio. (So as to know readily when any ratio
is the square of another, simply multiply the denominator of the ratio by itself; thus one can know

54

that, since the denominator of a tenfold ratio is ten, when 10 is multipled by 10, the number 100 results, and this is the denominator of the squared ratio of ten itself.) From this it should be apparent that Venus cannot cover the sun in any way, even if it were interposed between our sight and the sun, for it would cover only a hundredth part of that body, and this would hardly be noticed by us. *A fortiori* neither can Mercury hide the sun, since its diameter is much smaller than the visual diameter of Venus.

[32] You say: why then can the moon, being much smaller than the sun, occasionally eclipse it totally? I reply: this happens from the moon's being very near the earth and very far from the sun; so the visual diameter of the moon appears greater than the visual diameter of the sun, and thus the moon appears larger to us than the sun.

    [1] The heavens seem to be one of the simple
bodies or to be composed of them. First: because
wherever the same accidents are found the same nature should be there also; but the same accidents
are found in the heavens as in composed bodies;
therefore the same nature also. Proof of the min-
or: because light and heat are found in the heavens as its properties, also the perspicuity that
is proper to air, the kind of even surface and
joining of parts that cannot exist without water,
and finally the solidity that we see is a property
of earth.

    [2] Confirmation of the argument: [a] because
if the heavens had a nature different from the elements they would have this because of a distinctive
motion, for two simple motions cannot be proper to
one simple body, as Aristotle teaches; but this
does not prevent two simple motions from being
found in one simple body; therefore [the heavens
have the same nature as the elements]. [b] Proof
of the minor: elements can be considered in a twofold state: when some parts at least are outside
their proper place, and here their motion is properly rectilinear; or when they are perfect in their
own place, and then it is not inconsistent that
some elements at least move with a more perfect motion, such as the circular, as is apparent with
fire.

    [3] Add to this that the differentiation of
simple bodies is taken from active qualities. Confirmation of the same: because even animals, before
arriving at their perfect size, move with a motion
of augmentation and after that with more perfect
motions; therefore, just as several active qualities are proper to the elements, so too can several

                           81

motive powers be.

[4] Second: an active natural power ought to have a corresponding natural passive power of the same nature and proportion; but the heavens are related to lower bodies as an active natural power is related to natural passive powers; therefore the heavens should be of the same nature as compounds and elements.

[5] Confirmation of the argument: [a] because the heavens have been made by God for such inferiors and so they should not have a nature different from theirs; and [b] because each thing is an agent insofar as it is in act; but the heavens communicate to such inferiors warmth at one time, dryness at another; therefore they have these [in act] and, as a consequence, their principles, which are the elements.

56   [6] Third: no simple body has heterogeneous parts; but the heavens have heterogeneous parts; therefore they are not a simple body. Proof of the minor: because in the heavens some parts are luminous, others are without light.

[7] The first opinion was that of practically all ancient philosophers before Aristotle, who thought that the heavens are not different in nature from the elements; and this opinion originated with the Egyptians, as Albertus teaches in tract 1, chapter 4, of the first *De caelo*, the Egyptians thinking that the heavens were made of fire. For it is a property of fire to be carried upward, and then, when it can ascend no farther, to go around in a circle -- as is seen in flame, which, when it arrives at the top of a furnace, circles around. From this it is apparent that the heavens are fiery, for they have the uppermost place and are moved circularly.

[8] Anaxagoras does not depart much from this opinion, for he, as is gathered from Aristotle in the *Metaphysics* and the first *De caelo*, text 22, holds that the heavens are fiery. Empedocles also, as Plutarch notes in the second book of *De placitis philosophorum*, chapter 11, thought that the heavens are solid after the fashion of ice composed of fire and air, and therefore partly fiery and partly airy. Some, however, attribute to Empedocles the idea

that the heavens are earthy and heavy but do not
descend because the velocity of their motion is
the greatest, and that they are indissoluble, as
St. Thomas states in the First Part, question 68,
article 1, noting that friendship and not strife
is dominant in their constitution. Anaximenes,
from Plutarch as cited above, thought that the
heavens are nothing but the outer earthly circum-
ference. Democritus and Epicurus favored the view
that the heavens are made of atoms, which, being
rounder and lighter and forced out in the collis-
ion and mutual agitation of bodies, cohere and come
to the highest place and make up the heavens.
Others thought them to be of a watery nature.

[9] Plato seems to have agreed with the Egyptians: indeed, he did not wish that the heavens be
merely fiery, as St. Thomas improperly ascribed to
him in the place cited above [8], but that they
consist of the other elements or of the most ex-
cellent among them, and, as Proclus says, *Ex deli-
tiis*, particularly of earth and fire. And Plato
puts this as follows in the *Timaeus* and in the work
De natura et anima mundi: nothing can be visible
without fire or touched without earth; therefore,
since the heavens are visible and touchable, they
must be made of fire and earth; and because these
two extreme elements cannot be rightly combined
unless the remaining two, air and water, come in
between, [the heavens must be composed of all four
elements].

[10] From this one may gather that some have
improperly held that Plato did not disagree with   57
Aristotle, such as Simplicius in the first *De caelo*, comment 6, Proclus, and Ficino. All others,
following Philoponus in the work *Adversus Proclum*,
in the solution of the thirteenth argument, part
15; Taurus in the first of the commentaries on the
Timaeus; Plotinus in the book *De mundo* (as is apparent also from Porphyry on the *Timaeus*); Philoponus in the solution of the sixth argument, parts
1 and 14, and as above, part 1 and from 13 to the
end; Albertus Magnus in the first *De caelo*, tract
1, chapter 4; and others besides, maintain that
Plato, following the opinion we have exposed, generally disagreed with Aristotle. Those who follow
Plato include, among the Platonists, Taurus, Porphyry, and Plotinus; among the Greek Fathers, St.
Basil on the *Hexämeron* and St. [John] Chrysostom

in homily 10; among the Latin Fathers, St. Ambrose
in his *Hexämeron* and St. Augustine in the first
Super Genesim; and among the scholastics, St. Bonaventure and others.

[11] The second opinion was that of Aristotle,
who was the first of all, as Philoponus references
in the solution of the thirteenth argument, part
15, to think that the heavens are different in nature from the elements. Yet Plutarch says in book
2 of *De placitis*, chapter 11, that Aristotle
thought that the heavens were composed of a fifth
body, or from fire, or from a mixture of heat and
hardness -- but his citation was in error, since
it is apparent that Aristotle's opinion was otherwise. Likewise Plutarch, book 1, chapter 3 and
elsewhere, takes note of such a fifth body posited
by Aristotle as a nature distinct from the elements. This opinion of Aristotle has been embraced by all the peripatetics, Greek and Latin, and
by all the scholastics.

[12] I say, first: the heavens are a body distinct from the four elements. The conclusion is
Aristotle's, on this book, from text [5] up to 17.
First: because circular motion is simple and different from rectilinear motion; but a distinctive
simple motion is accounted for by a distinct simple body; therefore, since simple circular motion
is proper to the heavens just as rectilinear motion
is proper to the elements, the heavens must be a
simple body distinct from the elements. The major,
i.e., that circular motion is simple, is apparent
from texts 5 and 6 of this book; and likewise,
that it is different from rectilinear motion. The
minor is proved from text 7, where it is maintained that a simple motion is to be assigned to a
simple body, and from text 9, where it is held that
there is only one natural motion for one simple
body. What is assumed in the inference is apparent
to sense. Note here, however, that the entire
force of this argument depends on what is said in
text 5: nature is the principle of motion. From
this it is apparent that a different motion indi-
58   cates a different nature.

[13] Second: because the heavens, from text
10, move with a circular motion; therefore this motion belongs to the heavens either according to
their nature, and so the desired result follows;

or contrary to nature; or, as it were, above their
nature, communicated to them by a superior body.
But the motion is not contrary to nature and violent: for otherwise it would have to be attributed
to another body as in accordance with its nature,
and so there would exist a prior body that moves
naturally in circular motion, different from the
elements, and this would be the heavens.

[14] Moreover: if this motion were violent to
the heavens it could not be natural except to one
of the elements; but this cannot be, because each
element naturally has a rectilinear motion, and for
one simple body there can only be one simple motion.

[15] Moreover: if such a motion is contrary
to nature for the heavens, then the heavens have
another motion according to nature, and this cannot be other than rectilinear; but rectilinear motion is proper to the elements; therefore, not to
the heavens.

[16] Moreover, if a rectilinear motion were
natural to the heavens, violent motion for them
would be rectilinear in the opposite direction;
thus circular motion could not be violent for them,
because only one violent motion is opposed to each
natural motion.

[17] Finally: if circular motion were violent
for the heavens, the motion could not be perpetual, for nothing violent is perpetual.

[18] If you say the motion is above nature,
communicated by a superior body, there would exist
a prior superior body for which circular motion
would be natural; but this cannot be other than
the heavens, as we maintain, and if the heavens
must have a distinctive circular motion, necessarily they will be of a different nature. And from
this same teaching one may gather also that the
heavens are a body that is in a certain way prior,
more perfect, and more divine than the elements;
since their motion is circular, and this is prior
to and more perfect than the rectilinear., from the
eighth *Physics,* 75, the first *De caelo,* 12, and
the second *De caelo,* 23.

[19] I say, second: the heavens are not a
body composed of the elements. This is proved

from Aristotle, texts 7 and 8 of this book, where
he says that a composed body moves with the motion
of the predominant element; but the heavens move
naturally with no motion deriving from the elements, since they move with a circular motion;
therefore [they are not composed of the elements].

[20] Nor can you say that the heavens are composed of the four elements plus a fifth, and that
the latter, moving with a circular motion and being predominant in the heavens, makes the heavens
revolve naturally with a circular motion. For,
first of all: it would follow that a fifth body
distinct from the elements exists, and this cannot
be supported by any experience or argument; indeed,
to concede it would imply a fifth element combin-
ing with others in compounds, as is apparent from
what Aristotle says concerning the number of ele-
59   ments, for he holds that if there were a fifth
element above the heavens it would exist to no purpose, since it could never combine with the other
elements.

[21] Second: because, since every element undergoes at least alteration, as will be proved in
its place, it would follow that there would be alteration in the heavens; and yet the heavens never
undergo alteration and augmentation. Add to this:
the heavens cannot be the first and universal a-
gent, for then they would also be equal to the elements and neither prior to them nor ungenerable.

[22] Third: the heavens are eminent above all;
therefore they have a nature prior to all. Confirmation: the heavens include everything in their em-
brace; therefore they cannot be an element. For if
they were, they would most likely be fire; but fire,
being most mobile, is inadequate as a container,
and so they cannot be fire. Nor can they be composed, because it would not be proper that such a
body be located above all the elements; therefore
[the heavens are neither fire nor composed of the
elements].

[23] Fourth, from size: for the heavens are
the largest body; therefore they are not an element,
because they are over all others; nor are they composed, for a composed body cannot exceed in size
the elements of which it is composed. Confirmation:
because the heavens are an integral part of the

universe; therefore, just as the remaining bodies
making up the universe are simples, so also the
heavens, which are a principal part of the universe.

[24] Fifth: if the heavens were elemental
they would most likely be of the nature of fire;
but this cannot be, for otherwise they would already have burned up everything; therefore [they
are not elemental]. This is the argument Aristotle
uses against Anaxagoras, in the first *Metaphysics*.

[25] Sixth: the heavens are a body neither
heavy nor light, from the first *De caelo*, from text
17 to 20; since a heavy or light body has a motion
that is rectilinear, not circular, as is the motion
of the heavens.

[26] You reply on the authority of Aristotle,
first: in the twenty-fifth section of the *Problem-
ata*, problem 18, he states that the stars are hot
and the heavens are also hot, and therefore the
heavens have the nature of fire.

[27] Second, Aristotle again: in the third *De
caelo*, text 1, asserting that "substances and all
simple bodies, such as fire and earth and anything
of the same order, and whatever is composed of
them, such as the entire heavens and their parts,
and again, animals and plants, and their parts,"
etc. -- from which it is apparent that the heavens
and their parts are composed from those five as
from elements, just as are animals and plants.

[28] Third, Aristotle again: in the seventh
Metaphysics, text 5, maintaining that "animals and
their parts are substances and natural bodies, such
as fire, water, and earth, and that other individuals are either parts of them or are made from them
either partly or wholly, such as the heavens and
their parts, the stars, the moon, and the sun."

[29] To the first objection [26], I reply:
the stars and the heavens are hot by power or activ-   60
ity and not by quality, and this is sufficient to
solve that problem, as is obvious. And that the
stars and the heavens are not hot except by power
is apparent from Aristotle, in the first *Meteors*,
chapter 3, for if they were made of fire they would
have consumed everything. Moreover, from chapter 4

of the same book, since the heavens and the stars
move with much greater velocity than do fire and
air, if the latter motion would ignite fire and
air, *a fortiori* it would ignite the entire heavens
by reason of the stars, which move in the heavens
with a much greater velocity still. Apart from
this, as is stated at the end of the same chapter,
if the stars were made of fire and were hot, the
sun would be much more so; but this is not apparent, since it is white in color and not fiery.

[30] One may also reply that not all the problems treated in Aristotle are Aristotle's; and
moreover, that Aristotle does not speak in all matters from his own, but often from common, opinion.

[31] To the second [27] and third [28], Alexander replies, in the seventh *Metaphysics*, that by
the terms "entire heavens" are meant the "entire
universe" made up of the four elements and of the
heavenly body; thus the sense would be, especially
in the text cited from the *Metaphysics* [28], that
natural bodies and their parts are substances, and
from these bodies, either wholes or parts, are made
up all others -- the entire universe, from all bodies and their parts; the sublunary world, from corruptible bodies and their parts; the heavens, from
the entire fifth element and from its parts, namely, from the stars.

[32] Simplicius replies in the third *De caelo*
that when Aristotle says that "fire and earth and
anything of the same order" [27], by these last
words are to be understood water, air, and a fifth
simple body that is called an element by the same
title and so is said to be "of the same order" as
the other elements; and then Aristotle, adding "and
whatever is composed of them, such as the entire
heavens," etc., means that the heavens are made
from some one element just as are the parts of the
heavens, that is, from a fifth body.

[33] St. Thomas replies, in the third *De caelo*
and in the seventh *Metaphysics*, that when Aristotle
says "such as the heavens and their parts," etc.,
the "such as" does not refer to the immediately
preceding, so that, when speaking of compounds, his
example would be the heavens; rather it refers to
what he had said previously, namely, both in the
third *De caelo*, where he said that the simple bod-

ies are substances, and in the seventh *Metaphysics*,
that natural bodies are substances; for this reason, giving then the example of the simplest and
most natural bodies, he says "such as fire and
earth" and interjects concerning compounds that
they are composed of them; then he adds "such as
the heavens and their parts," as if he were to
say, "those too are simple and natural bodies, and
therefore they are substances."

[34] This exposition is confirmed from what
Aristotle teaches, in the beginning of the eighth
Metaphysics, where he repeats the same doctrine,   61
i.e., that natural bodies are substances just as
are elements, animals, and the heavens.

[35] To the first argument to the contrary
[1], I reply: from the fact that some accidents
are found in the heavens that exist also in these
lower bodies, one can only gather that the heavens
have some aspects in common with the lower, on account of which such accidents exist in them, not
that these flow from the ultimate differences of
simple bodies, but from something more common,
i.e., their corporeal nature.

[36] To the confirmation [2a], I reply: the
diversification of simple bodies with respect to
their active nature is gathered from active qualities; but, with respect to their simplicity, from
the diversity of simple motions.

[37] To the second confirmation [2b], I reply:
two simple motions cannot naturally be proper to
one simple body. For, although a change of state
that results in a different local motion must necessarily vary the intrinsic nature of the thing --
whereas the elements themselves, whether located
outside their place or constituted in their place,
are diversified only accidentally -- it cannot happen that the elements move naturally in their place
with a circular motion and outside their place with
a rectilinear motion; especially seeing that rectilinear motion cannot be subordinate to circular, or
vice versa, and that a simple motion terminates
with rest. This is why the elements do not move
in their place, as is obvious in the case of water
and earth; and this has been stated correctly by
Aristotle in the second *De caelo*, that the nature
of the elements consists more in being at rest than

in moving.

[38] Nor can you say that fire, moving continually as it does in its sphere with a circular motion, moves naturally with such motion; since nothing violent, from the first *De caelo*, 15, can be
perpetual. For fire does not move naturally in
its proper place; nor does Aristotle, as cited a-
bove, teach the contrary, maintaining only that
circular motion, being eternal and continual, is
the most suited of all motions to be proper to any
body according to nature.

[39] To the last confirmation [3], I reply:
the diversity of simple bodies can be gathered from
the diversity of local motions, but not from the
diversity of active qualities, since many of these
are compatible. Nor can it be deduced from the diversity of other motions of alteration and augmentation; for, although nature is the principle of
motion and of rest, it is especially the principle
of local motion. The latter is the most eminent
of all motions and is differentiated from others
in that it adds no intrinsic form to the movable
itself, and in fact is identified with it, as we
have shown in the books on the *Physics*.

62   [40] From this it is understood that local
motion presupposes that the thing moved be constituted in its perfect existence with respect to
everything that pertains to it, and thus it implies
a minimal change. And that is the reason why the
most perfect beings, of which sort are the heavenly bodies, move with local motion alone; for indeed
other motions add some intrinsic and inhering form
to the substances in which they exist, viz, generation, whether substantial or accidental, and alteration and augmentation; as a result they do not
come to a thing already existing in its complete
nature. From all of this it is understood that
the distinction of simple natures is rightly taken
from the distinction of local motions.

[41] Add to this: the motion of alteration
comes to be from something extrinsic and by reason
of matter; therefore, because matter of itself is
indifferent to many forms, the distinction of bodies cannot be correctly deduced from the kinds of
alteration. The same judgment cannot be made concerning local motion; for this comes not only from

within, by reason of matter, which is indifferent
to motion up or down; but also by reason of form,
which has a natural inclination to that kind of
motion.

[42] To the second argument [4], I reply: the
heavens and the other inferior bodies have the same
nature in some way and proportionately, since they
are physical substances.

[43] To the first confirmation [5a], I reply:
the heavens were made primarily that they might be
an integral part of the universe, and subsequently
that they might be a simple body distinct from the
elements; moreover, that they would exist for themselves principally, and then for lower bodies so as
to be a universal cause concurring in all genera-
tions; but from this it follows that they must be
incorruptible and therefore simple and different
from the others.

[44] To the second confirmation [5b], I reply:
according to some, the heavens share with hot bodies the virtual quality of heating, with cold, that
of cooling, etc., for matter's diversification.

[45] A better reply would be that the heavens
act on these lower bodies through light alone,
which heats by itself only through reflection.
And if one says that sometimes it moistens or drys
out, etc., this comes about accidentally, either
because the humid parts are taken out, or because
some humor that easily enters rarified bodies is
attracted by the moon with nocturnal light, or because the humid humors that are found in air cannot be boiled off by it.

[46] To the third argument [6], I reply, first:
from the fact that some dissimilar parts exist in
the heavens one cannot rightly deduce that the heavens are composed, since a compound is formed from
the diversity of qualities existing in the same
part; for compounds result from the fact that the
forms of the elements are in the same part of mat-   63
ter; or, as others prefer, because in one and the
same part of matter there is one form containing
many virtualities within it, and this requires many
qualities for its generation; but nothing like this
is found in the heavens.

[47] I reply, second: the diversity of parts
that comes about through different qualities each
of which is a distinct species, if it proves anything, proves only the distinction of forms; such
that each part has its own proper form, and the
whole resulting from them is some kind of totality
through aggregation. Thus the argument, if it
proves anything, proves only this, that the stars
have a nature different from the other parts of
the heavens; and this is defended by many as probable, following Aristotle.

[J] Fourth Question. Are the Heavens Incorruptible?

[1] The first opinion is that of Philoponus, holding that the heavens are corruptible of their very nature and that sometime they will finally come to corrupt; this is gathered from the solution of the sixth argument against Proclus, and from Simplicius who attributes this opinion to him. Philoponus assimilates to his view Plato, who thought that the heavens are corruptible of their nature but incorruptible by the kindness of God; this is apparent from the *Timaeus*, where he asserts that the world was generated and consequently is corruptible. In fact, what Plato did think concerning the incorruptibility of the heavens is a source of dispute among Platonists, for in partial agreement with Philoponus are Taurus, Apicus, Severus, Pleto, Plutarch, and Philo in the book *De incorruptibilitate mundi*; also very many of the Church Fathers, cited in the first question on the universe [C4], who hold that the heavens were said by Plato to be generated where previously they had not existed. Disagreeing, however, are Crantor, Plotinus, Porphyry, Iamblichus, and Simplicius in the first *De caelo*, text 20, where he asserts that it is taken to be generated by Plato, as above, from the fact that it is from another even though it existed from eternity. Aristotle and Alexander, however, understand Plato to mean that the heavens are not eternal.

[2] Philoponus proves his opinion by the following argument from Simplicius, eighth *Physics*, and from Averroës in the same place, from the twelfth *Metaphysics*, chapter 21, in the book *De substantia orbis*, chapters 5 and 7, and from the second *De caelo*, comment 71. This argument is found in Philoponus, chapter 6, where Philoponus uses it against Proclus: an infinite power cannot exist in a finite body, eighth *Physics*, 79; but since the

64

93

heavens are a finite body, if they were eternal
they would have an infinite power, namely, that of
enduring for an infinite time; therefore [they are
not eternal].

[3] Confirmation: to endure for ten years requires a certain power; for a hundred, a greater;
and so on; therefore, for an infinite time, an infinite power.

[4] Second confirmation: because, from Aristotle, eighth *Physics,* 69, and twelfth *Metaphysics,*
44, no power in a body can move for an infinite
time; therefore, *a fortiori,* neither can it give
existence to matter for an infinite time, since
existence is more fundamental than motion.

[5] The same result can be proved because the
heavens undergo alteration -- as is apparent in
the moon, which at one time is luminous and at another opaque; but whatever is alterable is corruptible; therefore [the heavens are corruptible].

[6] Again: because either [a] the heavens are
a completely necessary being in such wise that they
cannot be destroyed even by divine power, and this
is absurd; or [b] they are not so necessary that
they cannot be destroyed by divine power, and so
they are corruptible. Moreover, because nearly all
the Church Fathers thought this.

[7] Finally: it seems that Holy Scripture
teaches generally that the heavens are corruptible,
especially Isaiah, chapter 51, the heavens shall
vanish like smoke, and 34, the heavens shall fold
up like a book; David, in Psalm 101, the heavens
are the work of your hands and they shall perish;
John, in the Apocalypse, 6, the heavens receded
like a book unfolded; St. Peter, in the second
Epistle, last chapter, the heavens reserved for
fire will pass away with great impulse; and finally, Christ, in Matthew, heaven and earth shall pass
away, etc.

[8] The second opinion is that of Aristotle,
who was the first, as Averroës notes, to teach in
this book that the heavens are ungenerated and
therefore incorruptible. This was actually gathered from ancient writers; before Aristotle, Pythagoras and others thought that the heavens are un-

generated and indeed that they constitute a fifth
body distinct from the others, contrary to what
Philoponus says.

[9] And that this is the opinion of Aristotle
is apparent, first, from text 2 and following of
this book; and from the twelfth *Metaphysics*, text
5, where he states that the heavens are an eternal
substance; and from the eighth *Metaphysics*, texts
4 and 12, the ninth *Metaphysics*, 17, and the twelfth, text 10, where he says that in the heavens
there is no matter of contradiction.

[10] Second, from his principles: for, first,
Aristotle posits an eternal world, in the eighth
Physics, text 1, and in the first *De caelo*, toward
the end. He posits an eternal circular motion,
eighth *Physics*; but what is generable and corrup-   65
tible cannot be eternal; first *De caelo*, texts 121
and 122. Confirmation: if the heavens are generable, then a generating body precedes them; therefore the heavens are neither the first body nor
eternal. Confirmation: because whatever is generable comes to an end in time, from the fourth
Physics, texts 117 and 120; therefore it is not e-
ternal. Moreover: if the heavens are generable,
then the motion of the heavens is not the first;
but that it is the first Aristotle proves in the
eighth *Physics*, from text 54 onward. Moreover:
the heavens could not be the universal agent of
generation, as Aristotle maintains in the second
De generatione.

[11] Moreover: generation cannot take place
without elements, from the third *De caelo*, text 2,
and the second *De generatione*, text 1, and these
are totally incorruptible in themselves; therefore
the heavens must also be incorruptible. Confirmation: because whatever is ungenerable is incorruptible, from the first *De caelo*, 121 and 122. Moreover: the motions of the heavens ought to be without end, from the eighth *Physics*, because the generation and corruption on whose account the heavens exist are perpetual, from the second *De generatione*, text 56. Finally: the intelligences
achieve their perfection in moving the heavens,
and so the heavens must be incorruptible.

[12] For the solution of the difficulty [8],
note that in truth we can speak of the heavens,

just as we can of anything created, in two ways:
first, from their very nature, whether, namely,
they have by their nature some intrinsic principle
through which they can be corrupted; second, whether only through the absolute power of God, whereby
God can make everything return to nothing, they
are corruptible. The reason for this is that the
divine power does not require a corresponding natural potency making the thing corruptible of its
nature; sufficient for it is a kind of potency that
the theologians refer to as obediential, whereby
all creatures are subject to God. And so it follows that even if the heavens are said to be incorruptible, this does not mean that they are incorruptible necessarily; for in this way God alone, as
St. Paul teaches, is a completely necessary being;
and the Council of Constance defines that angels
and human souls are immortal by divine grace. Some
of the Church Fathers who say that the heavens are
incorruptible can be understood in this way.

[13] I now say, first: if we speak of the
heavens according to their nature, and if corruptible be taken to signify anything that has in itself a passive potency whereby it can be corrupted
by an active power proportioned to it, it is probable that the heavens are corruptible. The conclusion is proved from the arguments and reasons in
support of the first opinion [2-7].

66   [14] Second proof: because the heavens were
made especially for man; therefore they ought not
to be incorruptible, for otherwise they would be
more noble than man. Confirmation: because, as
some doctors say, the heavens must corrupt after
the Day of Judgment; for, since they were made for
man's use and for conserving sublunary things, when
such a function ceases they themselves ought to
cease.

[15] You say: if things are actually this way,
why do the heavens not corrupt and undergo change
even now? I reply: by the permission of the divine
will; since there is no agent powerful enough to
corrupt them, for the fire that is next to the heavens is of minimal action because of its rarity,
whereas the heavens are most solid and most dense,
and so have maximal power to resist contraries.
And this opinion should be supported particularly
by those who think that the heavens will one day

corrupt; for otherwise it would have been to no
purpose that God made them as they are, if they
would have to corrupt.

[16] To one inquiring, if the heavens were
corruptible what would their nature be: it might
be said that they would be of a fiery nature but
that they would not take their circular motion
from that nature, because such a motion would not
be proper to them, except in the way that philosophers say that the circular motion of fire is
proper to fire in its sphere, i.e., not violently.
For fire, when it moves with such a motion from a
superior body and does not leave its proper place,
cannot be said to be moved violently in circular
motion; so also, since the heavens would be moved
by an intelligence having a superior nature and
with a motion that would not remove them from their
place, they would not be moved violently.

[17] To one inquiring again, for what purpose
they would be moved, one might answer: for the
use and conservation of sublunary things, and especially for man.

[18] I say, second: it is more probable that
the heavens are incorruptible by nature. Proof of
this, first: because it is conformable to natural
reason, as is apparent from the arguments of Aristotle, from text 20 onwards. The first is that the
heavens move circularly. But circular motion has
no contrary motion; for if it had, this would most
likely be rectilinear motion, and there cannot be
two contraries opposed to the same thing; therefore
rectilinear motion is not contrary to circular.
From this it is apparent that if the motion of the
heavens has no contrary, neither do the heavens;
but whatever has no contrary is incorruptible;
therefore the heavens are incorruptible. The force
of the argument consists in this: a substance that
is corruptible -- since a subject as subject is not
corruptible (for corruption takes place within the
subject and is not of the subject) -- will be corruptible by reason of what exists in the subject,   67
namely, the form.

[19] From this it follows that every substance
that is corruptible is such that it is composed of
matter and form; and the form corrupts to the extent
that it leaves the subject. And this always comes

about from something else expelling it: for the
subject (i.e., the matter) does not drive the form
from itself, but always seeks to retain it; nor
does the form leave of itself, since it seeks existence and by leaving it would be corrupted; therefore it must be expelled by another. But a form is
expelled when something else is induced into the
subject where the form is, and which cannot coexist
with it -- for otherwise it would not be expelled;
from this it is apparent that corruption must come
about through the introduction of a contrary.
Moreover, since a substantial form in itself does
not have a contrary, nor is it active, it is expelled through qualities that are contrary to those
whereby it is produced and conserved in matter,
with the result that if there is to be corruption
it must be owed to some other form that has qualities contrary to the qualities of the initial form.

[20] From this it is also understood that
every substance that is corruptible must consist
of matter and form, and that there cannot exist in
matter another form having qualities contrary to
the qualities of the form already existing in it.
It is by these means that generation and corruption
come about; for when one agent induces its qualities so that it may induce a form, it necessarily
expels the contraries, and when these are expelled
the form is expelled also.

[21] From this one gathers that whatever undergoes corruption has a contrary, in the manner
explained; and therefore that the heavens, since
they lack contraries of this type, are incorruptible. That the heavens lack contrary qualities is
learned from the fact that local motion is an attribute of a substance that is already perfected.
And this substance, if it is such as to have a contrary, i.e., a form to be introduced with contrary
qualities, will also have a contrary motion that
follows from the qualities; but the circular motion
of the heavens is of such a nature that it can be
perfect in itself, for it is always the same in the
beginning, the middle, and the end, by its nature.
As a consequence, all that can be said of such a
body of its nature is that it can naturally be perfect, and hence it lacks a contrary; therefore, so
do the heavens.

[22] Confirmation: because just as rectilinear

motion is finite by its nature, so also the bodies
with which it is associated are corruptible; therefore, since the motion of the heavens is infinite,
it follows [that they are incorruptible].

[23] Confirmation of the same on the part of
contraries: because the qualities that are found
in the heavens, such as light, perspicuity, etc.,
do not have a contrary; therefore the heavens do
not have a contrary. For, if they were to have   68
qualities with a contrary, these either would be
elementary qualities or they would be others with
their own proper contraries: not the first, because
it has already been shown that the heavens are different in nature from the elements; nor the second,
for otherwise there would be six simple bodies --
the four elements, the heavens, and some other body
that would naturally have qualities contrary to
those of the heavens.

[24] The second argument of Aristotle is drawn
from experience: for it has been found over all
preceding centuries that no change whatever has
taken place in the heavens. And this argument has
the greatest force: for, since the motion of the
heavens is of maximum velocity such that it could
destroy even the most solid bodies, and since it
has endured for such a long time, preserving the
stars always at the same distance, opposition, and
magnitude, from this argument it is most certain
that the heavens are incorruptible.

[25] A third argument is drawn from the consensus of all peoples, that the heavens, as something immortal, have been made the abode of the
gods.

[26] Fourth, from the etymology of the word:
for they are said to be an aether from the fact
that they are always in motion.

[27] And from all this it follows that the
heavens are also unalterable: because alteration
requires a contrary, since alteration does not take
place without some corruption of an opposite quality; and because no alterative qualities are observed in the heavens; and finally because alteration is a disposition to generation and corruption.

[28] It follows, second, that the heavens are

not augmentable, because every augmentation and
diminution presupposes alteration and a contrary.
Yet Aristotle proves [a] that the heavens do not
increase or decrease from the fact that they are
ingenerable and incorruptible, and a thing undergoes increase in the same manner as it comes into
being. Similarly he proves [b] that the heavens
do not alter, for alteration comes about through
passible qualities, and whatever undergoes alteration in this way both increases and decreases.

[29] Of these the first argument [28a] is
valid only for strict augmentation, not for augmentation taken in a broad sense; for it is false
that whatever undergoes alteration through passible qualities undergoes increase, as is apparent in the elements; and yet it is true that whatever is altered increases or decreases [28b],
strictly or not. Hence it is apparent that Aristotle's argument is not good: because, first, the
heavens are not augmentable by strict augmentation, and so, arguing from augmentation taken in
the broad sense, one may not rightly conclude that
they are unalterable. Yet it can be said that,
when Aristotle proves that the heavens are not
69   augmentable, he is speaking of augmentation taken
in any way whatever; but he proves it particularly
for strict augmentation, and this is more appropriate to the heavens. Moreover, Aristotle proves
this using a type of argument that shows there is
no true augmentation in the heavens: for the force
of his argument reduces to the fact that the heavens lack a contrary, from which it results that
they can be neither generated nor increased; and
from this argument it follows also that the heavens are not augmentable by any augmentation, strict
or not; for both rarefaction and condensation and
augmentations and diminutions that are strict presuppose the actions of coldness and hotness, and
these are contraries.

[30] Second proof of the conclusion [18]: because it does not follow necessarily from Holy
Scripture that the heavens are corruptible or will
be corrupted, as will be apparent from the responses to the arguments.

[31] With regard to the arguments to the contrary: to the first [4], I reply with Simplicius,
Averroës, and St. Thomas that alteration is twofold:

58665

one corruptive and the other perfective. The first
is between contraries and involves corruption, and
this has no place in the heavens; the other involves no contrariety and is found even in spiritual
things -- for which reason it is found also in the
heavens. And from this the response to the argument is apparent.

[32] To the second [5a], I reply: the heavens
are corruptible in relation to God, just as are intelligences and rational souls and all creatures;
but by their own nature they are incorruptible.

[33] To the third [5b], I reply, first: the
response is apparent from what has been said; second: St. Augustine, in the twentieth and twenty -
fourth of *The City of God*, Bede on the second epistle of St. Peter, St. Jerome on the word of Isaiah
cited, St. Thomas and the theologians on the fourth
[*Sentences*], distinction 48, and scholastics there
also, think that the heavens will not be corrupted
in their substance on the Day of Judgment, but only
with regard to accidents. From this it is apparent
that for them the heavens are incorruptible.

[34] And this is confirmed by reasoning: because, if after the world had been destroyed another world were to be created, according to the
words of Scripture, "Behold I create new heavens,"
etc., either the world to be created would have the
same parts as this world, or not. If not, it would
not be a world except equivocally; if so, either
its parts would be of the same nature or they would
be different from the parts of this world. If the
same, then this world would have been destroyed to
no purpose. If different, the earth of the other
world would either be heavy, dense, cold, and dry,
in the middle of the universe, or not: if the first,
it would be of the same nature as the earth of this
world; if the second, it would not be earth. Therefore [the heavens are incorruptible]. And what has
been said of earth applies also to other parts of
the world.   70

[35] To the last [6], I reply to the citations
from Isaiah, David, and John, and others similar:
the heavens, according to the testimony of Holy
Scripture, will be changed from the state they now
have and will perish in a qualified way, i.e., with
regard to motion, influence, power to heat, to gen-

erate, etc., but not with regard to substance; and
neither will the elements. That this will not be
impossible for God in the future is apparent from
what has already happened; for at the time of Josh-
ua the sun stood still, and the fires, with God
restraining their action, did not consume the three
boys; and it will be apparent in the case of glori-
fied bodies. To the text from St. Peter, I say
that the word for heavens means air, as St. Augustine notes in the twentieth of *The City of God*,
chapter 18; this is apparent from what St. Peter
said, for, speaking there of the heavens reserved
for fire, he says it is these that perished in the
flood. To Christ Our Lord, I reply that this is to
be understood conditionally: its sense is that
heaven and earth will pass away sooner than that my
words be false; or, heaven and earth can indeed
pass away by my power, but my words can never be
false.

[36] To the basis of Philoponus's argument
[2], I reply: the heavens have finite power but
they can, by finite power, endure for an infinite
time. To the confirmation [3], the response is obvious: for although enduring more or less goes with
greater or lesser power in things having a contrary, this is not so in things not having a contrary. Hence it also cannot happen that a moving
power lodged in a body move over an infinite time,
for it must have a contrary and a resistance, as
will be proved in its place.

[K] Fifth Question. Are the Heavens Composed of
            Matter and Form?

    [1] The first opinion is that of Averroës, who
holds that the heavens are a simple body and that
this body is not said to be matter by reason of
quantity and the remaining accidents and local motion, but that it nonetheless is matter actually
existing by itself and perfect. So maintains Averroës in the first *De caelo*, texts 5, 20, 22, and
95; the second *De caelo*, texts 1, 36, 40, and 71;
the third *De caelo*, text 25; the first *Physics*,
comment 63, the eighth *Physics*, comment 79; the
eighth *Metaphysics*, comments 4 and 12, and the
twelfth *Metaphysics*, 15; and extensively in the
book *De substantia orbis* throughout the entire
work.

    [2] Averroës proves his opinion, first: be-
cause if the heavens were composed of matter and
form they would be generable and corruptible, since
they would have a potency to substance; but potency   71
to substance is one of contradiction, i.e., to being and non-being; therefore the heavens would be
corruptible. This argument is taken from chapters
2 and 6 of the book *De substantia orbis*, where he
tries to prove that to be composed and to be generable are convertible; and from the eighth *Metaphysics*, 12, where he says that the heavens do not
contain matter, for otherwise they would be generated, since transmutation is what indicates matter.
He repeats the same thing in the first *De caelo*,
text 5.

    [3] Second: because it would follow that the
heavens would have a contrary, since a form that
exists in matter has a contrary; for otherwise it
would follow that the potency of matter would be
frustrated, since the proper operation of the potency of matter is generation and corruption, which

                    103

is effected through contraries. From this it follows that if there were in matter a form not having a contrary, the potency would never have its
own operation. Averroës uses this argument in the
second *De caelo*, text 20, and in the book *De substantia orbis*, chapter 3.

[4] Third: because in the heavens there is potency to place alone; therefore the heavens are
not made of matter and form, for otherwise they
would have a potency to substance. This argument
is taken from the first *Physics*, 63.

[5] Fourth: because from the eighth *Physics*,
at text 79, one gathers that no power in matter can
be infinite, and therefore a thing composed of matter and form cannot have infinite power; and this
is to be understood, says Averroës, equally of potency or of active and passive power. The heavens, however, receive an infinite motion from their
intelligence; therefore they cannot be [composed
of matter and form]. And this argument is used in
the book *De substantia orbis*, chapter 2.

[6] Note here, for a better understanding of
this opinion, that this simple nature of the heavens is sometimes called matter in act, as in *De
substantia orbis*, chapter 2; sometimes however, and
more correctly, it is called a subject, there and
in the eighth *Metaphysics*, 12, because matter signifies potency; at other times, something intermediate between potency and form, because it has
something in common with matter, something with
form, as is apparent from the Paraphrase on the
first *De caelo*. For it is similar to matter in
that it is sensible, has a potency to place, and
is corporeal; it is similar to form, on the other
hand, in that it exists in act, not in potency --
from which it is apparent that it has more in common with matter. Hence, in the ninth *Metaphysics*,
text 17, Averroës states that the heavens are matter and that they cannot be form, because they are
mobile and quantified, or divisible.

[7] Nor can you object that in the heavens a
moving part can be distinguished from a moved part,
and therefore form from matter: for Averroës replies that the moving part in the heavens is a form
that is abstract and does not constitute the heavens, since the heavens have quantity before receiv-

ing their form, and so only motion is to be at-   72
tributed to the form. And if it is said that the
form contributes *esse*, this happens because it
contributes motion, without which the heavens
could not exist.

[8] Averroës confirms this opinion in *De substantia orbis*, chapter 5, and the eighth *Metaphysics*, 12, following Themistius, who says that the
sun, the moon, and the stars are either forms or
dimensions without matter, i.e., spiritual bodies,
or, if they have matter, this is not the same kind
as that in things below. And certainly Themistius,
in the third *Physics*, text 3 -- although he had
said that composites of matter and form are partly
in act through form and partly in potency through
matter -- states that the heavens are in act solely because they do not change their form, and that
they are in potency merely by reason of motion.
Simplicius holds the same in the same place.

[9] This opinion, so proved and explained, is
followed by Durandus in the second [*Sentences*],
distinction 12; Scotus in the way of Aristotle on
the second [*Sentences*], distinction 14, question 1;
John of Bacon and Lychetus in the same place; Antonius Andreas on the eighth *Metaphysics*, question
4; Marsilius on the second, question 8, article 1;
Jandun on the first *De caelo*, question 23, on the
eighth *Metaphysics*, question 7, and on *De substantia orbis*, question 1; Cajetan on the first *Physics*, question 21; Zimara, propositions 103 and 108;
and all Averroists, some of whom even invoke Alexander in support of their opinion, in the first
Quaestiones naturales, chapters 10 and 15, and the
second *Metaphysics*, last chapter.

[10] Proof of this opinion: first, from Aristotle, who excludes potency and matter from the
heavens, as is apparent from the ninth *Metaphysics*,
text 17, where he says that nothing eternal is in
potency since every potency is one of contradiction; from which it follows that whatever is in potency is corruptible. He concedes, however, that
there is a potency to place "in eternal things,"
viz, in the heavens; and so he says that one ought
not to fear that they will suffer fatigue, for
their motion does not arise from a potency of contradiction.

[11] Confirmation of the same, also from Aristotle, third *Physics*, 32, teaching that in eternal things existence and capability are one. From this it is readily understood that there is no potency to substance in the heavens as eternal; there would be such a potency, however, if they were composed of matter and form, for then heavenly matter would have an aptitude to receive form, and aptitude is nothing more than potency. This would be contrary to Aristotle, who excludes matter of contradiction from the heavens but not their mobility to place, as is apparent from the eighth *Metaphysics*, texts 4 and 12, ninth *Metaphysics*, 17, and twelfth *Metaphysics*, 10.

[12] Second proof, again from Aristotle: because if the heavens were composed it would follow that they would be corruptible -- proofs both on the part of matter and on the part of form.

[13] On the part of matter: because for Aristotle all potency is one of contradiction, i.e., to being and non-being, as he holds in the ninth *Metaphysics*, 17, and the first *De caelo*, 136. In the same texts he also says the same of matter, again in the seventh *Metaphysics*, 22 and 53, and in the first *De generatione*, 54; he implies the same in the eighth *Metaphysics*, 4 and 14, where he states that whatever cannot be transformed does not contain matter, but the heavens are not transformed; and finally in the second *De generatione*, 34.

[14] Confirmation, again on the part of matter: because whatever has matter must also have a contrary, from the book *De longitudine et brevitate vitae*, chapter 2; but things that have a contrary are not eternal, from the same chapter; therefore [the heavens are not composed of matter].

[15] Confirmation: because the first *Physics* teaches that matter is the subject of contraries, and the fourth *Physics*, 84, and the second *De generatione*, 6 and 34, that matter can never be separated from contrariety but always has one contrary or another. But the heavens lack a contrary and are eternal; therefore [they do not contain matter].

[16] Proof of the same on the part of form: every natural form can be the end or form of some

natural change, as is apparent from the first *De partibus animalium*, chapter 1, for there form is said to be for the sake of something; but a form of this type is generable and corruptible; therefore [the heavens have no natural form].

[17] Confirmation from the first *Physics*, 83, with regard to physical and corruptible forms, and from the third *De caelo*, text 1, which states: "Natural substances are bodies and whatever are generated and corrupted along with bodies." From this it is apparent that every natural form is corruptible and therefore that the heavens, if composed of matter and form, would be generable and corruptible.

[18] Moreover, from the first *De generatione*, 54, things that have a form in matter are passible, i.e., they act and are acted upon; on the other hand, things that do not have a form in matter are impassible. But the heavens are impassible, since they are not alterable, from the first *De caelo*; therefore [they do not have a form in matter].

[19] Finally, Aristotle, in the twelfth *Metaphysics*, 30, proves that intelligences lack matter because they are eternal; and, if this argument is correct, since the heavens are eternal, they must lack matter. Nor can you say that Aristotle proves only that intelligences lack incorruptible matter, a kind that is not in the heavens; for then it would follow that Aristotle had not proved that intelligences are absolutely immaterial, since such a proof would still allow that intelligences subsist in the type of matter found in the heavens.

[20] Third proof of the same opinion, on the part of matter: if the heavens were composed of matter and form, it would follow that they would be corruptible; because matter is potency, and essential potency, and therefore one of contradiction also. Explanation of the argument: if the heavens were constituted essentially of matter and form, the matter would be in essential potency to the form, for otherwise they would not make a unity *per se*. Therefore, considered in itself, the matter would lack the form and have annexed to it the form's privation. But wherever there is privation there is potency to being and to non-being; therefore [the heavens cannot be composed of mat-   74

ter and form].

[21] Confirmation: matter as potency is prior, at least by nature, to the form of the heavens; in the heavens, however, the prior matter does not have a form, and so it has a privation; therefore [there is no such matter in the heavens].

[22] Further confirmation: matter, if in potency to form, does not have that form and so receives it from another; therefore, since it receives form, it can also be deprived of form; therefore the heavens are corruptible. Confirmation: matter is in potency to form and receives it from another; therefore the form is produced in matter and is educed from the potency of matter; and so the heavens are generated.

[23] Another proof on the part of matter: the matter of the heavens is either pure potency or potency by reason of a specific act; therefore it has an aptitude to receive some specific act, since it has an aptitude to be perfected and determined in some way; as a result such matter, together with the form of the heavens that it has, has a potency and privation to other forms that it lacks; and consequently the heavens are by nature corruptible.

[24] Another proof, also on the part of matter: there are in the universe some things that are composites of matter and form, and these are corruptibles; there are others that are perfect by reason of form only, and these are intelligences; therefore there must be yet others that are perfect by reason of matter alone, and these are the heavens.

[25] Confirmation: form and matter are correlatives; but there are some forms that need matter, such as corruptibles; there are other forms that are perfect without matter, such as intelligences; therefore there must also be matter that is without form, such as the heavens -- especially since the forms that exist without matter, as forms, give assistance to these heavens.

[26] Proof of the same on the part of form: every natural form is generable and corruptible, from Aristotle; so the heavens, being incorruptible, cannot consist of matter and form.

[27] Second proof: either the form of the
heavens moves the heavens, or not; if not, it is
not a natural form, for such a form is by nature a
principle of motion. Moreover, whatever gives existence gives everything that follows on existence;
thus if a form were to give existence to the heavens, it should also produce motion and the operations that follow on that existence, especially
since other qualities, such as light, etc., come
with existence. And if you say that motion is not
produced because a corporeal power cannot move for
an infinite time: to the contrary, for this would
happen if the power were to suffer fatigue; but it
does not do so, because fatigue comes from a contrary and from resistance, and these are not present in the heavens.

[28] Confirmation from the ninth *Metaphysics*,
17: here it is held that one need not fear that the
heavens will be fatigued because their motion does
not involve a potency of contradiction; therefore   75
such a form can be a mover, even for an infinite
time. And if it is such a mover, it follows first,
against Aristotle, that a corporeal power can move
for an infinite time, which Aristotle denies in
the eighth *Physics*, 79. It follows moreover that
such a form is corruptible; because in moving it
moves *per accidens*, since it exists in matter; but
anything of this kind is corruptible, from the
eighth *Physics*; therefore [so is such a form]. Finally, it follows at least that intelligences are
not necessary to move the heavens, and so the entire argument Aristotle proposes in the eighth book
of the *Physics*, when investigating the first mover,
is destroyed, and yet again, his method of investigating intelligences is vitiated or severely re-
stricted.

[29] Proof of the same conclusion on the part
of the heavens. First: the heavens are incorruptible and thus they are not composed; for everything
that is composed is of its nature dissoluble, since
it has two parts that are really distinct and so
can be separated. If they are not separated because there is no agent that is able to effect the
separation or for some other reason, it follows
that the heavens are indissoluble extrinsically but
corruptible intrinsically.

[30] Confirmation: because composition is ap-

parently instituted by nature so that things can
be dissolved; and if the heavens were to be forever indissoluble, it would be in vain that they
were naturally constituted of two parts. Add to
this that we do not detect composition except
through transformation and corruption; on this account anything that is not transmuted or corrupted
cannot be known by us as composed; but the heavens
are neither transmuted nor corrupted; therefore
[they are not composed].

[31] Confirmation: because the heavens lack
contraries; but transformation comes about through
contraries, just as composition comes to be known
through transformation.

[32] Second proof of the same: the heavens
must have the simplest motion and shape; but this
comes from a nature that is extremely simple, simpler even than that of the elements. But the elements have no composition except that arising from
matter and form; therefore the heavens must lack
even this, for otherwise they would not be simpler.

[33] Third proof: the heavens must be a universal agent; therefore they must be active to the
highest degree, such that they cannot be acted
upon by inferiors. From this it is apparent that
the heavens must be in act simply.

[34] Final proof: the heavens are intermediate between intelligences and sublunary bodies;
therefore, as they differ from intelligences and
share with sublunaries in their being bodies, so
they should differ from sublunaries and share with
intelligences in their being simple bodies.

[35] Confirmation of the argument, for composition is threefold: first, from subject and accidents, which is found even in immaterial things;
second, from quantitative parts, which cannot exist except in a body; and third, from essential
76   parts. Therefore, just as intelligences have only
the first type of composition, and sublunaries all
three types, so the heavens should have the first
two.

[36] Confirmation: because all beings are led
back to God, and in a special way through the intelligences and the heavens. So, just as all forms

are led back to God through the intelligences,
which are the most perfect forms lacking matter,
all matter should be led back to God through the
heavens, the nature that is simple and perfectly
free of every form.

[37] The second opinion is that of those who
think that the heavens are of an elementary nature,
regarding the heavens as a composed body. So
thought the Egyptians, Plato in the *Timaeus*, the
Stoics, and others, of whom more below [38]. Also
Alexander, in the twelfth *Metaphysics*, chapter 34
and at text 48, where he holds that each heaven
has a proper form and soul apart from its intelligence; and in the first of the *Quaestiones naturales*, chapter 10, where he states that if matter
is defined as a subject that is receptive of contraries, the matter of the heavens is not included
within this definition; if it is defined, on the
other hand, as something first and unformed, it is
included. But if there is an unformed subject in
the heavens, there will be a form there also, and
thus composition.

[38] That Alexander was also of this opinion
can be confirmed from what Averroës takes from
Alexander, in the eighth *Physics*, 79, that the
heavens are corruptible on account of their mover;
and if they are corruptible they are also composed;
therefore [they are composed]. Philoponus also
held the same, because he thought that the heavens
are corruptible and because he placed matter and
form in the heavens, in the first *Physics*, 50, and
the third *Physics*, text 1; likewise Simplicius in
the eighth *Physics*, 79, in the first *De caelo*, comments 6 and 8, and in the second *De caelo*, text 50.
Also all the Arabs, with the single exception of
Averroës, attributed composition to the heavens; so
Avicebron in the book *Fons vitae*, from Albertus and
from St. Thomas in the First Part, question 66, article 2; Avempace, from the first *De caelo*, tract
1, chapter 3; Avicenna, in the first of the *Sufficientia*, chapter 3. So did a great number of the
Latins, such as Albertus Magnus, in the first *Physics*, as above, the eighth *Physics*, tract 1, chapter
13, and in the book *De quatuor coaequevis*, question
4, article 3, where he teaches that Rabbi Moses was
of the same opinion; St. Thomas, in the First Part,
as above, in the eighth *Physics*, lecture 21, and in
the first *De caelo*, lecture 6, although in the sec-

ond [*Sentences*], distinction 13, question 1, article 1, he does not disagree with Averroës; and likewise all Thomists, as Capreolus, on the second [*Sentences*], distinction 12; Cajetan, on the First Part, as above; Soncinas, on the twelfth *Metaphysics*, question 7; and Ferrariensis, on the third *Contra Gentes*, chapter 30. Add to these St. Bonaventure, on the second [*Sentences*], distinction 12; Giles of Rome, in the same place and in the special question *De materia caeli*, 1; Achillini, in the first *De orbe*; Mirandulanus, in book 11 of *De eversione singularis certaminis*, section 16; and Scaliger, in his *Exercitationes*, 61.

77

[39] However, the cited authors disagree among themselves. First, because some of them wish to define the matter of the heavens differently from the matter of inferior things. So Alexander, in the first of the *Quaestiones naturales*, chapters 10 and 15; Simplicius, in the first *Physics*, 68, comment 63; Albertus, in the first *Physics*, tract 3, chapter 11, and in *De quatuor coaequevis*, question 2, article 6; and St. Thomas in the places cited above [38]. But others contend that heavenly matter is the same in kind as sublunary matter; so Philoponus, Avicenna, Avempace (as Averroës notes in the book *De substantia orbis*), Avicebron, Giles, and Scaliger -- yet with the qualifications that Philoponus thinks that the heavens are corruptible and that they will eventually corrupt; Avicenna and the Arabs, that they are corruptible *per se* and intrinsically, but considered from without they are incorruptible; Giles and Scaliger, that they are incorruptible *per se*. The corruptibility and incorruptibility of the heavens has been treated above [J1-36].

[40] Second, they disagree in this: that some of them want the heavens to be composed of matter and a form that is an intelligence, as Mirandulanus and Achillini, who also think that the matter of the heavens is not in potency *per se* but in act, and nonetheless that it takes an intelligence as a form; all the others, on the other hand, place some kind of form in the heavens. Concerning this, however, in its proper place [L1-41].

[41] Proof of the opinion of those thinking that the matter of the heavens is different in kind from sublunary matter: because Aristotle claims, by

the words he uses in some texts, that the heavens
do not have the matter inferior bodies have, and
practically all peripatetics teach that the matter
of the heavens is matter only equivocally when compared with the matter of these inferiors; and because otherwise it would follow that the heavens
are corruptible. But concerning this, below [130-
170].

[42] The opinion of those thinking that the
matter of the heavens is the same in kind as sublunary matter is proved by these arguments by
Giles. First, because the matter of the heavens is
either pure potency or act: if it is act, a unity
per se and essentially would not result from matter
and form; for when a unity *per se* results from a
duality, as Aristotle asserts in the second *De anima,* text 2, and the eighth *Metaphysics,* text 15,
one of these must be related as act, the other as
potency. If on the other hand it is pure potency,
then it is the same in kind as sublunary matter,
since the difference of each matter is the potency
through which that matter is made distinctively
substantial.

[43] Confirmation: because, if pure potencies
were multiple, they could not contain anything by
which they would be differentiated. Nor can you
say that pure potency is said of the matter of the
heavens and of sublunary matter for different reasons; because each is potency and in the same genus, namely, that of substance as ordered to a specific act. Add to this: it would otherwise follow   78
that there were different degrees of pure potency,
and this is absurd.

[44] Confirmation: because the matter of the
heavens, like the matter of inferiors, must be in
potency to every kind of specific act; for a potency that is not to every kind of act is comparable with others on the basis of the act to which
it is not in potency; just as the intellect is the
potency of matter not to every act but only to
those in the genus of intelligibles, and the eye
to those in the genus of colors, and so these potencies can be something different in act. Therefore, since the matter of the heavens is not in
act, it must be a potency that is in potency to
every kind of act, and therefore it is similar to
the matter of inferiors.

[45] Second proof: because every distinction
is made through act, from the seventh *Metaphysics*,
49; but neither the matter of the heavens, considered in itself, nor the matter of these inferiors
has an act; therefore, no distinction either.

[46] Confirmation: because wherever there is
a distinction there is also an ordering; but all
ordering is to form; therefore [the matters in
themselves are not distinct].

[47] Third proof: because all entities are of
a particular nature based on a kind of regression
from the highest and first being, namely, God, just
as all species of numbers are constituted by a similar distance from unity; therefore it is impossible that the matter of the heavens and of sublunaries differ essentially from each other. For
things that are equally distant from a first being
are of the same species, just as numbers that are
equally distant from unity are of the same nature;
but the matter of the heavens and the matter of inferiors are equally distant from God, since each is
pure potency; therefore [they are the same in kind].
Nor can you say that they differ from each other
insofar as one is ordered to a nobler form than
the other; for it would follow that one matter
would be closer to God than the other, and so each
would not be the pure potency that is totally distant from the simplest form, which is God.

[48] Fourth proof: because matter is intermediate between being in act and nothing; but between
being in act and nothing there cannot be any intermediate other than a single species; because when
we move from such an intermediate we fall directly
into nothing or into being in act; therefore [the
matters are of the same species].

[49] Fifth proof: because the matter of the
heavens and of these inferiors have similar attributes, such as quantity, etc.; therefore they are
similar in nature also.

[50] Confirmation from the seventh *Physics*,
text 29, and from the second *De anima*, text 26:
here it is held that no thing is simply receptive
of any other, but each thing receives some particular kind first; from this it is apparent that,
since the heavens and these inferiors are receptive

of the same attributes, they have the same nature
also.

[51] Confirmation from the second *De generatione*, 37: here it is held that things that are
comparable in quantity are reciprocally transmutable, and so they have matter of the same kind;
but the heavens are comparable in quantity with   79
the elements, for we say that the first heaven has
a particular ratio to the sphere of earth, of fire,
and so on, based on quantity.

[52] Sixth proof: because Aristotle, in the
second *De generatione*, 51, says, "equal in number
and of the same kind are the principles in eternal
and corruptible things," viz, matter, form, and
agent; therefore the matter of the heavens is the
same kind as the matter of sublunaries.

[53] Confirmation: because Aristotle knew
only a single matter, which he defined in the first
Physics; therefore, if there is matter in the heavens, it is of the same kind as Aristotle defined;
but Aristotle defined the matter of the sublunaries:
therefore [the matter of the heavens is of the same
kind].

[54] Confirmation: because in the first *Physics* Aristotle is concerned with principles that are
common to all natural things; therefore, also with
matter, particularly since nowhere else did he
treat of the matter of the heavens.

[55] Another confirmation: because things that
differ in matter differ also in genus, from the
eighth and the twelfth *Metaphysics*; but the heavens
and sublunaries belong in the genus of body and of
substance; therefore they do not differ in matter.

[56] Finally: because if the matter of the
heavens and of sublunaries differed *per se*, it
would follow that the heavens would be constituted
from some common element and from a *differentia*;
but this is false; therefore [the two matters do
not differ *per se*].

[57] I say, first, following the common opinion of the peripatetics: the heavens are composed
of matter and form, whatever the matter may be.
The conclusion is proved from Aristotle, who, in

the first *De caelo*, text 92, raises the difficulty
why there cannot be many heavens. The reason be-
hind the difficulty is that a heaven is a unity of
things that are singular and sensible; for to be a
heaven is not the same as to be this heaven, since
the first is a form while the second is a form in
matter; but things that have a form in matter can
be multiplied numerically; therefore the heavens
can be also. In solving this difficulty Aristotle,
in texts 93, 94, and 95, says that the heavens are
not so multiplied, because they are composed of
total matter. From this it is apparent that the
heavens, according to Aristotle, are composed of
matter and form.

[58] Those opposed reply that Aristotle in
these texts takes the heavens to mean nothing more
than the universe, which he was proving to be one.
But, to the contrary: first, the entire universe
is nothing more than the heavenly bodies together
with the elements; but by far the greater part of
the universe, as is obvious, is the body of the
heavens; therefore, to state that the universe is
composed of matter and form and is not multiplied
because it uses up a total matter is nothing more
than to state that the elements, and particularly
the heavens, are composed of matter and form, and
of total matter. From this it is apparent that if
the heavens did not contain matter, Aristotle's
difficulty and its solution would be useless and
futile.

[59] Second proof: similarly, the same reason
80   Aristotle gives for saying that the universe is a
form in matter is true also of the heavens, for
Aristotle proves this from the fact that the universe is singular and sensible; also, in the eighth *Metaphysics*, text 3, he teaches that sensible
substances contain matter; but a heavenly body is
singular and sensible; therefore [it contains mat-
ter].

[60] Those opposed reply that, when Aristotle
says that a heaven signifies a form and that this
heaven signifies a form in matter, he means by a
form any nature at all and by a form in matter a
nature that is singular and existent; with the result that, since a heaven is singular, Aristotle
intends nothing more than to distinguish the nature
of a heaven generically from the nature of a heav-

en as singular and existent; therefore the nature
of a heaven can be multiplied numerically. But, to
the contrary: first, what Aristotle says of a heav-
en he does not prove from the fact that the heaven
is singular but from the fact that it is sensible;
and from this he infers that it is singular, that
it exists in matter, etc.; and so for it to exist
in matter does not mean it is singular matter, because he infers that it is singular from the fact
that it is matter. Moreover, in solving the problem he states that a heaven is not multiplied because it is composed of a total matter; and by matter here he means a proper matter, not an existent
and singular matter; therefore, even in proposing
the difficulty, he takes matter to mean true matter.

[61] Confirmation: from the fact that Aristotle often admits that there is matter in the
heavens but that this is mobile, as in the eighth
Metaphysics, 12, the ninth *Metaphysics*, 17, and
the twelfth *Metaphysics*, 10, where he also asserts
that everything that undergoes change contains matter; this he likewise holds in the first *De generatione*, text 1, and he says that this is true in
every change, even one according to place; but the
heavens undergo change; therefore [they contain
matter].

[62] Second proof of the same: from the second *De generatione*, 51, where it is stated that
principles the same in kind and equal in number are
found in eternals and corruptibles [52]; but the
latter are composed of matter and form; therefore,
so are the former.

[63] Confirmation: because the principles of
natural things that are treated by Aristotle, as
is apparent from the first and second *Physics*, are
matter and form; similarly, nature, as it is defined in the second *Physics*, is matter and form; therefore, since the heavens are natural, they must be
composed of matter and form.

[64] Further confirmation: because natural
things are like the curve of the nose, i.e., they
are said to be in matter, second *Physics*, 19 and
21; first *De anima*, 17; third *De anima*, 35; and
sixth *Metaphysics*, 2. But the heavens are a natural body; therefore [they are in matter also].

[65] Confirmation from Theophrastus: because, as Simplicius indicates in the first *Physics*, at the beginning, Theophrastus maintains that all natural things are composed of matter and form.

81

[66] Third proof: from the first *De caelo*, where Aristotle, proving the nature and simplicity of the heavens, says that they are simple bodies in the same way that elements are simples; but elements have matter and form; therefore [so have the heavens]. Nor can you say that the motion of the heavens, from which Aristotle proves their simplicity, is simpler than the motion of the elements because it is circular; for circular motion is indeed more perfect than rectilinear, as is apparent from the eighth *Physics* at text 54 and the first *De caelo* at text 12, but it is not on this account simpler. Add to this: just as the motion of the heavens can be said to be simpler than the motion of the elements in a particular respect, so a heavenly body can likewise be said to be simpler than the elements in the sense that it is composed of matter and an indissoluble form. And if you say: Aristotle explains this simplicity of the heavens without their being composed of matter and form, since he proves the heavens to be ingenerable and incorruptible; I reply to the contrary: because incorruptibility can coexist with composition. Moreover, if Aristotle did think that the heavens are completely simple, he could easily have shown them to be incorruptible *a priori*, i.e., because they are simple; but he did not use this middle term, but proved it *a posteriori*, i.e., because they lack contraries; therefore he assigned to the heavens nothing more than the simplicity found in the elements.

[67] Confirmation: because Aristotle proves the simplicity of the heavens from motion, and so he proves a kind of simplicity to exist in the heavens that can permit motion; but motion cannot involve a simplicity that rules out a composition of matter and form. For, if the heavens move, this requires that they contain matter, as is apparent from the seventh *Metaphysics*, 12, the twelfth *Metaphysics*, 10, and the first *De generatione*, text 1. Moreover, the heavens are so moved that they are determined to a particular movement; but such a determination comes only from nature; therefore they have a form by which they are determined.

Moreover: the heavens are moved; therefore they
are not pure potency and matter, from the fifth
Physics, 8, nor form alone, from the same, text 3;
and so motion necessarily requires composition.

[68] Proof of the same by an argument taken
from Aristotle: because all substance is either
matter, or form, or a composite, from the second
De anima, text 2, the seventh *Metaphysics*, text 7,
the eighth *Metaphysics*, text 3, and the twelfth
Metaphysics, text 14; but the heavens are neither
matter nor form, which is sufficiently proved from
their motion; therefore they are composites.

[69] You say: this division applies only to
corruptible substance. To the contrary: first, it
is a division of predicamental substance, as is apparent from the second *De anima*, text 2, and is
gathered from the seventh and eighth *Metaphysics*,
where Aristotle divides the categories and treats
of substance.

[70] Second: in the twelfth *Metaphysics*, text
5, Aristotle divides substance into sensible and
immaterial; he then subdivides sensible into corruptible and eternal, and at text 10 proves that
every sensible and eternal substance, from the fact
that it undergoes transformation, contains a form   82
in matter; then at text 14 substance is divided in
the aforesaid manner; therefore [the argument is
valid].

[71] Third: in the eighth *Metaphysics*, text 1,
Aristotle states that the obvious natural substances
are the heavens and the parts of the heavens, animals, elements, etc.; and at text 2, treating of
obvious substances, that these are sensible; and
at text 3 he teaches that every sensible substance
contains matter; and then he further divides substances in the foregoing manner; therefore he includes the heavens in his division. He proceeds in
practically the same way in the seventh *Metaphysics*,
beginning at text 5.

[72] Those opposed reply: in this division
Aristotle takes matter broadly, just as he does
form, in such a way that form can even mean intelligences, and by the term matter can be meant something that is in potency, and something that, while
simple, is nonetheless corporeal, as are the heav-

ens. But, to the contrary: first, Aristotle defines matter to be what is in potency and what is
not *hoc aliquid*, as is apparent from the second *De
anima* and the eighth *Metaphysics;* therefore he does
not include the heavens under the definition.

[73] Confirmation: because, though intelligences might be included under the word form -- for
it could be that when Aristotle defined form he
meant the act also found in intelligences -- the
heavens can in no way be said to be potency and not
hoc aliquid. Moreover: intelligences are not included under the division, because that is a division of either predicamental substance or sensible
substance, as is apparent from the texts cited;
but intelligences, according to many, pertain to
neither type; therefore [this is not Aristotle's
meaning].

[74] Proof of the same from another argument
taken from St. Thomas, as above [38-39]: either the
heavens are act or they are something having act,
for it is certain that they are not potency; but
they are not act, for, if they were act, since
they are subsistent *per se* they would be simply intelligible and indivisible, that is, abstract and
immaterial forms; but the heavens are sensible and
quantified; therefore they are not act but rather
something having act, and therefore, composed of
act and of something having act, i.e., of form and
matter.

[75] Those opposed reply: not everything that
is not in potency is either act or having act, but
there is an intermediary, namely, substance existing in act. But, to the contrary: apart from what
has already been said in the argument above [74],
the heavens are a type of species that is more in
act and more determined than any inferior species.
This is apparent: because the heavens effect more
action, but action comes from what is in act;
therefore, since things below are either act or
something having act, much more is this true of the
heavens, which are more in act.

[76] Those opposed reply, second: a thing is
not act from the fact that it is intelligible and
abstract, as is apparent with accidents, e.g.,
whiteness; indeed there can be, they say, an act
83   that is not in matter and nonetheless is not an

abstract form, such as accidents that are in the
soul, and virtues. Moreover: according to them
there can be a substantial act that is not an abstract form, as is apparent in the case of a material form. And they add finally: since the heavens
have quantity they cannot be an abstract form. But
to the contrary: the instances they adduce are all
instances of an act that exists in another; but
the heavens, if they are an act, are an act such
that they do not or cannot exist in matter or in
any other subject. For that something is an abstract and intelligent form does not follow from
the fact that it is simply in act, but from the
fact that it is *per se* subsistent in act, since
this is the reason why we assert that separated
forms are intelligences.

[77] To what they also say about the heavens
having quantity [76], I reply that this works against them too: for quantity follows on matter, and so
it is that, if the heavens have quantity, they have
matter also. And if they say that the heavens are
in act, and so cannot have quantity, to the contrary: for Averroës, in *De substantia orbis* and
elsewhere, maintains that acts and forms that are
united to a subject before quantity are immaterial
forms; but this act of the heavens is in the heavens before quantity, because it is identical with
the heavens, and quantity is an attribute that is
received in the heavens; therefore, since such an
act is prior to quantity, it must be immaterial.

[78] Confirmation of the argument: because the
heavens are not purely in potency, because they
cannot undergo change, from the fifth *Physics*, text
8; nor are they pure act, for motion is the act of
a being in potency; therefore they are composed of
act and potency, of form and matter. And practically the same argument can be drawn from nature in
the following way: the heavens are natural, therefore, they are either nature or merely according to
nature; but they cannot be nature, because nature
is a principle in natural substance and the heavens
are a natural body; nor are they merely according
to nature, for the properties and operations of
natural things are of this type; therefore they are
bodies having a nature and consequently constituted from matter and form.

[79] Third proof of the conclusion, from an

argument based on accidents: in the heavens there
is quantity; but quantity is a proper attribute of
matter and a condition for it insofar as it is the
subject of other accidents, as is apparent from
what is said in the first *Physics*; therefore matter
exists in the heavens.

[80] Confirmation from the seventh and eighth
Metaphysics: from these passages, on the testimony
of Averroës himself, one may gather that length,
width, and breadth are in matter, and that when
these are taken away, so is it also.

[81] Further confirmation: because each attribute has only one subject. And not only is the
argument valid when based on quantity but also when
based on other accidents, for rarity and density
exist in the heavens; therefore the parts of the
heavens can be compared to each other in respect to
84   rarity and density also; but what is compared according to quantity contains matter, from the second *De generatione*, text 37; therefore, matter
exists in the heavens.

[82] Fourth proof of the conclusion, from an
argument taken from many indications that there is
composition in the heavens. The first is: the
heavens are sensible, therefore they have matter;
they are intelligible, therefore they have form;
the inference is obvious from Averroës, first *De
caelo*, 91 and 92.

[83] Second: the heavens have sensible accidents; therefore, since they are suited to receiving accidents of this type, they must also be suited to receiving a material form; for the reception
of accidents is ordered to the reception of form.

[84] Third: the heavens possess quantity,
therefore matter also, since quantity is its property; they have light, therefore form also, since
light is its property.

[85] Fourth: the heavens are corporeal and
sensible, therefore they contain matter; they are
determinate and finite, and have finite and determinate accidents; therefore form also, since determination comes from form, from the fourth *Physics*,
14.

[86] Fifth: the heavens are moved by intelligences; therefore they contain matter. They move inferiors and act on them, as is apparent from the first *Meteors*, chapter 2; therefore they have form, from the second *De generatione*, 53.

[87] Sixth: motion requires matter and form, as has been said above; therefore, since the heavens are in motion, they must be composed of matter and form.

[88] Confirmation: because the heavens are moved with a natural motion; therefore, by a natural principle and by nature; but nature is either an unformed subject, second *Physics*, 7, or a form in matter, the same, text 12.

[89] Seventh: in the heavens there is a physical composition made up of a subject and attributes, which nonetheless is *per accidens*; but such a composition presupposes a composition *per se*, since it must be reduced to that -- for whatever is *per accidens* is reducible to the *per se*, from the second *Physics*, 66; but composition *per se* is from matter and form; therefore [the heavens are composed of matter and form].

[90] Eighth: we experience that all other bodies are composed of matter and form; therefore we must make the same judgment of heavenly bodies, if indeed we come to the knowledge of things that are unknown from things that are apparent, through analogy; therefore [the heavens are composed of matter and form].

[91] Confirmation: because nothing prevents there being composition in the heavens, as will be proved by the following argument; therefore [there is composition there].

[92] Last proof of the same: because nothing rules out composition in the heavens; therefore [there is such composition]. Proof of the antecedent: for if anything were to rule it out, it would be either [a] that the heavens are incorruptible, or [b] that Aristotle denies that there is potency and matter in eternal things. But the first [a] is not obviating, because although the heavens are composed, they are nonetheless composed of matter of a different kind, as we will ex-

85

plain below [130], which is in potency only to a
heavenly form; from this it follows that such a
form does not have a contrary and such matter does
not have privation, and hence that the heavens are
incorruptible. This is confirmed by Averroës, in
chapter 1 of *De substantia orbis*, where he clearly
states that forms that exist in a subject not having a contrary are neither generable nor corruptible, and similarly that their matter is not in
potency to many forms but to one only. Nor is the
second alternative [b] obviating: for in eternal
things no potency lacks act, nor does any potency,
being ordered to many acts, have one act at the
same time as it has an aptitude for another; but
if the heavens contain matter of a different kind
in the way already indicated, and if such matter
is always with form, none of these consequences
follow. That some potency can exist in the heavens, however, St. Thomas proves in the eighth
Physics, lecture 21; and this is obvious: because
in the heavens there is at least a body that is
subject to accidents, as to quantity, light, etc.,
to which it has a potency but not in a way that
will make it corrupt. When, on the other hand,
Aristotle denies matter to the heavens, this is because he denies that there is in the heavens matter
of the same kind as the matter of lower bodies.

[93] Note here that I do not hold this opinion as demonstrative, but only as highly probable;
because, with the single exception of Averroës, it
is that of practically all of the peripatetics,
and because there is nothing that contradicts it,
while there are many things in its favor, as is apparent from the fourth argument [82]. Note also,
however, to overturn the foundation of the opposition's argument and to strengthen our own position,
that it is indeed true that the existence of matter
is not discovered except through transformation
[30], as is apparent from the first *Physics*, 62,
and which Averroës also teaches in the first *Physics*, 63, the fourth *Physics*, 38, and the eighth
Metaphysics, 12; once matter has been discovered
through transformation, however, one can know it
to be necessary not only for transformation but also for other reasons, even though no transformation
occurs. Place likewise, from the fourth *Physics*,
texts 3 and 32, is not discovered except through
change of place; nonetheless afterward, once the
nature of place is known, we assign a place to some

immovables, such as the earth, whereas to other movables, such as the heavens, we do not.

[94] Likewise from the nature of matter we know it to be necessary for other reasons also: as, for example, that it be the subject of a material act. Because, if an act does not exist in matter but subsists *per se,* straightaway it is immaterial and indivisible, because act of itself bespeaks no potency and imperfection. Again, straightaway it must be intelligent: because every act must have a proper operation, and if it does not exist in matter it must have an operation that is without matter; but an operation of this kind is of the intellect and will. Since we gather therefore that matter is necessary for there to be a material act, and in the heavens there is a kind of material act, such a subject must also exist. This is confirmed from the first argument [57], from the second of St. Thomas [74], and from Aristotle: the latter, since he attributed so much to form that he wished all accidents to derive from it, and since everything is found much more perfectly in the heavens, doubtless did not deny a form to the heavens.

86

[95] I said that I defend this opinion as highly probable [93]: because that the heavens are simple is capable of some defense, following Averroës, for those opposed find it harder to defend the composition of the heavens than to reject their simplicity. And second: there is as yet no compelling reason to reject this view, which has some probable arguments in its favor.

[96] Of these, the first is the most powerful: because composition seems to be instituted by nature so that things might corrupt, whence the absolutely simple is more perfect than the composite; from this it follows that, unless something else prevents it, nature will make a thing simple rather than composite. The simple, moreover, has more in common with the incorruptible, just as the composite has with the corruptible; whence it is understandable that, if nature made the heavens incorruptible, it should also make them simple, since simplicity is compatible with incorruptibility. Hence we see that incorruptible intelligences are simple, whereas sublunaries, in view of their being corruptible, are composed of matter and form.

[97] Confirmation of this argument: because
an intelligence is a simple form perfect in itself,
for which the heavens serve as matter, such that a
unity results from both; so therefore an intelligence is a simple form subsisting *per se* and perfect, such that, since matter pertains to the same
order as form, the heavens will be perfect matter,
and so on.

[98] The second argument: because, if the
heavens were to have a proper form apart from their
intelligence, they should be moved by that form,
not by an intelligence, contrary to Aristotle.

[99] Third: because it seems that Aristotle
is more in favor of this opinion, never indicat-
ing a composition in the heavens, and often denying matter in them.

[100] Confirmation: because Aristotle and the
peripatetics, accepting intelligences as forms of
the heavens, say that the heavens are animated.

[101] To the arguments in favor of Averroës's
opinion, I reply to the first [2], following Aristotle: Aristotle means by potency whatever is properly a potency of contradiction [10] because in
such a case it seems truly a potency, since it
bears on being and non-being; similarly by matter
87   he means whatever has a potency of contradiction;
therefore he does mean that a matter truly ordered
to opposites exists in the heavens, but that no
generable matter exists there. For the matter of
the heavens has no potency of contradiction with
respect to its form; yet it is the matter of something changeable, for there is a potency of contradiction with respect to place in the heavens, since
the sun can either be in the east or not.

[102] I reply, second: Aristotle denies to
eternal things any potency not having an act [5];
there is no doubt, however, that a potency of some
kind should be assigned to eternal things and to
the heavens -- but not one of contradiction, rather
one determined to a single act. This is obvious:
because, though the heavens are posited as simple,
and yet accidents that are really distinct exist in
them, and also motion, and an intelligence as an
assisting form, all of which are separable from
them, there must be some potency in them for receiv-

ing all these things; but since this is not one of contradiction, it is not mentioned by Aristotle.

[103] To the second: to the authorities on the part of matter [13], it is apparent from what has already been said that only matter that is in potency to many forms has a potency of contradiction and is susceptive of contraries.

[104] To the authorities on the part of form [16], I reply, first: the definition of a physical form consists in this, that it is a form only rationally separable from matter, as Aristotle teaches in the second *Physics*, 12 and 26, in the first *De anima*, text 17, and in the first *Metaphysics*, text 2, and the eleventh *Metaphysics*, summary 3, chapter 1; as a consequence the definition of a physical form is not that it is corruptible and generable. It is indeed true for the most part, however, that forms that are only rationally separable are corruptible, and so Aristotle sometimes teaches that physical forms are generable and corruptible; but this is to be understood for the most part, not absolutely. The form of the heavens, although inseparable in reality, is nonetheless rationally separable, and therefore is physical.

[105] I reply, second, in particular, to the argument from the first *De partibus animalium* [16]: the sense of Aristotle in this text is that abstract things do not pertain to physics, for in abstract things there is no end, and the form of the heavens is their end.

[106] To the argument from the first *Physics* [17], I reply: since Aristotle in the first *Physics* has treated of the matter that is in corruptibles, he goes on to state that he will be treating of corruptible forms that correspond to this corruptible matter.

[107] To the argument from the third *De caelo* [17], I reply: by the things he says are generated along with bodies he could mean composites, especially animated composites, just as by bodies he meant simples. Simplicius seems to indicate this, and it is confirmed from the first *De caelo*, where, since he states almost exactly what he does in the third, he says of natural substances that some are bodies, some are things having a body -- and here   88

by bodies he means simples, by having bodies,
things that are animated. Similarly, therefore,
in the third *De caelo* he says that certain things
are bodies, i.e., elements, others are generated,
i.e., animated composites.

[108] To the argument from the first *De generatione* [18], I reply: Aristotle there means that
things having the same matter both act and are acted upon; for in text 53 he had said that things
that do not have the same matter do not interact,
and again, text 54, those that have matter, i.e.,
the same matter, do react; whence, explaining what
this same means, he says that he means matter that
is the same subject of opposites.

[109] To the proof from the twelfth *Metaphysics* [19], the reply will be given below [117].

[110] To the arguments, to the first on the
part of matter [20]: I reply that matter in the
heavens has no potency of contradiction or of privation, for the reasons already given [101-103].

[111] To the confirmation [21], I reply that
the consideration of matter, which, as prior, is
without form, is a type of metaphysical consideration, and therefore that a kind of metaphysical
privation exists there, but not a real and physical privation that supposes matter without form,
and which does not exist in the heavens. Confirmation: for otherwise it could be said that the
heavens have a privation for their accidents and
a motion whereby they are in potency to them; and
the heavens are prior to accidents.

[112] To the other confirmation [22], I reply:
according to Aristotle's opinion the form of the
heavens was coeternal with their matter, but in
actual truth the matter and form of the heavens
were created at the same time; moreover, the form
of the heavens is not generable, because it does
not have dispositions associated with it whereby
it can be educed from the potency of matter.

[113] To the second argument [23], I reply:
the matter of the heavens is indeed in pure potency
by reason of specific act, but it is determined to
such an act by its proper nature alone; just as
many subjects are also in pure potency by reason of

an accidental act, though they are not in potency
by their nature to any particular accident.

[114] To the third [24], I reply: it is more
fitting to reject whatever implies an impossibility;
but it is impossible that matter exist in act without form, for -- granted that a perfect form can
exist, since form, as such, bespeaks act -- matter
cannot, because it bespeaks potency.

[115] To the argument on the part of form: to
the first [26], this is already obvious from the
foregoing [104].

[116] To the second [27], I reply: the form
of the heavens is not an active mover even though
it is a natural form; for it is a passive principle
of motion, and it gives a spherical shape to the   89
heavens whereby they are adapted to circular motion. Yet it is not a mover, because no form that,
when moving, is moved *per accidens*, from the eighth
Physics, can be a mover for an infinite time; but
concerning this argument, more below. Moreover, if
the forms of the heavens must be movers, the heavens must also be movers if they are regarded as
simple, since they are also perfect bodies both in
act and as natural, especially since accidents such
as quality, light, etc., flow from an act of that
kind.

[117] To the last text from Aristotle [28], I
reply: perhaps Aristotle only proved that intelligences lack corruptible matter. You say: then intelligences are not completely immaterial. Some
would concede that. Nonetheless it is better to
say that the immateriality of intelligences has
been proved in the eighth *Physics*. I reply, second: Aristotle proved first that intelligences are
movers in act, and then, from the fact that they
are eternal and movers in act, he argues that anything that must move for an infinite time does not
exist in matter in any way; for nothing can move
for an infinite time if it exists in matter. I
reply, third: intelligences, if they existed in
matter, would exist in corruptible matter. Because a form is in matter for its operation; but
the proper operation of an intelligence is intellection; therefore intelligences must be in matter
for intellection, and so in a matter that can contribute to it by providing senses and the organs of

sense; but these cannot exist except in corruptible matter, as is apparent from the *De anima,* for
anything sensitive must be composite.

[118] To the arguments made on the part of the
heavens, to the first [29], I reply: not every composition is for dissolution, as is apparent with
genus and difference. And if you say that the latter is a metaphysical composition, I say: there is
a type of physical composition that is not for dissolution, such as the composition of subject and
accidents in the heavens, and also that of the heavens themselves and intelligences. Composition for
dissolution therefore exists because of the imperfection of material things, which prevents their
having existence perfectly in a single act or by a
single part.

[119] To the second [32], I reply: this shows
that the heavens are a more perfect, but not a simpler, body than the elements.

[120] To the third [33], I reply: for this it
suffices that the heavens have matter of a different kind.

[121] To the last [34], I reply: such a cor-
respondence implies an impossibility and so is to
be rejected.

[122] For anyone defending the opinion of
Averroës, to the argument made for the composition
of the heavens one may reply as follows: to the
first proof [60], the sense of this is that things
that are material and corporeal can be multiplied
within the same species, since multiplication and
division arise from corporeality or from material-
ity and quantity. Thus Aristotle means by form the
nature and substance of a thing, and by form in
matter the singular nature of a thing insofar as it
is corporeal and natural; as, for example, the complete nature of man considered in itself vs. the
nature of man as individual because arising from a
particular corporeality and from particular material accidents. That this indeed is to be so understood, and that matter is not to be taken for part
of a composite, is apparent: because the origin of
the difficulty, namely, that some thing can be multiplied in species, arises not only from matter
that is part of a composite but directly from the

90

fact that the thing is corporeal and material; and
because Aristotle solves the difficulty, text 95,
[by saying] that the heavens are not multiplied
because they are composed of total matter. By total matter, moreover, he means a sensible whole
and a material body, as he teaches in the same
text; hence he also proves that the heavens are
composed of total matter by showing that there are
no natural bodies outside the heavens; but a natural
ural and sensible body is not the matter of the
heavens, to which form would correspond as a part.

[123] To the second proof [62], I reply: there
is matter and form in the heavens, as these are
understood to have intelligences assisting.

[124] To the confirmation [63], I reply: this
is proper to corruptible things, as are practically
all the things explained in the eight books of the
Physics, and according to a certain analogy it can
be applied to the heavens also, in the sense that
they are composed of a sphere and an intelligence.

[125] To the third [66], I reply: Aristotle
acknowledges this simplicity in the first *De caelo*
when he teaches that the heavens are ingenerable
and incorruptible; but he does not prove this from
the fact that there is matter in the heavens, lest
he seem to beg the principle or to argue from
things less known. Rather he proves it from the
fact that the heavens lack a contrary, as from
something more known; from this it therefore follows that the heavens lack matter, for where matter is there must be a contrary.

[126] To the arguments, to the first [68], I
reply, first: since Aristotle alone posited that
the heavens are distinct in nature and simple, he
did not interpose a fourth member in the common
definition of substance to allow for the heavens;
especially since this did not serve his purpose,
and that would not be the place to dispute whether
the heavens were a fifth essence. Moreover, it
would work against the common division of substance
into three, deriving from the Pythagoreans. It may
also be said that the heavens can be included under
the term matter, since they are material and since
they are related to the intelligences as potency.

[127] To the second argument [74], I reply:

91   for an act to the intelligent and immaterial it
does not suffice that it be *per se* subsistent, as
is apparent with the first and proper act of primary matter; what is also required is that it be an
incorporeal act; but the heavens are corporeal;
therefore [they do not have intelligent and immaterial forms].

[128] To the third [79], I reply: quantity
takes its origin from corporeal act, and this is
found both in the heavens and in matter.

[129] To the fourth [82], I reply: this shows
merely that a simple heaven is equivalent to matter
and to form. To the last [92], I reply that, as
opposed to this, incorruptibility is not always
found to accompany composition.

[130] I say, second: the heavens are not composed of matter of the same kind as the matter of
inferior bodies. Proof of the conclusion, first,
from Aristotle: in the eighth *Metaphysics,* texts 4
and 12, the ninth *Metaphysics,* text 17, and the
twelfth *Metaphysics,* text 10, he expressly teaches
that the matter found in generable things does not
exist in the heavens. Indeed, often when speaking
of the matter that is in inferior bodies Aristotle
denies that all natural things [have the same] matter, as in the places cited, the second *Metaphysics,* last chapter, and the first *De generatione,*
43; there he reproves Diogenes for positing one
common matter so that all things might be transformed into one another, teaching that there is
not one matter except in those things that are so
transformed. He provides the same judgment in the
eighth *Metaphysics,* 14, and hence he says, first
De generatione, 53, 54, and 87, that things that
share a common matter interact with one another.
Moreover, in the first *De generatione,* in the
places cited and in 43, he teaches that things that
communicate in matter act with each other and interact; but the heavens, being unalterable, do not
interact with inferior bodies, from the first *De
caelo,* 21; therefore they do not share a common
matter.

[131] Giles replies that all these things are
to be understood of a matter that has a privation
annexed and a form having a contrary. Hence he
distinguishes a twofold subject: one that has a

form having a contrary and so has a privation, for,
since contraries are apt to succeed each other in
the same subject, a subject possessing one contrary has the privation of another and a potency to
it; another, in which there is no form having a
contrary, nor is there privation properly speaking
and a potency to it. Thus when Aristotle says that
things that communicate in matter act and react
with each other, Giles wishes him to be understood
as meaning matter in the first sense; similarly,
when Aristotle denies that matter exists in the
heavens, Giles again states that matter considered
in itself is not the subject of transformation, but
only when understood in the first sense. For
things that have such a matter can, according to   92
Giles, be transformed into one another; but in the
heavens there is no matter that is the subject of
substantial change, only of local motion.

[132] But, to the contrary: the matter of the
heavens, even according to Giles, considered in
itself is in potency to all forms; therefore, when
possessing the form of the heavens, it remains in
potency to the forms it does not possess, and so
is deprived of them. Hence it follows also that
the matter of the heavens is the subject of substantial change, because it has privation and because such matter is of itself apt to be transformed into any other form; for otherwise it would not
be in potency to other forms. And if it cannot be
so transformed because it would then possess a form
lacking a contrary, this would be *per accidens;* of
itself it would always be a subject apt to be transformed.

[133] Confirmation: because Aristotle defines
matter through generation; and, again, all [his]
texts prove that the heavens are corruptible on the
part of matter.

[134] Proof of the conclusion from reason: if
there were in the heavens matter of the same kind
[as here below], it would follow that the heavens
would be intrinsically corruptible; for the matter
of the heavens is in potency to all forms, and this
potency, as Giles also attests, is of the essence
of matter; therefore the heavens have a potency to
other forms so long as this potency remains. Again:
through the reception of the heavenly form the form
of matter is not changed, and so the same potency

remains; thus, while existing with that form, it can still receive others; therefore the heavens are corruptible.

[135] It can also be proved similarly that the heavens are generable. For the matter, for example, of water and fire is the same in kind as the matter of the heavens; therefore it is in potency to the form of the heavens in the same way as they are; thus this potency either will always be frustrated or at some time it will be reduced -- or at least it can be reduced -- to act; therefore either the heavens will be generated or they will be generable.

[136] Giles replies that the cause of corruption is sometimes attributed by Aristotle to form, as in the first *Physics*, 68, and the first *De generatione*; sometimes also to matter, as in the seventh *Metaphysics*, 53; sometimes finally to privation, as in the first *Physics*, 80; indeed the root of corruption is privation, for corruption signifies privation. And hence it is apparent why matter is the cause of corruption by reason of privation, and not *per se*, as Aristotle teaches in the first *Physics*, 82. For, if matter is the cause of corruption, it is the cause insofar as it seeks a form other than the one it has; for it is in this way that it corrupts what it has; moreover, it has no appetite for another form except insofar as it is deprived of the earlier one; therefore it has the appetite and is the cause of corruption by reason of privation. Form likewise is not the cause of corruption, except by reason of privation. For the cause of corruption is nothing other than a form that has a contrary from which corruption can take place; for a form having a contrary entails the privation of the contrary. And so corruption comes about because the form exists in matter which it informs in a somewhat diminished manner, namely, with the privation of another contrary; hence the matter remains deprived, and is in potency to another form and therefore has an appetite for it; then corruption results.

93

[137] From the foregoing it can be seen why privation is the source of corruption, and why privation arises from the fact that a form has a contrary. And hence it follows that matter is not in potency to all forms according to its essence, but only to some by reason of privation. For this

reason, wherever a form exists that lacks a contrary, there can be no privation in matter, and therefore the matter will not be in potency nor will it have an appetite for other forms. Such a matter, however, exists in the heavens. Nor should it be feared that a potency of matter would be frustrated in the heavens: because matter of itself has no appetite for another form, for if it did, it would have an appetite to be deprived of its own existence; and if it has such an appetite, this is by reason of a contrary or of privation. Indeed, since these do not exist in the heavens, no potency exists there either.

[138] And from the foregoing it is seen that the heavens are incorruptible and ungenerable: because matter that possesses a form having a contrary, such as the matter of earth or of fire, is not in potency except to forms that have a contrary, and so it is not in potency to the form of the heavens.

[139] Against this reply, first: it follows that Giles is self-defeating. For, in the same question, when he argues against St. Thomas, he assumes that the potency of matter to all forms is of the essence of matter and so is always found with it. Therefore matter is not in potency to some or other forms from the fact that it possesses a form having a contrary and a privation, but by reason of its own nature. And if Giles should say that he is speaking of a physical potency through which matter can actually receive form, for this it is necessary that it possess such a form with a contrary, and so the solution is not to the point. For we have shown here that the heavens are incorruptible of their nature, although extrinsically and by divine power they can be corrupted.

[140] Second: I prove also that the matter of the heavens, while possessing its form, has a potency to others. Matter receives all forms; therefore of its nature it is adapted to receiving them, for otherwise it would not do so, since the union of matter and form is immediate. Therefore there is something intrinsic to matter itself by which it is said to be adapted to forms and in potency, and so it is not in potency to forms because it possesses a form having a contrary; therefore, even

94

when it possesses forms without a contrary, it is
in potency to all forms.

[141] Confirmation: matter, before receiving
a form, is adapted to receive a form with a contrary and one without; for otherwise it would at
the same time be apt only for a form without a contrary and for another with; but, from the fact that
it receives a form with a contrary or one without,
it is not changed; therefore no matter what form it
has, it still remains in potency to all forms.
And from this it is known that the root of corruption is not privation, but matter in potency to
many forms; for from the fact that matter of itself is adapted to receive many forms it happens
that, while possessing one, it still is able to,
and is adapted to, receive others. Hence Aristotle
attributes the corruption of the whole to matter,
first *De caelo*, 136; first *De generatione*, 24;
seventh *Metaphysics*, 22 and 53; eighth *Metaphysics*,
14; and ninth *Metaphysics*, 17.

[142] Another confirmation: because, from the
tenth *Metaphysics*, last text, corruptible and incorruptible are either of the essence of a thing
or they follow from it immediately; therefore the
cause of corruption must be said to be an essential
part, namely matter, and not something extrinsic,
i.e., matter might or might not possess privation,
and so [privation cannot be the essential cause].

[143] Understand, second, that if the opinion
of Giles were true the heavens would be corruptible, and indeed could *de facto* be corrupted; because a form which is in matter with privation must
necessarily have a contrary, as Giles admits, for
otherwise the potency of matter would be frustrated; and because matter is in potency to the dispositions and qualities of any form to the extent that
it is in potency to that form. Therefore, if the
matter of the heavens is in potency to other forms,
it will be in potency to their qualities also; as
a consequence, if through inducing other dispositions it could corrupt, similarly, if the matter
of earth has a potency to the form of the heavens
it has a potency to its dispositions also, and
therefore it could be generated; thus the heavens
would be generated and corrupted by local motion.

[144] Confirmation: because the end and the

means are sought by a potency with one and the same
appetite; therefore the form and the dispositions
to it are sought by the same appetite also, especially since a passive potency corresponds to any active potency in matter, from the third *De anima*,
text 17.

[145] Indeed, to this argument one could reply:
the heavens are corruptible by reason of form, because the form of the heavens fulfills the total potency of matter; and this will be on account of
either [a] the nobility of the celestial form, or
[b] its virtuality, or [c] its causality, or [d] its   95
incorruptibility. But, to the contrary: first, the
potency of matter is ordered to the form of the
heavens and to all others precisely insofar as they
are specific acts determining the potency of matter;
from this it is apparent that the potency of matter can never be exhausted except through these
very forms.

[146] Second: this cannot happen on account of
the form's nobility [145a]: because the soul, at
least the rational soul, is a nobler form than the
inanimate form of the heavens; and because it is
known that matter with a nobler form may still seek
an ignoble form and be changed into it.

[147] Nor can it happen on account of the form's
virtuality [145b]: because the form of the heavens,
being inanimate, does not include animate forms virtually; and because matter has an aptitude for formal act in itself, but the form of the heavens does
not contain all forms formally.

[148] Nor can if happen on account of the form's
causality [145c]: because matter is in potency not
to the causality of the form, but to its formal act.

[149] Nor, finally, on account of the form's
incorruptibility [145d]: because matter receives
form by reason of act, not by reason of duration.

[150] Second proof of the same [149]: because,
if the matter of the heavens is of the same kind
and is of itself in potency to all forms, for it to
receive the form of the heavens and not another it
must be determined by appropriate dispositions and
qualities; therefore the form of the heavens is
educed from the potency of matter, and so the heav-

ens are generated; for a form's being educed from
the potency of matter is nothing more than its being produced, through qualities and dispositions,
in a naturally apt subject.

[151] Third proof of the same [149]: this matter differs from that of inferiors by reason of potency, of reception, and of determination, because
the matter of the heavens receives its form in such
a way as not to remain in potency or to be undetermined, whereas inferior matter receives forms in
such a way that it remains in potency and is indeterminate; therefore they differ from each other
essentially, since the notion of potency and inde-
termination, as Giles himself agrees, is essential
to matter.

[152] To the arguments of Giles, to the first
[42], I reply: although both matters share the common definition of matter in that they are potency
to a specific act, they still differ in that they
are potency to different kinds of act.

[153] To the second [45], I reply: this is
true in the composite, but not in matters, for
these differ from each other.

[154] To the third [47], I reply, first: some
things can be equally distant from God and nonetheless differ specifically, to the extent that they
are distant, even though equally, in a different
genus according to different perfections; and yet
this cannot happen in numbers, because the regress
is based on one formality alone. I reply, second:
96   although all matters are equally distant in that
they are matters and pure potencies, nonetheless
the matter of sublunaries is more distant according to its proper formality, because it is more
potential, since it looks to many forms.

[155] To the fourth [48], the reply is obvious
from the foregoing [154].

[156] To the fifth [49], I reply: from the
fact that certain accidents of the heavens and of
inferiors are common, one can only infer that some
common perfection is found in the heavens and in
inferiors from which such accidents emanate, as the
perfection of body. To the text from Aristotle
[51], if that argument proves anything it proves

that the heavens are transmutable along with the elements. I reply, second, from Philoponus: the sense of Aristotle in this text, contrary to Empedocles, is as follows. If the elements are compared to each other, as Empedocles concedes, and are said to be equal, this is not to be understood according to size, because the amount of air is much greater than that of earth or water; rather it is to be understood in this way: earth is equal to air in the sense that, if it were rarefied to the degree that air is, it would be of the same quantity as air. This comparison cannot be known except from the fact that if earth were transformed into air, one palm, for example, would equal as much as ten of air. Thus, when compared in this way, they are convertible with each other.

[157] To the sixth, and to the text of Aristotle from the second *De generatione* [52], I reply: one can gather from this only that there is matter and form in the heavens just as in inferiors, and so an equal number of principles also, and of the same genus, though analogous. To the argument of Aristotle in the first *Physics* [53], I reply that there he is instructing about the principles of corruptible things; but the matter of the heavens, if there is such, is deduced only from a type of analogy with inferior matters. It is of the latter that he has treated in the first *Physics;* nonetheless what is of interest is the note peculiar to the former matter, from what Aristotle says, that the heavens are ungenerable. To the argument from the tenth *Metaphysics* [55], I reply, first: according to some authorities the heavens are not in the same category as corruptibles. But how these authorities are to be understood has been explained by us in "On the Categories."

[158] To the last [56], I reply that the matters differ from each other, as Alexander rightly teaches in the first of the *Quaestiones naturales,* chapter 15.

[159] You inquire here: on what basis do these matters differ? Capreolus thinks they differ by different forms, Cajetan in themselves alone. I say, first: they differ essentially in nothing but their matter, for otherwise, considered in themselves, they would not seem to be essentially the same, and they do so appear.

97

[160] I say, second: they have in common that
they are imperfect acts in potency to specific
acts; but they differ in that the heavenly matter
is of such an act and entity that it is in potency
only to a heavenly form, whereas the matter of sublunaries is such that it is in potency only to the
form of inferiors. It could also be said that
these matters differ likewise in relation to forms:
for the potencies differ in kind because they are
related to acts and forms of different kinds.

[161] I say, third: although the heavens are
composed of form and matter of a different kind,
they are nonetheless not corruptible intrinsically.

[162] For the explanation of this conclusion,
note, first: a substance that is completely simple
is necessarily incorruptible of its nature, because
what exists *per se*, insofar as it exists and subsists *per se*, cannot be corrupted. For, if it were
corrupted, it would corrupt insofar as it were made
up of a subject and of something that exists in the
subject; from this it is known that whatever corrupts is composite. Indeed, whether for something
to be corruptible it is sufficient that it be composite, or whether something else is required, is
not well enough established. Certainly, if corruptible signifies that for which dissolution is
not incompatible because it has two components,
whatever is composed in this way is also corruptible; and in this sense we say that dissolution is
impossible for anything that is completely simple.
Moreover, if by corruptible we mean intrinsically,
in the sense of having some intrinsic principle,
active or passive, inclining to corruption, from
which corruption can also naturally result -- for
in this way compounds are said to have within themselves an active principle of corruption insofar
as they are composed of contraries that mutually
corrupt each other, and elements are said to have
a passive principle insofar as they have a matter
inclining to corruption -- then being a composite
will not be a sufficient condition for intrinsic
corruptibility, unless in addition to this there
is composition from some substantial part that inclines toward corruption. For the corruptible, being either an essence or something flowing from the
essence, if corruptible of itself must have a principle inclining to corruption that is an essential
part of it.

[163] Note, second: if it be established that
the heavens are a simple body just as are the elements, and if they be regarded as composite, for
them to be corruptible they must have some part,
either form or matter, inclining of its nature toward corruption. Form cannot be this part, neither
in the heavens nor in a simple body, since form of
itself inclines to informing: it is in this way that
it has existence, which is sought by each thing;
since from the very fact that it would cease to inform it would cease also to exist -- for I am speaking of a material form. We conclude, therefore,
that if anything inclines to corruption in a simple
body it is matter, particularly because it is po-   98
tency; for potency bespeaks negation, and so inclines to corruption. From this it follows that,
since every composite has a subject that is in potency with respect to an act, it is corruptible;
for, wherever there is a matter existing *per se* in
potency, there must also be matter not having a
form, and therefore a negation of form, which is
the intrinsic principle of corruption. Indeed, it
is noteworthy here that matter does not incline to
corruption simply from the fact that it is a potency; nor, from the fact that it is potency to some
act, does it incline to the latter's corruption.
For matter as potency, if it is inclined, is inclined to receive the act whose potency it is, and
also the existence that such an act gives; it is
not inclined, on the other hand, to the opposite
non-existence; for, as potency, it is never inclined to leave its act, since the formality of potency
is that it be the subject of an act and that it be
perfected by it. Hence it follows that, if any
matter is in potency to one act alone in such a way
that it has no inclination apart from receiving and
possessing that act, it never inclines to corruption; for, if it were inclined, it would be inclined to non-act and to being without a form, and it
would seek non-existence, which is absurd.

[164] Note, third: since matter is potency and
potency is ordered to act, *per se* and primarily matter inclines, not to non-existence, but to the existence it acquires through act; secondarily, however, it sometimes inclines to non-existence. This
happens when a potency by nature inclines to several acts that are specifically distinct; for then,
because *per se* and primarily it inclines to all
those acts, when it possesses one it inclines also

to another; and because it cannot have that unless
it leave the one it has, it inclines secondarily
to the latter's non-existence. And so, when something is composed of one form and a matter that is
in potency to other forms, such a composite must
be intrinsically corruptible, for it has an essential part inclining to corruption.

[165] Note, fourth: the same doctrine we have
treated concerning the matter of corruption is true
when applied to the actual case of corruption. A
thing is corrupted by reason of qualities; for,
when a composite has matter that is in potency to
many forms, if this potency is not to be frustrated, such forms, not being able to coexist at the
same time, must be able to expel each other. Thus
these substantial forms must have contrary qualities through which they are generated and corrupted, assuming that contrariety is not found in the
forms themselves. Moreover, matter is in potency
to many forms; therefore, for it to receive one
rather than another it must be determined by qualities. But qualities have a contrary; therefore,
the form that is induced in such matter through the
determination of qualities can be corrupted by contrary qualities, which expel the proper dispositions. When, on the other hand, a composite is
composed of matter that is in potency to one form
alone, and this entails an intrinsic incorruptibility, it is not corrupted through qualities.
For, since such matter is ordered to only one form,
no other form should be able to expel this, lest
the matter's potency be frustrated. Moreover, this
form should not be united through qualities that
determine the matter, for the matter of itself is
determined only to that form; thus no contrary can
expel the determining dispositions by which the
form is induced in matter, since the matter is disposed of itself to such a form. And for this reason, being by nature immutable, it can never be
otherwise disposed to receive another form.

[166] Note, fifth: the same result can be established by going back from form to matter. For
there are certain forms that can unite themselves
to matter without dispositions, and certain others
that cannot, such as those that are educible from
the potency of matter, since these have dispositions through which they are educed. The latter
are also able to be removed from matter, because,

99

being united through dispositions that are qualities and so have a contrary, they can be expelled
when these dispositions are corrupted. Hence it
happens that they entail an intrinsic principle of
corruption; for, being united through dispositions,
they must have a matter that is in potency to many
forms, since dispositions exist in order to determine matter. Dispositions, moreover, have a contrary; therefore, wherever a form is induced with
these dispositions there can be contrary dispositions, since contraries come to exist in the same
subject. Finally, because otherwise it would follow, since such a form can be expelled, that matter would have to be without a form if it were not
in potency to other forms. The complete opposite
is the case wherever there is an act that is united
to matter by itself. For first, it is not educed
from a subject, since it does not have dispositions;
second, it cannot be taken away from the subject,
because it has no dispositions that can be corrupted; third, it presupposes an intrinsic principle
of incorruptibility, namely, matter that is in potency only to such an act, because, being united
by itself alone, it has no need of anything determining matter, since the matter to which it is united is already determined to it.

[167] Note, finally, the consequences that
can be gathered from the foregoing. First: not
every potency is one of contradiction, but only   100
that ordered to many acts; for this so inclines to
one act and to the existence conferred through it
that it also inclines, granted *per accidens*, to
non-existence insofar as it inclines to another
act. For when a potency is ordered to a single
act it is not one of contradiction, since it inclines only to the existence that is given by that
act, and the same should be understood of a potency that has a privation.

[168] Second: the intrinsic explanation of
corruptibility is matter with a potency to many
forms; hence Aristotle many times in the places
cited reduces corruption to matter; moreover, matter also explains why a thing is actually corrupted. For, if matter is in potency to many forms,
it is also in potency to their dispositions, and
these are contrary to each other; so, wherever such
matter exists, there can be actual corruption. It
is customary, however, for corruptibility and cor-

ruption to be associated with form also, to the extent that any form united to matter through dispositions has a contrary, and so becomes corruptible; nonetheless this reason is secondary, since it presupposes something prior, though it is more known to us. Hence, even though it could happen that this secondary reason can be valid, i.e., that some form not have a contrary, the primary reason would be, i.e., that matter would be in potency to many forms, and so the composite would still be corruptible by nature. Indeed nature never allows a form not having a contrary to exist in matter that is in potency to many forms, for, as Aristotle holds in the first *De caelo*, this would entail that matter could be frustrated. And therefore Aristotle says the same thing in the book *De longitudine vitae*, chapter 2, that it is impossible that something containing matter not have a contrary in some way; and in the same *De caelo* he states that the ingenerable and the incorruptible are convertible. From all of this one may gather that what we have said is true: if the heavens are intrinsically incorruptible, they cannot be made of the same kind of matter as inferiors.

[169] Third: wherever there is potency to one act alone, in such a composite there is no intrinsic principle of corruption. And from this it is obvious that the heavens are composed and yet are incorruptible intrinsically, since they are constituted of a matter determined of its nature to one form and of a form united to matter by itself and not through dispositions. From this it is also known that the heavens have no extrinsic principle of corruption.

[170] You inquire here: what is to be said of the matter of the heavenly spheres, whether this is one or many just as the spheres are many. We say that if the heavenly spheres differ specifically from each other, the matter of any one sphere is different in kind from the matter of another, as Albertus thinks in *De quatuor coaequevis*, question 2, article 6, and Cajetan on the First Part, question 66, article 2. Capreolus holds the contrary in the second [*Sentences*], distinction 12, question 1, article 3, as do Soncinas in the tenth *Metaphysics*, question 10, and others.

101

[171] The latters' argument is that just as

the definition of matter in general consists in
its aptitude to being made actual through form, so
different definitions of matter arise from the different ways in which matter is actuated by forms.
Therefore, just as all inferior matter is so actuated by any form that its potency and privation remain unfilled, with the result that all matter under any inferior form is of the same kind; so too,
since heavenly matter is so actuated by any form
that its entire potency is fulfilled and no privation remains, it must be of the same kind, no matter what form it is under.

[172] Our proof of the first opinion [170]:
because, if there were only a single matter in the
heavenly bodies, and their forms were to differ
specifically among themselves, and their matter
were to be in potency to many forms, with the result that, when existing under one form the matter
would be in potency to another and deprived of it,
there would be an intrinsic principle of corruption
in the heavens.

[173] Capreolus and others reply: this does
not happen because the matter of the heavens is not
an apt subject of privation and the form of the
heavens informs in such a way that it removes all
potency. But, to the contrary: first, this reply
is open to all the objections we have made against
Giles [131-158]. For, if the matter of the sun,
for example, is the same as the matter of the moon,
since the matter of the moon is in potency to such
a form of its nature, the matter of the sun will
have the same potency; but the matter of the sun,
receiving the form of the sun, is not changed of
its nature; therefore it still retains a potency
to the form of the moon. Moreover, if the matter
of the sun is the same as the matter of the moon,
and when receiving the form of the sun is no longer
in potency to the form of the moon, the same could
be said of inferior matter. For, even if heavenly
matter were the same as sublunary matter, nonetheless it takes on a heavenly form so actuating it
that it is no longer in potency.

[174] Nor is the objection that Capreolus offers valid, viz, that the argument is not the same
because sublunary matter can admit privation whereas heavenly matter cannot. For, to the contrary:
first, because matter is apt to receive privation

by reason of its potency to many forms, and so, if
the matter of the heavens is in potency to many
heavenly forms, it can be the subject of privation.

[175] Second: if this is not the reason why
matter is a subject of privation, Giles could say
102   that matter of the same kind as inferior matter is
such a subject, not from its nature, but from the
fact that it takes on a form with a contrary.

[176] To the argument to the contrary [171],
I reply: although all celestial forms are united
to, or actuate, matter in the same way, i.e., without dispositions and of themselves, nonetheless it
does not follow that this matter is one. For, being united of themselves, they require matters determined to these forms by themselves, and since
matter and form are correlatives, second *Physics*,
26, a different matter requires a different form;
thus, if there are many celestial forms, there
must be many matters.

[177] We say, second: according to Aristotle
the celestial spheres differ from each other in
species, for Aristotle posited intelligences different in species because of the heavenly bodies
being different in species.

[178] From the foregoing it is apparent, [a]
first, that one planet differs essentially from another, since planets are identical with their
spheres; [b] second, all the stars of the firmament
are the same in species.

[179] You object against the first [178a]: all
planets move with a circular motion, and this is
of the same identical kind, so they cannot differ
from each other in species. I deny the consequence:
for, although the motion of the planets is of the
same kind, nonetheless the planets differ in species for a different reason; for even though different kinds of motion always indicate natures different in species, the same kind of motion does not
always indicate the same nature. This is apparent
in the case of progressive motion, which is found
in many animals that nonetheless differ from each
other in species.

[180] You object, second: stars have the same
shape and luminosity, and thus they do not differ

specifically. I deny the consequence: because such
accidents flow from them by reason of their genus,
not their species.

[181] You object, against the second [178b]:
the fixed stars have some operations and influences
that the spheres to which they are affixed lack,
and therefore they have different specific natures
that can be known from their operations. The reply
to this argument will be apparent from what is to
be said concerning the influence of the heavens;
meanwhile I say that not every difference of operation indicates a different nature.

[182] You object, second: if the stars of the
firmament do not differ from it specifically, then
they differ numerically. But, to the contrary:
numerical multiplication is for the conservation
and perpetuation of species; but stars are incorruptible and are not composed of elements, as is
apparent from the above; therefore [they are not
numerically distinct]. Our reply is that numerical multiplication is not merely for perpetuity;
it is also for the beauty of the universe.

[183] You object, third: the stars of the firmament provide illumination, whereas its other
parts do not; therefore [they are not all of the
same species]. I reply: the stars give illumination, not from the fact that they are different in
substance from other parts of their spheres, but   103
from the fact that they have a greater density; and
this is a condition *sine qua non*, for a transparent
body such as the heavens cannot contain light that
is visible to us. That this response is valid is
apparent from the fact that a lesser or greater
density in the elements does not vary their species; so, for example, water frozen as ice, granted
that it is more dense and indeed more lucid and
visible to us, does not differ specifically from
other water. So, for the same reason, since the
stars of the firmament are related to their spheres
as knots in a table and as denser parts with which
they are continuous, they do not differ in species.

[L] Sixth Question. Are the Heavens Animated?

[1] Having explained what pertains to the matter of the heavens, it remains for us to consider what pertains to their form.

[2] The first opinion is that of certain ancient philosophers who posited a vegetative soul in the heavens because they wanted them to be nourished, for there cannot be nutrition without a vegetative soul. So felt Heraclitus and the Stoics, according to Plutarch, who said that the heavens are nourished by exhalations. Plato also, as Plutarch references in the same place, was of this opinion, as was Philolaus the Pythagorean, chapter 1, and Hesiod, who thought on this account that the heavens consume nectar and ambrosia.

[3] The second opinion is that of others who posited a sensitive soul with an external sense in the heavens; so Simplicius in the second *De caelo*, who held that this soul indeed lacks taste and smell but that it has touch, since the heavenly bodies touch each other, as well as hearing and sight, since they also hear the sound they put forth and see everything that happens. Proof of this opinion: because it is more perfect for a body to sense, see, and hear than to lack these senses; second, because even the viler animated bodies have them.

[4] The third opinion is that of others who posited a soul with an internal sense, i.e., imagination, in the heavens; this opinion is attributed to Avicenna, who in the ninth *Metaphysics*, chapters 2 and 3, thought that there would exist in the heavens, apart from moving intelligences, some other type of soul that would be related to the heavens as man's soul is to his body. He teaches that this soul is necessary because for mo-

104

tion to occur in the heavens it is not enough to
have an intelligence understanding and willing a
universal motion; the imagination of such motion,
e.g., of daily rotation, is also necessary, and
this cannot come from an intelligence whose understanding is universal and invariable.

[5] Finally, the fourth opinion is that of
those who posited an intellective soul in the heavens, concerning whom we shall treat below [10-28].

[6] I say, first: there is no vegetative soul
in the heavens. First: because, from Aristotle,
third *Metaphysics*, text 15, what requires food is
not eternal. The reason for this: because what is
nourished must have an organ, and so requires a
body that is not simple; it must change food and
convert it into its own substance, lest it become
weak; but what has these characteristics is corruptible; therefore [the heavens would be corruptible
and not eternal]. Second: on the part of the food.
If the heavens are nourished they are nourished by
something either corruptible or incorruptible; if
corruptible, then they themselves would be corruptible; if incorruptible, they could not convert it
to their own substance; moreover, the nourishment
would finally run out at some time; therefore [the
heavens again would not be eternal].

[7] I say, second: in the heavens there is no
sensitive soul having either [a] an internal or
[b] an external sense. Proof of the conclusion
with regard to the second part [b]: first, because
the sensitive soul presupposes both the vegetative
soul and touch, from the second *De anima*, 17; but
touch consists in primary qualities, which do not
exist in the heavens, any more than does the vegetative soul; therefore [the heavens have no sensitive soul]. Indeed, there cannot be touch in a
simple body, as Aristotle rightly teaches in the
third *De anima*, texts 60, 62, and 66. Second: if
there were a sensitive soul in the heavens there
would be organs also, and thus the heavens would
be composite bodies, they could move themselves,
and they would not require intelligences; and all
of these consequences are opposed to the truth.
Third: because senses would exist in the heavens
to no purpose; for they are not necessary for conservation because the heavens are incorruptible;
nor for intellection, because, as we shall show,

the heavens do not possess an intellective form;
nor for motion or for guidance, because they are
moved and governed by intelligences.

[8] To Simplicius [3], I reply: the heavens
are indeed in contact but not by a sensitive touch,
since they lack primary qualities; and although it
is more perfect that a body sense than not, nonetheless it is impossible that a simple and incorruptible body sense, just as that it see and hear.
Add to this: the heavens are most perfect only under the formality of being a body, not in an unqualified way.

[9] Proof of the conclusion with respect to
the first part [7a]: because an internal sense presupposes an external sense, for the imagination can
never know anything unless this exists previously
in an external sense, and so even Aristotle, second
De anima, text 161, specifies that the imagination
is moved by a sense when reduced to act. Second:
because there is no reason why such an imagination
should be posited in the heavens. Nor does what
Avicenna says [4] have any necessity, for an intelligence knows motion as an effect when knowing itself as a cause, since it knows the entire eternal
motion that it effects, and the parts of this motion are not actually divided in it, since the motion is one and perpetual.

[10] I say, third: the entire difficulty of
this question revolves around how the heavens can
be animated by an intellective soul. For that it
is so animated was held by Plato, in the *Philebus*,
the *Phaedo*, the second book of the *Republic*, and
the *Timaeus*, and by Timaeus also in his work, *De
natura et anima mundi*, by Aristotle, and by some
Church Fathers such as Origen and St. Jerome; St.
Augustine, however, is doubtful on this, and St.
Basil and Damascene deny it.

[11] First, therefore, concerning this problem there was the opinion of some who thought that
there ought to exist in the heavens, apart from intelligences, some kind of proper intellective souls;
thus Alexander, in the twelfth *Metaphysics*, texts
30 and 49, comments 20 and 24, maintaining that intelligences move the heavens in the order of final
causality and proper souls in the order of efficient causality, to the extent that the latter are

105

brought to bear on the intelligences by their appetite. Algazel, Rabbi Moses, and Isaac seem to
feel the same, as Albert mentions in the eleventh
Metaphysics, tract 2, chapter 10.

[12] Proof of this opinion: because God and
the intelligences, according to Aristotle, move by
a motion of appetite and desire; therefore there
ought to exist in the heavens something capable of
having appetite and desire, and this is nothing but
the proper souls of the heavens; therefore [there
are proper intellective souls in the heavens].

[13] The second opinion is that of others
thinking that the intelligences themselves are
forms informing the heavens. That this is the o-
pinion of Aristotle St. Thomas teaches in the second *Contra gentes*, chapter 70, and Ferrariensis in
the same place, and Aquinas seems to indicate the
same thing in the first *De caelo* at text 13; St.
Bonaventure also teaches this in the second [*Sentences*], distinction 14; as does Achillini in the
first and third *De orbibus*, Mirandulanus in book
21, section 6, and Balduinus in inquiry 11. These
three think that the heavens are composed of an intelligence, a form informing, and the heaven itself, which is matter in act that receives its animated being from the intelligence. They explain
their opinion as follows. Matter is twofold: one
kind is in potency to existence alone and is united to form without dispositions; this entails that   106
the form united to it, coming as it does before
dispositions and quantity, remains immaterial, indivisible, immobile even *per accidens*, and incorruptible, and indeed gives existence to matter --
not receiving it from matter, because it is abstract and does not inhere in matter. The other
matter is in potency to existence and to non-existence, and is united to form through dispositions
and quantity; this requires that the form coming
to it be quantified, material, and corruptible, because it comes after quantity, and so it gives
existence to matter in such a way that it also receives existence when it inheres in matter. In the
heavens, therefore, matter and form are present in
the first way, not in the second. From this it
follows that the intelligence gives animated existence to the heavens first and then operation and
motion, but in such a way that it itself is moved
neither *per se* nor *per accidens* when the heavens

move, since it is abstract.

[14] Proof of this opinion: first, because the soul, which is a form giving existence, is the act of an organized body having life potentially, from the second *De anima*, 17; but an intelligence is an act of this kind in relation to the heavens. For a heaven is a natural body, an instrument apt to receive an operation from an intelligence; and an intelligence is its act, as is apparent from Aristotle, at text 24 of the second *De anima*, teaching that when any operation is found in two things, and in the one on account of the other, the one is form and the other matter. Therefore, since to live, to sense, and to understand goes with the soul, and with the body because of the soul, it follows that the soul is form and the body matter. In the same way, however, the intelligence's motion goes with the heaven, on account of the intelligence, and also with the intelligence itself; therefore the intelligence is act and the heaven matter.

[15] Second: the heavens are animated, from the second *De caelo*, texts 13 and 63; but, if they are animated, they are animated by a soul that gives existence; and indeed, from the second *De anima*, 17, life is existence for living things.

[16] Third: the heavens are alive, from the first *De caelo*, 10, and the second *De caelo*, 6; but whatever is alive lives by a soul; therefore [the heavens have a soul].

[17] Fourth: the proof that the soul of the heavens is intellective. The heavens move with an eternal motion; but such a motion cannot come from a material soul because a soul in matter moves in a finite time; therefore [the soul of the heavens is immaterial and intellective]. Confirmation: because man's soul is intellective, and thus the soul of the heavens must be even more so.

[18] Fifth: the proof that this intellective soul is an intelligence. An intelligence is commonly said to be the form of the heavens; thus it is also the soul of the heavens, as is apparent from the second *De caelo*, text 6; but the soul is the quiddity of the thing ensouled, from the second *De anima*, text 8; therefore [the intellective soul of the heavens is an intelligence].

[19] Sixth: intelligences are the nature of
the heavens, and nature must be either matter or
form; but intelligences, as is apparent, are not
the matter of the heavens; therefore they must be
their form.

[20] Seventh: in everything that is moved and   107
in every physical thing four causes may be found,
from the second *Physics*, 70; but, unless an intelligence is said to be the form and both the final
and the efficient cause of the heavens, the four
causes of the heavens cannot be assigned; therefore
[an intelligence is the form of the heavens].

[21] Eighth: if an intelligence is not the
form, then there must be an extrinsic mover; but
what moves from without moves with a violent motion, from Aristotle; thus the motion of the heavens would be violent.

[22] Ninth: the heavens and intelligences make
one in number; thus the first is matter, the second, form.

[23] Finally: whatever gives operation also
gives existence; but intelligences give operation
to the heavens; therefore [they give existence al-
so]. Nor can you say that an intelligence is merely an assisting form, for this kind of form was not
known to Aristotle. Second: it would follow that
intelligences would be united to the heavens only
when moving, and would then make them move, whereas
they continually animate the heavens. Confirmation:
because intelligences give many things to the heavens that could not be in them from assisting forms
alone; for by reason of intelligences the heavens
are said to move themselves, to understand, to desire, and so on; and these operations cannot come
from an assisting form. For the latter would be
related to the heavens only as a sailor is to his
ship, and no one would say that the ship moves itself, understands, and is animated because of the
sailor.

[24] The third opinion is that of others thinking this the opinion of Aristotle: the intelligences
simply assist the heavens, nor are there other souls
apart from these. St. Thomas holds this in the
First Part, question 70, article 6, and in the question *De creaturis spiritualibus*, Jandun in the twel-

fth *Metaphysics*, question 12, and the second *De
caelo*, question 4, and Zimara in proposition 70
and on question 12 of Jandun.

[25] I say, first: apart from intelligences
no other souls are constituent in the heavens.
Proof: because, if apart from intelligences the
heavens were to have a soul, the latter would be
of the same kind as the human soul in its body and,
as a consequence, would presuppose a sensitive soul
so that it could gather knowledge by means of the
senses; and this has already been refuted [7].

[26] Second: such souls would be in the heavens to no purpose. For they would not be needed
to give existence to the heavens, because the heavens are in act by their very selves, since they are
simple; nor do they need a soul to have existence,
since for that any form is sufficient. Nor would
they be necessary for operation: they are not needed for understanding, for understanding cannot be
exercised by a form existing in a simple body,
since it requires phantasms and senses; nor are
they needed for motion, since an intelligence is
sufficient for this. Confirmation: because, if
there were a soul in the heavens imparting motion,
it would move *per accidens* with the motion of the
108   heavens; but thus it would be corruptible, from the
eighth *Physics*, 72. And if you say that it is made
eternal by the intelligence, to the contrary: because what is corruptible of its nature cannot be
made incorruptible by another, according to Aristotle. Confirmation: because, from the eighth
Physics, 78, a power that resides in a body cannot
move for an eternal time; therefore this kind of
soul cannot give the heavens a perpetual motion.

[27] Third: if there were such a soul it
would pertain either to physics or to animastics;
but Aristotle never takes note of this; therefore
[there is no such soul].

[28] Finally: Aristotle's argument contained
in the eighth *Physics*, showing that there is a first
mover, is based on a mover moving efficiently, not
finally; on this account he also differentiates in
the heavens a part moving from a part moved, and
the moving part he proves to be immobile and immaterial; therefore intelligences are the movers of
the heavens not only finally but also efficiently.

[29] I say, second: although it may not seem
completely improbable, according to Aristotle, that
intelligences are forms simply informing, neverthe-
less, according to Aristotle and the truth, it is
much more probable that they are assisting forms.
The first part of the conclusion is obvious from
the arguments already given [14-23], and from the
fact that respected authorities teach that Aristotle was of this opinion.

[30] Proof of the second part: first, because
St. Thomas in the places cited, St. Cyril in the
second book *Contra Iulianum*, Scotus, Durandus, and
other scholastics teach that Aristotle thought
this. The same seems apparent also from Alexander,
who, if he had not thought from Aristotle's opinion that it was quite certain that intelligences
are not informing, would never have posited other
souls apart from intelligences. This is also confirmed from what Simplicius wrote, second *De caelo*,
chapter 3.

[31] Second: because this agrees with what
Aristotle has written concerning intelligences.
For he teaches, first, that intelligences are separated from matter and exist apart from bodies;
from this it is apparent that they are not informing. And that Aristotle teaches this is apparent
in many places, especially from the eighth *Physics*,
text 78, and from the twelfth *Metaphysics*, texts
30, 35, and 41, where he proves this.

[32] Those opposed reply: one can gather from
Aristotle only that intelligences do not depend on
matter for their existence. To the contrary: first,
Aristotle's statement that intelligences are separated from matter and exist apart from bodies clearly asserts that they are not informing forms. Confirmation: because in text 78 of the eighth *Physics*
he proposes to demonstrate later that intelligences
do not exist in bodies, and he refers to that in
text 86, and he repeats the same in the twelfth
Metaphysics, 41; but if they were informing forms
they could truly be said to be parts of a body, and
to have a body for a subject, and so to exist in
it. Add to this: though Aristotle always maintains   109
that intelligences exist apart from bodies, he never
states that they inform.

[33] Nor can you say that Aristotle sometimes

holds that intelligences are in the heavens: for
he says that they are in the heavens either as in
a kind of proper place, and this from the common
consent of mankind, or that they are in the heavens as movers; so also, in the eight *Physics*, 84,
he states that the first mover is in the equinoctial circle because the greatest velocity is most
apparent there. From these statements, however,
one cannot correctly infer that intelligences are
informing forms.

[34] Nor again can you hold that what Aristotle says, that intelligences exist apart from bodies, must be understood of the first mover alone
and not of other intelligences; or that this is
definitely not to be understood of things that move
efficiently, but only finally. For, though in the
eighth *Physics* Aristotle speaks of the first mover,
nonetheless in the twelfth *Metaphysics* he asserts
the same of all intelligences. Moreover, in the
eighth *Physics* Aristotle treats of the first efficient mover; for this reason he divides the heavens into a part moving and a part moved, and shows
that the moving part is immovable outside of bodies; thus he is not speaking only of things moving as final causes.

[35] Confirmation of the argument from the
first mover: for, since Aristotle proposes the same
argument for the first mover and for other intelligences, if the others are informing forms, the
first mover will be also; but this cannot be maintained. For it would follow that there would then
be potentiality and imperfection in God; because,
if the first mover is a form, then it has a potency
to informing, and, as a part, a potency for making
a single whole when taken together with another
part. But a part, precisely as part, implies imperfection, for it is a part from the fact that it
is not a perfect *quid per se*. And from this it
would also follow that God is not pure act, as Aristotle holds.

[36] Moreover, the first mover would not be a
first cause, because a first cause must depend on
no other. But the first mover, if it were a form,
would depend on matter. For, though it would not
receive existence from matter, nonetheless, insofar
as a form requires a subject, it would depend on
it, just as the rational soul, though not receiving

existence from matter, is dependent on a material
cause; also because the first cause would actually
be the first composite heaven, and not the intelligence. Similarly, the first composite heaven
would be a totally perfect and complete being,
whereas the intelligence would be related to it as
part to whole and would communicate to it, as form,
its act and everything that flows from it. Again,
the heaven itself would be the agent acting on inferior bodies by its motion and light; for the
whole heaven would be the agent that would effect
the motion.

[37] Confirmation from the first *De anima*, 64:   110
here Aristotle states that it is more correct to
say that man understands through his soul than that
the soul understands, even though the intellective
soul is an immaterial form. So, for a like reason,
it would be more correct to say that the heaven
acts on inferiors through an intelligence than that
the intelligence is the first cause that acts itself.

[38] Confirmation of the same on the part of
the rational soul: the latter is a form that does
not inhere in matter; in fact many even think that
according to Aristotle it is merely assisting, as
does Averroës, and yet Aristotle never speaks of
the rational soul as he does of intelligences; rather he teaches that it can be separated but that
it cannot exist completely apart from bodies. From
this Aristotle seems to indicate that intelligences
are even more separated from matter than is the
rational soul.

[39] Final confirmation: because Aristotle
seems always in doubt whether the rational soul is
a form, from the mere fact that it understands,
granted through phantasms; and yet he never expres-
ses doubt whether an intelligence could be the form
of the heavens. Still there seems to be more reason for doubting in the case of the intelligence,
because its operation, namely, intellection, is independent of the body not only subjectively but
even objectively. From this it is apparent that
Aristotle thought that an intelligence is not a
form.

[40] Aristotle teaches, second [cf. 34], that
intelligences are immobile even *per accidens*; and

this is gathered from the eighth *Physics*, 52, where
he holds that anything that, when moving, moves
per accidens cannot move for an eternal time. From
this text it is apparent that intelligences are not
forms, because a form moves *per accidens* with the
movement of the body.

[41] Those opposed reply: from this text one
can gather only that an intelligence is not a form
inhering in matter, for the latter moves *per accidens*. To the contrary, first, Aristotle in the second *Topics*, chapter 3, argues against those holding
that ideas are immobile: ideas are in us; but, when
we move everything that is in us moves; therefore
[they move too]; and yet it is certain that ideas
do not inhere in matter and are separate; therefore [forms that do not inhere in matter also move
per accidens]. Second: the rational soul is an immaterial form and yet it moves *per accidens* with
the movement of the body; therefore [immaterial
forms move *per accidens*]. Third: an intelligence
is an informing form; therefore it communicates
its act to the heavens; but the resulting composite moves while having the act of an intelligence;
therefore the act moves *per accidens* at the same
time [as the heavens move].

[Tractate on Alteration]

[First Question. On Alteration]

[0] [Alteration is what takes place when a
thing "alters" or changes in some respect. The
term itself has many usages, and can be taken in a
very broad sense to mean any transformation, in a
less broad sense to mean any change that is sensible and successive, in a proper sense to mean any
change that involves contraries, and in a most
proper and fundamental sense to mean any change
between primary qualities. Depending on whether
qualities are perfective or corruptive, moreover,
alterations are also spoken of as perfective or
corruptive; the first involves qualities that only
perfect or complete the subject, such as light,
knowledge, and virtue, whereas the second involves
qualities whose change can bring about the corruption of one substance and the generation of another, such as primary qualities. Again, since different kinds of change are specified by their
characteristic termini, the various types of alteration can be made precise by identifying the
terminus of each.]

[1] [This understood, I say, first: if alteration is taken in its broadest sense for any type
of transformation whatever, its terminus can be
substance or any one of the accidents. I say,
second: if alteration is taken less broadly for
any type of successive change, its terminus can be
any accident that terminates motion *per se*, viz,
quantity, quality, and location. I say, third: if

159

alteration is taken in a proper sense for that
which takes place in contrary or intermediate attributes with the subject remaining sensibly the
same, the terminus can be only a quality of the
third species. It cannot be a quality of the first
and second species, for these are not sensible nor
do they necessarily involve contraries, nor can it
be a quality of the fourth species, figure or
111   shape, for this is really identified] with quantity, which being indivisible and not susceptive of
contraries, cannot terminate generation.

[2] I say, fourth: if alteration is taken for
what takes place amjng primary qualities, its terminus is a tangible quality, for primary qualities
are perceived by the sense of touch. Hence Aristotle, in the first *De generatione*, 24, maintains
that the alteration most proper to man terminates
with tangible qualities.

[N] Second Question.   On Intension and Remission

[1] It is certain and obvious to the senses
that alteration takes place not only when something
changes in quality, but also when a thing varies
according to more or less while retaining the same
quality, as Aristotle teaches in the fifth *Physics*,
19. From this arises intension and remission in
qualities, which we are about to explain: first,
because they are found in practically every alteration, and so one cannot understand how alteration
comes about if he does not understand intension
and remission; and second, because almost every
action comes about through intension and remission,
and so to understand action it is first necessary
to understand remission and intension.

[2] Authors who have treated this matter are:
St. Thomas in the first *Sentences*, distinction 16,
question 2, article 2, in the First Part of the
Second Part, question 52, article 2, and in the
Second Part of the Second Part, question 24, article 5; Capreolus, on the first *Sentences*, distinction 17, question 2; Herveus in *Quodlibet* 6, question 11; Gandavensis in *Quodlibet* 5, question 19;
Soncinas on the eighth *Metaphysics*; Giles on the
first *De generatione*, question 19, in *Quodlibet* 5,
question 13, and in *Quodlibet* 2, question 14; Burley in the tract *De intensione et remissione*; Durandus in the first *Sentences*, distinction 17,
question 7; Gregory, same place, question 4, arti-   112
cle 1; Scotus, same, question 4; Ockham and Gabriel, question 7.

[3] Note, first: two things can be considered
in intension and remission. One is what is formally defined as intension and remission, the other,
the mode these terms signify. Concerning the
first: as in quantity there is extension and large
and small, and in every genus perfect and imperfect,

161

so wherever there is any notion of form or of quality there is more or less; and this denominates not
the qualities but the subjects, as is gathered from
the seventh *Physics*, 29. Hence it is said that
comparisons are made in the lowest species and that
more or less does not vary the species. Concerning
the second, intense and remiss can be taken in two
ways: first, in the sense that intense is said in
comparison with remiss, and hence whatever is less
can be said to be intense with respect to something
lesser, and conversely; second, they can be taken
absolutely and *per se*, and so intense and remiss
require some latitude of which they themselves may
be considered the extremes, and on this account if
there is a medium degree of any quality, whatever
would be above it would be said to be intense, below it, remiss. And from this can be understood
how intense and remiss differ when compared to larger and smaller and perfect and imperfect.

[4] Note, second: the existence of intension
in qualities can be proved, first, from the senses,
which establish that the same object when less hot
can later become more hot; and this does not arise
from the fact that some part previously not hot
becomes hot, but from the fact that what was completely hot previously becomes hotter later. Aristotle also teaches and confirms the same, for in
the category of quality he asserts that it is a
property of quality to be susceptive of more and
less, and, in the fifth *Physics*, text 19, he concedes that there can be a kind of alteration in the
same quality according to more and less. And here
it is understood that, having undergone this intension, contraries can be together and intermingled
in some way. For if there were no intension contraries would be simples and would always exist
integrally; as a result, either they could never
be mixed and come together, or they would exist together and be perfect, and consequently they would
not act on each other. Hence Aristotle explains
mixture through intension and remission, as is apparent from the first *De generatione* and especially
from the second, text 48.

[5] From the foregoing it is apparent that intension permits a comparison that involves a latitude in the same species, and moreover that altera-
113   tion is successive not only from the fact that the
subject is altered in one part and then in another,

but also by reason of form insofar as the remiss
comes to be intense, and conversely, in the same
part of the subject. The existence of such a successive intension may be proved: because, even when
the subject has been altered in its entirety, there
may yet follow an alteration that comes to be successively. Moreover: there are some kinds of alteration that do not take place successively on the
part of the subject, since all of its parts are altered together, as is apparent from the first *Physics*, 23 -- an example of this, according to Aristotle, is freezing; and nonetheless it is certain
that some of these alterations take place successively; therefore they do so by reason of form, as
Alexander rightly notes from Simplicius, fourth
Physics, comment 23 on text 22.

[6] Nor can you object: Aristotle sometimes
states that alteration is continuous only on the
part of the subject, from which it appears to follow that there is no succession on the part of the
form and hence no intension either. For, from what
has been said concerning the continuity of motion,
the reply should be obvious: changes cannot be continuous intrinsically on the part of the form, but
they can be on the part of the subject and of time;
in addition, since Aristotle obviously grants that
in quality there is intension, he must also admit
that in alteration there is succession, apart from
that taking place on the part of the subject.

[7] Note, third: intension is proper to quality, although some wish to locate it in substance
and others in quantity; this is apparent from Aristotle in the *Categories* and from common opinion.
Indeed, intension can take place in quality in two
ways: first, consecutively, and in this way, for
example, health is intensified and diminished with
the intension and remission of the qualities that
go to make up temperament -- in this way also relation is said to undergo intension and remission
by reason of its foundation; second, *per se* and
properly. The latter again takes place in two ways:
first, through admixture with a contrary, and in
this way, for example, the less hot always has some
cold mixed in with it; second, without the admixture of a contrary, as happens with light, where
there is more and less either on the part of the
agent as it is more or less a light source, or on
the part of the subject, for a subject that is less

disposed receives less light and, if successively
disposed, is more and more illuminated.

[8] Intension properly speaking is what is
found in true alteration and with the admixture of
a contrary; concerning this there arises the difficulty how intension takes place in alteration.
It should be noted that we can estimate an intension to have taken place in an alteration in two
114   ways: first, extrinsically, when no change has
taken place in the quality but only in something
else -- and this can take place again in two ways,
for the quality can be intensified through the
greater disposition of the subject or through the
expulsion of a contrary; second, intrinsically,
when some change has been made in the quality that
is intensified -- and this also can take place in
two ways, through a new production of the quality
or in some other way.

[9] I say, first: intension does not take
place through an extrinsic change alone -- that is,
either an intension follows in the quality itself
when some extrinsic change has been made, for then
the intension takes place not through the disposition of the subject or through the expulsion of
the contrary but through an increase on its own
part; nor, second, does it take place through the
expulsion of the contrary or the disposition of
the subject, with the quality itself remaining in-
divisibly the same.

[10] First: because it would follow that the
quality is indivisible and itself always the same;
but the same thing when remaining the same always
acts the same, and as a consequence it always af-
fects the subject in the same way; moreover, the
action of the quality is always the same whether
it is intense or remiss, since action follows from
the quality in itself; and finally, the senses
should perceive the intension and remission in the
same way, for the senses perceive a quality the way
a power apprehends its object.

[11] Second: it would follow that there is no
true intension in the quality; indeed one cannot
say of a quality that it is remiss and not remiss,
etc., since contradictories cannot be truly predi-
cated of the same thing.

[12] Third: it would follow that intension
would not be alteration, the contrary of what Aristotle teaches, nor would it be motion or change
either. For alteration is an acquisition or at
least a transmutation of the form that is being altered, and motion is nothing more than a *forma fluens;* but here the form remains completely unchanged; therefore [intension would be neither alteration nor motion]. And if one should admit that
there is some motion or alteration here, it would
not be in the quality that is said to intensify but
in its contrary, if the intension takes place
through expulsion, or it would be in the dispositions of the subject, if it takes place through
dispositions. Confirmation: because it would follow that the quality is acquired in an instant.

[13] Fourth: it would follow that contraries
cannot exist together because, if they were together, they would be integral and perfect, and this
cannot happen.

[14] Finally: in the production of a quality
and in intension the agent remains and operates in
the same way -- this is apparent with fire, which
always acts by the same principle, namely, heat,
and by the same action, namely, heating -- and thus
it would always act the same; so, for example, just
as it was producing heat in the beginning, it would
also produce heat later. Therefore, if it either   115
expels the contrary or changes the disposition of
the subject, since it would do this through heat
it would be effective secondarily for the production of heat, or, if it acts through some quality
distinct from that through which it first produces
the quality, which then is increased, the alteration
would not be one motion, but there would be two alterations and actions.

[15] Proof of the same result in particular,
against dispositions, an opinion that Giles seems
to favor when he treats this as above [2] and in
Quodlibet 6, question 9: first, because it would
follow that a very weak agent, e.g., heat, would
produce an intenser heat in a subject that is well
disposed, e.g., straw, than a very strong agent,
e.g., a very intense fire, would produce in a subject that is quite indisposed, e.g., iron, and this
is false.

[16] Second: because, if intension comes about through the dispositions of the subject, when the agent intensifies heat, for example, it would do nothing but dispose the subject more; yet a disposition cannot be effected except through some action whereby a particular quality is produced in a subject, and so this quality either is produced all at once or successively; if all at once, then intension takes place in an instant; if successively, the disposing quality will then undergo intension either through the intrinsic mutation from which the intensity results, or through another disposition, and so there would be a disposition of a disposition to infinity.

[17] And if you should say that the subject is more and more disposed not through an intension of the same disposition but through different qualities successively produced, the later of which disposes more than the earlier, to the contrary: because, when fire warms and increases the heat, if it disposes and does not dispose through heat because it then would produce heat, it disposes only through dryness, since it has no other active power, and so it would not be able to effect the various dispositions. Moreover, the disposing quality would be produced in an instant, for, if successively, it would already have its proper intension, and so it never happens that there is any one type of continuous intension, but many.

[I say, second: intension takes place through the addition of a new part to the quality. This is so because intension cannot take place, nor is it at all intelligible, if there is no addition of a new entity. This new entity or part is then combined with the quality already existing in such a way that the two make up one integral and perfect quality, which is the terminus of the process of intension.]

[18] I say, third: in intension the prior part of the quality does not perish. First proof: because no cause can be assigned why it should perish. For there is no contrary present, and the subject remains the same; nor is a conserver needed if the agent is actually present; nor does a quality require a conserver, except for light. Nor is it possible, for example, for the first degree of heat induced by a heater into cold water to be

116

corrupted, for then water would act by itself;
moreover, contraries would never exist together,
for even if all extrinsic agents were removed they
would corrupt each other.

[19] Nor is it corrupted because a subsequent
degree is produced, for the subsequent degree can
be united to the prior in the same way as a quantity can be united to a pre-existing quantity.

[20] Nor is it corrupted because the second
degree contains the first in itself virtually, for
such containment is found wherever there are forms
that are different in species, since then the higher contains the lower virtually, but this cannot
occur in qualities of the same species.

[21] Nor is it corrupted because the earlier
degree is the *terminus a quo* from which the alteration must recede, because the *terminus a quo* in
intension is the contrary, as Aristotle teaches in
the fifth *Physics*, 19, and, although the first degree could be said to be the *terminus a quo*, nonetheless it would be such a terminus not in its entity, but formally, because it is remiss, and so
it would suffice that it recede in this way; just
as in augmentation the smaller quantity does not
perish really, but only formally, because it is
the smaller.

[22] Nor, finally, is it corrupted because,
if it should remain, at the end of the alteration
an infinite quality would be acquired, for, since
such an acquisition takes place successively, at
the end a quality is finally acquired that is potentially infinite but actually finite; and in this
way philosophers also speculate about time and motion.

[23] Second proof, on the part of the contrary: for if someone intensifying heat in water corrupts the earlier degrees, he either corrupts the
coldness all at once or he first corrupts one degree and leaves the others; if in the second way,
the same mode would be served in inducing [heat]
also, that is, one degree would be produced and
would remain, and so on; if, on the other hand, he
immediately corrupts all the coldness, then he also
immediately produces all the heat, since all the
cold cannot be corrupted except by its complete

contrary, and, in view of the fact that nothing is
left to resist when all the cold is corrupted, all
the heat must be produced immediately, for succession arises from impotency.

[24] Perhaps you say: fire first corrupts all
the cold, for example, eight degrees, and then produces seven; for cold can be produced from a contrary, since it is then produced *per accidens* and
as a means to the production of the contrary qual-
117   ity. But, against this: for, in whatever way that
come about, the hot would in no way have within
itself the power to produce a coldness of seven degrees. Add to this: fire acts only to corrupt coldness and produce heat, and, as a consequence, when
it corrupts cold initially it does not produce it
again, especially since the cold so produced would
not be conducive to producing heat but to impeding
it.

[25] Third proof: because it would follow
that, just as fire corrupts all the coldness of water, so, since the thing acted upon itself reacts,
the water in reacting would corrupt all the hotness; but when all the heat in the fire and all the
coldness in the water have been corrupted, no agent
can be assigned that could produce seven degrees of
coldness in the water and seven of heat [in the
fire]. Add to this: even a reagent that is remiss,
as, for example, a cold object of two degrees, when
reacting with fire hot to eight degrees, would corrupt the eight degrees of heat and generate seven
of cold, and this is completely absurd.

[26] Fourth proof: because otherwise there is
no way for motion and alteration to come about.
First: since the alteration would not have any unity, because for it to be numerically one there must
be a form that is numerically one, fifth *Physics*,
34.

[27] Second: because either the degrees that
are produced and that corrupt the others are produced in single instants -- but if this is said,
then alteration would not be continuous, since instants cannot be produced successively; or they are
produced successively -- and then either the first
degree, having been produced, will remain only until the second is entirely produced, and then some
part of the second degree would be superadded to

the remainder of the first, and so in this way the
whole alteration would come about; or, if the first
degree does not remain for a time and nothing of
the second degree is added to a pre-existing degree,
it would follow that in alteration quality is successive in the same way as is motion and time, and
so nothing of it would exist except at an instant,
because in the preceding time that quality would
not exist, and so forth.

[28] Therefore one must conclude that intension comes about through the production of a new
quality in such a way that, when the later part
comes, the earlier remains. And this again can
take place in two ways: first, the later degrees
that are added are produced in single instants, and
in this way the intension would be discrete, as the
Thomists prefer; second, in such a way that the intension comes about successively by a type of continued action.

[29] I say, fourth: intension comes about continuously. First proof: for otherwise it would
follow that alteration is not a single motion,
since the instants are not continuous but time intervenes, nor is it motion, since it would not be
the act of a being in potency, as has been proved
in the *Physics*.

[30] Second proof: because, if a form or qual-
ity is produced through instants, either the agent   118
does nothing in the time intervening between the
instants, or it does something. If it does nothing, this is absurd: for the agent then has been
applied and has sufficient active power, and the
reagent is well disposed; therefore it will act
with full vigor, since no reason can be assigned
why it should have acted a little previously and
then stop acting. If, on the other hand, it does
not act with full vigor, this is because some time
must have elapsed between the first and the second
action, to prevent continuity; but for this any
time at all is sufficient and, however little is
assigned, still less is sufficient, and so to infinity; thus a determinate time can never be assigned, and so there will never be action. And
if the agent does act, either it produces something
of the quality, and thus successively, or it merely
disposes. But setting aside that it cannot always
be shown that the agent disposes or how it disposes,

if it disposes it induces some quality in the
thing; therefore this disposition and quality is
induced either successively, and the quality is
successive, or through instants, and then the initial question returns.

[31] Nor can you say with the Thomists that
heat having been produced, at the same instant it
is then extended to the other parts of the subject:
for the first part in which heat is already produced is closer to the agent, and so the agent, having finished with that, will not act on the more
distant part. Add to this: it would follow that
the agent would act no less on the closer parts
than on the most distant, nor would it initially
induce the first degree in the closest part rather
than in the most distant. Confirmation: because a
form is produced successively by reason of the resistance of the contrary, and so it cannot be produced through instants alone, for it would otherwise follow that each part would be produced in an
instant and, as a consequence, without resistance
and all at once. Therefore one must conclude with
Simplicius on the eighth *Physics*, 12, at text 23,
Giles on the first *De generatione* at text 20, Jandun on the eighth *Physics*, question 8, and others,
that intension and remission come about continuously.

[32] To anyone, however, who objects from
Aristotle, eighth *Physics*, 23, that alteration does
not take place continuously, he should be met with
the argument, based on Simplicius's interpretation,
that Aristotle is there arguing against those who
thought that all things are in motion perpetually;
and Aristotle shows this to be false in augmentation and in alteration as well. Concerning alteration, moreover, he teaches basically two things:
first, it is not the case that, if the subject altered is divisible to infinity, alteration also
takes place successively through the parts of the
subject, for sometimes the entire subject is altered in all its parts, as is apparent in freezing;
second, he teaches that since alteration is between
contraries, it should not be said that alteration
119   takes place continuously, that is, that a thing is
altered perpetually, for the thing is finally changed through alteration to the contrary, and there
it stops. These considerations, however, do not

preclude that, in the time in which the alteration
takes place, it come about continuously through
the intension of the quality.

[0] Last Question. On the Parts or Degrees of
       Quality

[1] Note, first: in a quality one can consider
essential degrees through which the quality is constituted such and such in its species; based on
these degrees it is certain that the quality is indivisible in the sense that, if any of them should
be changed, it itself would also change. Second,
one can consider degrees through which it is constituted hot or cold, etc., and so can be more or
less perfect; on this account the quality has a
certain latitude over which there are a number of
degrees that do not vary the essence. That the
latter degrees are found in a quality is obvious
both from the senses, which are the arbiters of
qualities, and from action, which is greater at
one time, less at another.

[2] Intension comes about through new degrees
or parts of a form, as is apparent from Aristotle,
fourth *Physics*, 84, where he states that, just as
the cold comes to be from the hot, so the more hot
comes to be from the less hot; but the former comes
to be from the new eduction of a quality, therefore
the latter also. To understand this, note that
Aristotle wishes to explain how -- since matter is
in potency to contraries, as, for example, to hot
and to cold -- a thing can come to exist anew not
by the addition of something extrinsic but solely
from the fact that the same matter that was in potency comes to be in act. For in this way the cold
is said to come to be from the hot and the more hot
from the less, not by having any extrinsic hot added or by having any part heated that was not heated
previously while it was less hot, but because what
was in potency comes to be in act; and from this
text of Aristotle is gathered that intension can
come about through the new eduction of a quality.
The same is confirmed from Aristotle, fifth *Physics*,

172

19, where he holds that intension is a true alteration and a motion from contrary to contrary, and
thus is a true production.

[3] Note, second: this latitude of quality is
in some way similar to that found in quantity, for,
just as in quantity there is a latitude over true   120
parts outside of parts, so also in quality there is
a latitude of intension over several distinct degrees. They differ, however, for in quantity the
latitude is over a multitude of parts one of which
is outside the other, and on this account it is
properly called extension; in quality, on the other
hand, there is a kind of latitude in that several
degrees are found in the same part, and for this
reason it is called intension. Hence it comes a-
bout that the latitude of a quantity is perceived
not only when the quantity is acquired successively but also when it arrives at being that quantity,
with the result that its latitude is more obvious.
The latitude of quality, on the other hand, is
perceived only in coming to be, where first there
is one part and then another, but not in the com-
pleted state, since the senses cannot distinguish
a number of degrees when the quality is at rest;
from this one can see why such a latitude is not
obvious.

[4] Note, third: since quality always exists
in a quantified subject, apart from its own degrees
it also participates in the latitude of quantity
and can be divided into quantified parts. Moreover, if the degrees and parts of quality are compared with the parts of quantity, either there will
be equal degrees of quality in each part of the
quantity, and then the quality is said to be uniform; or there will be unequal degrees, and then it
is said to be difform. And if the excesses of the
parts are equal, such that, if there are two degrees in the first part, four in the second, six in
the third, and so on, in such a way that the excess
is always by two, the quality is said to be uniformly difform; if on the other hand the excesses
are unequal, it is said to be difformly difform.
Again, if the excesses are said to be unequal in
such a way that, in the first part, for example,
there are four degrees, in the second six, in the
third nine, and so on, then the quality is said to
be uniformly difformly difform; if on the other
hand the excesses are not proportional, it is said

to be difformly difformly difform. Since there
can therefore be a twofold latitude over qualities,
proper and extrinsic, there can also be succession
and continuity over quantity in two ways; and, if
a contrary is further present, given a proper latitude there will always be continuous alteration;
but it is not always necessary that continuity a-
rise by reason of quantity. Note, however, that
Aristotle has given greater consideration here to
this proper latitude as more obvious, and for the
other reasons mentioned above.

[5] Note, fourth: intension in quality -- being, as we said, continuous -- comes about through
a single continuous eduction and has a single corresponding quality in act. Yet we divide this e-
duction and the educed quality into a number of de-
121   grees. For a degree signifies any part of a quality that can exist *per se* and less than which cannot be found *per se*; the lesser parts into which
degrees can be divided, on the other hand, are said
to be degree-like parts, through which the form is
intensified by a kind of continuous eduction. In
such intension two things are considered, the intension itself and the eduction, for these, while
being the same in reality, differ in definition
and formally. Eduction signifies a proper production and its termini are privation and form, whereas intension signifies formally the increase of
quality and has as its termini the pre-existent
part and the produced part. Hence it follows that
eduction is prior by nature to intension, since a
thing's being educed is prior by nature to its being intensified.

[6] Note, fifth: it can be gathered from the
above that intension does not come about by addition alone; and so, if heat, for example, while
pre-existing outside matter were added to heat existing in matter, such would not be intension.
This is what Aristotle himself holds in the fourth
Physics, 84, where he states that the more hot
comes to be from the less hot, by something made
hot in the matter that previously was not hot.
Rather intension requires that, in any part in
which heat pre-exists, another [degree] be educed
from its potency, with the result that the entire
heat becomes more intense and, consequently, occupies the subject more. And St. Thomas can be
understood in this manner, as above [N2], when he

holds that intension does not come about from the
fact that two parts of a quality are united as two
pre-existing parts, but from the fact that the
subject is intensified through the eduction of some
form that contains the quality, with the result
that the quality is said to be educed and so also
more rooted [in the subject].

[7] Note, finally: since intension comes about
through the addition of a new degree, properly
speaking it is not the intension of the pre-existing
degree, for that remains while another is added.
The subject, however, is more intensified because
it acquires more quality from each degree; thus it
results that the subject is properly said to be intensified and is denominated as more intense through
the quality, as, for example, it is said to become
hotter, etc.

[8] Nonetheless, the quality itself is said to
be intensified also. First, because the degree-
like parts of the quality are the same in essence.
Second, because they do not truly differ numerically, since before one is produced it is not another,
and when it is produced it exists in the same subject and makes one quality, whereas if it had existed previously it would already be numerically
distinct. They do differ in a certain way, however, in the sense that one is already produced
whereas the other is not. Third, because they are
united; and they are united for no other reason
than the fact that, being of the same nature, the
subsequent degree does not exist but is produced,   122
and it does not come to exist except in something
that existed previously. From these considerations
one may conclude that the quality also can be said
to become more intense; for, by way of example,
throughout its entire intension the essence remains
always the same, and it is increased in entity
through parts that, when joined, make a numerical
unity *per se*.

[9] One may inquire here whether intension
comes about in such a way that one degree is first
produced in an instant and then the others successively, or whether even the first degree is induced
successively; and similarly, whether in alteration
there is a first part of the subject that is altered all at once and the rest of it then altered
continuously. However, this depends partly on what

we have said in the sixth *Physics* and partly on
the question whether there is a minimum in natural
things and in elements, which question is to be
treated below [U9-80], and so [we shall not reply
to it here].

Tractate on the Elements

[1] The following have written on the elements in general: Aristotle in the last two books of *De caelo*, in the second *De generatione*, in the book on *Meteors*, and all his commentators in these places; among the physicians Hippocrates in the book *De natura humana*, from which Galen took what he wrote on the elements; Galen also wrote many things concerning them in the eighth book of *De placitis Hippocratis et Platonis*; Avicenna in the First Part of the First, doctrine 2, on which text all the physicians have commented; the Conciliator in difference 11 and following; Contarenus and Achillini in their books *De elementis*; St. Gregory of Nyssa in the third book of his *Philosophy*, and Algazel; Carpentarius, in the second book of the *Descriptio naturae*, and Valeriola; Cardanus also wrote many things about them in the second book of *De subtilitate*.

[2] The first thing to be understood is the nominal definition of element. On this account, note, first: this word, as can be seen in Aristotle, fifth *Metaphysics*, 4, is equivocal. It is this fact that has caused all authors to argue among themselves as to the meaning of the term and as to what it is best applied; and this foolishly, since names, on the authority of Aristotle in the first *Perihermenias*, chapter 2, signify *ad placitum* and not from the nature of the thing. The result is that the individual's personal acceptance of the

123   term element permits it to be applied to a variety
of things.

[3] For this reason some, on the testimony of
Aristotle in the same text, accomodate it to anything that is a principle of another in any way,
and on this account they refer to points and units
as elements.

[4] In a second way others, same place, take
it for all things that enter into the composition
of a thing in any way but without being distinct
from each other; so universals, i.e., genus and
difference, which enter into metaphysical composition, are said to be elements.

[5] Third, it can be taken for principles that
function together in the production of a thing;
and so Aristotle, in the twelfth *Metaphysics*, 23,
says that the elements are three, i.e., matter,
form, and privation.

[6] Fourth, [it can be taken] for that which
functions in any way as matter; and so Aristotle
in the first *Posterior Analytics* refers to immediate propositions as elements, and in the second
Physics, 31, he calls suppositions the elements of
a conclusion, and in the same place, he refers to
syllables as elements -- also in the fifth *Metaphysics*, text 4, and the seventh *Metaphysics*, last
text.

[7] However, on the authority of Galen at the
end of the first commentary on Hippocrates's *De
natura humana*, all these are said to be elements
improperly. For this reason, if we are to speak
of the elements of natural things, the meaning of
this term is fourfold, as the Conciliator correctly notes in difference 11 and as is gathered from
Galen in the first *De elementis* and in the first
commentary on Hippocrates.

[8] The first meaning, therefore, is that an
element signifies the intrinsic causes composing a
thing, i.e., matter and form. These seem especially apt to be called elements because from them a
thing is first composed and into them it is ultimately resolved, and they are not in turn composed
of others nor are they resolved into others; and
this can in no way be said of the other meanings.

Such causes, on the authority of Eudemus, based on
Simplicius in his introduction to the *Physics*,
were first called elements by Plato; the same usage was taken up by Simplicius, Philoponus, Averroës, and Albertus on the first chapter of the
first *Physics*. For this reason Averroës, in the
third *De caelo*, comment 31, says that Aristotle in
the books of the *Physics* treated of the universal
elements of all simple and composed bodies. Thus
Philoponus, in the first text of the second *De
generatione*, gives the reason why Aristotle, in
the third *Physics*, 45, the second *De generatione*,
first text, and the second *De partibus* [*animalium*], chapter 1, calls the four simple bodies elements. He gives the reason: because, he says,
these bodies are not really elements themselves,
since they are composed of other things that are
prior, i.e., matter and form, which are most properly elements. For, although elements in this
sense are said of any intrinsic cause, more com-   124
monly and more properly they are said of matter,
as is apparent from Alexander, Eudemus, Simplicius,
and St. Thomas on the first chapter of the first
Physics. Since, however, matter is manifold, the
first and most common matter of all, says Averroës,
third *De caelo*, 31, second *De generatione*, text 6,
first *Metaphysics*, text 4, and tenth *Metaphysics*,
text 2, is primarily and most properly said to be
an element, for elements are like the material
parts of a thing; and this is the first meaning.

[9] The second is: element is taken for the
four simple bodies, fire, [air, water, and earth,]
which are commonly called elements because these
are the first things known to us, for other principles are less known; also, these enter into composition and are the elements of other things,
while themselves being bodies actually and existing *per se*. On this account the ancient philosophers held for these alone as elements, either
all or one or some. Even Plato, though holding in
the *Timaeus* for an unformed matter of all things,
thought of elements especially as these four, which
he constructed out of surfaces. In this understanding Aristotle also uses the term element rather frequently, and this principally defines element.

[10] Third, it is taken for the four humors
of animals. Fourth, it is taken for similar or

dissimilar parts. But these two meanings do not
pertain to us, and so we are treating of elements
only in the second meaning.

[11] Note, second: as is gathered from Aristotle in the second *Physics*, text 21 -- and in that
place all the Greeks note it -- elements may be
such according to composition alone, when they are
so conjoined that they never are corrupted or
changed, such as the components of a house. Only
in this way did the ancients think of elements, for
they wished generation and corruption to come about
through aggregation and segregation. Second, elements may be such according to corruptive alteration alone, and not according to composition, such
as blood coming to be from food, and flesh from
blood. Third, according to both composition and
alteration, such as components that are not corrupted completely and yet do not remain unchanged completely, but rather are altered, as oxymel made
from wine and honey.

[12] Our [four] elements can indeed be said
to be such in the first way, since they enter into
the constitution of the entire universe, and in
this sense even the heavens are referred to as an
element, following Aristotle; also in the second
way, as when an element is changed into another;
and again in the third way, as they enter into the
125   composition of compounds, for, even if there is
some doubt as to how elements remain in compounds,
nonetheless all are agreed that they remain in some
way, actually or potentially.

[13] Note, third: these four elements are sometimes called simple bodies, to distinguish them
from the compounds that are composed of them, and
sometimes they are called by the names of the qualities themselves, hot, cold, etc. -- as in the
fourth *Meteors*, summary 2, and by Hippocrates in
the book *De natura humana*; also by Galen, even
though he corrected the Athenian, who wished the
elements to be qualities only. Galen notes the
same in the book *De simplicium medicamentorum compositione*, distinction 3, chapter 1. Finally, they
are sometimes referred to by the names of motive
qualities.

[14] Note, fourth: from Galen in the eighth
De placitis, chapter 2, the word element is a rela-

tive term, since an element is said with respect
to that of which it is an element. So Averroës
also, in the third *De caelo*, comment 31, says that
it is incidental that something be called an element, for an element is said in relation to that
of which it is an element. From this is apparent
the terminological distinction that obtains between
matter and form and these four bodies: for, since
matter and form do not have existence properly
speaking except in the composite and insofar as
they are parts, they are said to be elements essentially; these four bodies, on the other hand, have
actual existence *per se*, since they have been *per
se* ordained by nature to compose the universe and
compounds, and for this reason they too are properly and *per se* said to be elements. On this account
if we attend to the nature of an element, first and
properly the term element is applied to matter and
form; if, on the other hand, we attend to the common way of speaking and to appearances, to these
four bodies.

[15] Of these four alone shall I treat in the
following, and this entire treatise we shall divide
into four parts: in the first we shall treat of
their essence in general, in the second, of qualities and their other accidents, in the third, of
the individual elements in particular, and finally,
in the fourth, of the same as they enter into compounds; all this pertains to the question, *propter
quid*. We shall say nothing of the question *an sint*,
for from common consensus it stands to reason and
experience that some such do exist.

[1] The substance of anything is conveniently
explained through its causes, and chiefly through
the intrinsic causes, i.e., matter and form; so we
shall explain these at present. Before all else
the definition of an element should be treated.
For this reason there is the

First Question. On the Definitions of an Element

[2] Note, first, that natural things can be
defined in two ways: first, metaphysically, through
genus and difference; second, physically, through
their causes, for we know something physically when
we know its causes, first *Physics*, text 1, and
eighth *Metaphysics*, last text; third, they can be
defined either absolutely or relatively.

[3] In each of these ways, therefore, element
can be defined. In the first way it is defined as
follows: an element is a simple corruptible body.
It is said to be corruptible to differentiate it
from the heavens; simple, to differentiate it from
compounds.

[4] In the second way it is described as follows: it is a body composed of primary matter and
a simple form produced by God for the perfection
of the universe.

[5] In the third way, finally, it is defined
variously by the authorities. The first definition
is Aristotle's, fifth *Metaphysics*, text 4: it is
that from which a thing is composed, primarily, existing in it, indivisible in kind into other kinds.

182

[6] The second definition is also his, seventh *Metaphysics*, last text: an element is that into which an existent is divided as matter.

[7] The third is from the third *Metaphysics*, 10, following Empedocles: elements are those things from which entities come to be and exist in them.

[8] The fourth is from the third *De caelo*, 31: an element is a kind of body into which other bodies are divided, which exists in them potentially or actually.

[9] The fifth is Galen's definition in the first *De elementis*, chapter 1, and the eighth *De placitis*, chapter 2: it is the smallest particle of the thing of which it is an element. Gregory of Nyssa's, in book 3, chapter 2, practically agrees with this: it is a certain minimum part for constructing bodies.

[10] The sixth definition is Avicenna's, in the sixth of his *Metaphysics*, chapter 4: it is that from which a thing is composed, different from itself, existing in it essentially, and not divided through form. And in the First of the First, doctrine 2 in the beginning, he says that elements are bodies or the first parts of a body, which cannot be divided into bodies of different forms, and from their intermingling the species of various animated things come to be.   127

[11] The seventh is that of the Stoics, from Laërtius: an element is that from which things first come forth when they spring into being, and into which they are last resolved.

[12] Note, second: of the foregoing definitions the more common is the first [5], and this we shall explain completely. The first particle is "from"; although this frequently signifies the relationship of an efficient cause or of a *terminus a quo*, here it signifies the relationship of a material cause. Elements are the matter of compounds and on this account are here defined in relation to composition, for it is clear that an efficient cause, or a *terminus a quo*, does not enter into composition.

[13] The second is "which," meaning body, as Aristotle himself explains in the third *De caelo*,

31, and in this definition the sense ought to be
the same as in other definitions of an element.
So matter and form are excluded from this definition, because they are not bodies.

[14] The third is "is composed." Composition
can be twofold: either substantial, the way in
which elements compose the universe; or alterative,
through alteration, mutual action, and intermingling. Here it is taken in the second way only,
because an element is defined in relation to mixing. By this expression is excluded the matter of
alteration, which does not compose but is transmuted; also excluded are primary matter and form,
which are neither mixed nor altered but united.

[15] The fourth particle is "primarily"; this
is to distinguish it from things that do indeed
compose, but themselves are composed of others,
and of this kind are similar and dissimilar parts.
You say: elements are not primary components because they themselves have a prior composition of
matter and form. I reply: they indeed are not primary components in an absolute way, but they are
first in the genus of body, since they are not composed of other bodies; for the definition, as I
said, is understood of the composition of bodies.

[16] The fifth particle is "existing in it";
for even bodies have some mode of existence in the
compound, either actually or potentially, as Aristotle explains in the third *De caelo*, 31. Which of
these modes is meant here we shall explain in treating of compounds.

[17] The sixth particle is "indivisible in
kind into other kinds," i.e., an element is not
further resolved into any other specific and existent natures, as happens with similar parts, although it may be resolved into matter and form,
which are not species but parts of species. And by
this particle, whatever others have said, matter
and form are also excluded, for it signifies that
an element must be one in species, and this is not
true of matter and form. Should one wish to state
this definition in clearer form, he may say that
an element is the first body of which others are
composed.

128

[R] Second Question. On the Material, Efficient,
and Final Cause of the Elements

[1] Note, first: the efficient cause of the
initial origin of the elements, according to truth,
is God, who created all things from nothing. Regarding Aristotle, there is some doubt as to what
he thought, but this question is explained elsewhere.

[2] Concerning the particular efficient cause,
in view of the elements being generable and corruptible according to parts, there is a single problem: must this cause always be univocal, i.e., must
fire always come to be from fire, water from water,
and so on; or can an equivocal cause suffice, for
example, can fire be produced by friction or in
some other way. Some moderns hold that fire can
be produced by a univocal cause alone, because, if
equivocal, it would not be of the same species; and
they gather this from Aristotle, first *De generatione animalium*, last chapter, where he states that
animals, if produced by an equivocal cause, would
not be the same in species. They also add: when
fire is produced by light or in some other way,
the motion and the light merely dispose the matter,
whereupon the fire that is in the surrounding medium or in an adjoining compound produces the form
of fire.

[3] But these considerations notwithstanding,
it should be said that elements can be generated
by an equivocal cause, since motion is capable of
igniting, second *De caelo*, 42, and first *Meteors*,
and since fire is produced by the reflection of
rays. Nor can you say that the fire is produced
by the [surrounding] air, since air does not have
the form of fire; nor again, by a compound, since
the form of fire is not actual in it or, if it exists in some way in diminished actuality, it is not

185

apt to produce the more intense form, for nothing
acts beyond its powers. Again, the proposition,
"similars are produced by similars," is not universally true, not even for plants and animals; so
Aristotle, in the second ·De anima, text 24, says
that it is a property of perfect living things to
produce offspring similar to themselves. This also
129   is apparent in plants and imperfect animals, which
come to be from putrified matter. In reply to
Aristotle [2], therefore, his inference is valid
only for perfect animals.

[4] Note, second: the intrinsic end of the
elements is the proper operation of each, whereas
the extrinsic end is the composition of the universe and the generation of compounds.

[5] Note, third: with respect to matter, Empedocles had said that elements do not have a common matter; others think that one element is the
matter of another; still others, that their matter
is one body that exists actually but is different
from them. Democritus favored atoms; Plato seemed
to say that the elements are constructed from surfaces -- which Galen explains in the eighth De
placitis, chapter 3, and Nyssa, in book 3, chapter
3; but Aristotle opposed him, third De caelo and
first De generatione.

[6] It should be said that the common matter
of all the elements is primary matter as affected
by primary qualities. That they have a common matter is indeed obvious, since they all act and react with one another and undergo mutual transmutation; but things of this type must share a common
matter, from the first De generatione, 53 and 54,
as Aristotle proves in the fourth De caelo, 37,
and the second De generatione, 37 and 46. That
this is primary matter is obvious, for the elements
are first and simple bodies and so are not composed
of other bodies. That it is not nude [i.e., that
it is affected by primary qualities], I suppose
proved in the first De generatione.

[S] Third Question. What are the Forms of the Elements?

[1] I suppose it to be demonstrated elsewhere, contrary to the ancient philosophers, that elements have forms that are substantial and not merely accidental. The only question remaining is: what are these forms?

[2] The first opinion is that of Flaminio Nobili, in the first *De generatione*, doubt 11 on chapter 3, saying that the forms of the elements are something made up of primary qualities and a kind of substantial form. But this is unintelligible, nor does he seem sufficiently to understand the nature of a substantial form.

[3] The second opinion is Achillini's, in the third *De elementis*, doubt 2 on statement 7, who adduces Averroës in support of his opinion; it also seems to be Alexander's in his first *De anima*, chapters 1, 2, and 3. They say that the forms of the elements are motive qualities, such as gravity and levity, and prove this from the third *De caelo*, last chapter, where Aristotle says that such qualities are properly speaking the differences of the elements.

[4] The third opinion seems to be Alexander's, in the book *De sensu et sensili*, chapter 4, who holds for primary qualities; there, answering the difficulty of how it can be true that substance has no contrary, he replies that a total substance has no contrary, but that contrariety can exist by reason of form. He holds the same in the first *Meteors*, 2, in the first *De anima*, chapter 2, in the first of the *Quaestiones naturales*, chapter 6, and in the second, chapter 4. The same opinion Averroës also attributes to him in the fifth *Physics*, 10, and the eighth *Metaphysics*, 5, as does Themis-

130

187

tius, in the fifth *Physics*, text 9.   Indeed this
opinion seems to be common to all the Greeks: so
Porphyry, at the end of the category of substance;
Dexippus, in tract 2 of the *Categories*, chapter 5;
likewise Simplicius on the category of substance,
comment 11, and in the fifth *Physics*, comment 11,
and also Ammonius on the *Categories*; Philoponus,
in the second *De generatione*, comment 40, and in
the second *De generatione*, from comment 4 onwards.
The same opinion is favored by the Conciliator,
difference 13, and he says this was the opinion of
Nicholas the Peripatetic.   Finally, all the physicians, as Hippocrates in the book *De natura humana*
and Galen, differentiate the elements through these
qualities.

[5] First proof: from the authority of Aristotle in the second *De generatione*, 6, where he
states that elements are generated from contraries;
in text 7 he says that qualities are the first elements; in 16 he holds that they are the elements of
the elements; and in 24 he states that they are the
differences of the elements.

[6] Second proof: each thing is constituted by
the characteristic through which it produces what
is similar to itself; but an element produces what
is similar to itself through its qualities, following Aristotle in the book *De sensu et sensili*, chapter 4, where he states that fire does not act as
fire but as hot; therefore [elements are constituted by their qualities].

[7] Third proof: if qualities are not the forms
of the elements, they must be subsequent forms; but
this cannot be, because, since the prior is conserved without the subsequent, forms would have to be
conserved without qualities; but this is contrary
to experience; therefore [qualities are the forms
of the elements].

[8] The fourth opinion is that of those saying
that the forms of the elements are substantial forms
hidden from us [but knowable through their] qualities.   This is the position of St. Thomas, Albert,
and the Latins, in the second *De generatione*, 16,
and the third *Metaphysics*, 27; likewise the Conciliator, difference 13; Giles, on the first *De generatione*, question 19; Jandun, *De sensu*, question
25, and the fifth *Physics*, question 4; Zimara in the

131

Table; and Contarenus in the first and seventh *De elementis.*

[9] I say, first: proper alterative qualities are not the forms of the elements. First proof, on the authority of Aristotle: what is an accident in one case cannot be a substance in another, from the first *Physics,* 27 and 30; but such qualities are accidents of compounds and animals, according to everyone; therefore [they cannot be substantial forms]. Moreover, in the third *Metaphysics,* 17, Aristotle expressly teaches that qualities are not the forms of the elements but that they are accidents; and in the second *De generatione,* 54, he proves that qualities are the instruments of elements and that, apart from these, there are also substantial forms by which elements are constituted; and in the *Categories,* in the chapter on substance, he holds that substance has no contrary. [Second proof, from reason: qualities are sensible *per se,* and this is not true of substances. Moreover, qualities are active immediately with an action that is true and proper, and this cannot be said of substances. Again, there can be successive change in the order of quality, but not in the order of substance or of substantial form. Yet again, in other substantial composites the substantial form is never a quality or something immediately sensible, and so this cannot be true of elemental composites either. Finally, there are only two active qualities in any element; as a consequence, either both would be substantial forms, or either one or the other. Not both, for then elements would not be simple bodies; not one or the other, for no good reason could be found for selecting between them.]

[10] Nor are all the Greeks cited above [4] of the same opinion. For most obviously Dexippus, in tract 2 on the *Categories,* chapters 25, 30, and 32, says that hotness, etc., are accidental qualities differing from substantial forms, which have neither a contrary nor more and less except insofar as they are the subjects of such qualities; and Ammonius teaches the same, as does Simplicius in explaining the expression, "substance has no contrary" -- read Simplicius in his commentary on the *Physics.* Porphyry says that coldness is not the substance of water; similarly Philoponus in the second *De generatione* distinguishes hotness from fire and states

that elements have no contraries in themselves but
only as they are formed, i.e., in their qualities.

[11] I say, second: motive qualities are not
the forms of the elements, for the reasons given
in the preceding conclusion [9]; also, because they
are subsequent to alterative qualities, and because
Aristotle, in the seventh *Physics*, 11, fifth *Metaphysics*, 19, second *De partibus* [*animalium*], and
elsewhere, clearly teaches that gravity, etc., are
qualities.

[12] Achillini [3] replies that gravity and
levity can be understood in two ways: in first act,
and so they are the substantial forms of the elements; or in second act, i.e., by reason of gravitation and levitation, and so they are said to be
qualities. But, to the contrary: gravitation and
levitation are in the category of action and passion; therefore they are not qualities. Add to
this: there is gravity and levity in the Most Blessed Sacrament, and yet there is no substance there.
He replies: God makes gravitation and levitation to
be there in place of the gravity and levity that
are not present. To the contrary: new miracles are
not to be multiplied without necessity.

[13] To the text of Aristotle [3], I reply:
Aristotle says that gravity and levity are most
properly differences because they take the place
of the ultimate substantial differences that are
unknown to us. You object: gravity and levity are
principles of motion and of rest; thus they are
natures, and therefore forms. I respond: gravity
and levity are merely instrumental principles of
motion; but principles [of this kind are accidental, and so are not natures].

[14] I say, third: each element has a proper
substantial form that is distinct and different
from its alterative and motive qualities. This is
obvious from its various operations and properties,
which must proceed from different forms. Finally,
it follows from all the arguments given in the
first *Physics* proving that there is such a thing as
substantial form.

[15] To the first argument [5], I reply: Aristotle, in those texts, is speaking with respect to
us, for whom the forms and the ultimate differences

132

of the elements are unknown, whereas qualities are most obvious; and second, by qualities he means the principles from which qualities flow.

[16] To the second [6], I reply: elements act principally through their own forms but instrumentally through their qualities. This text of Aristotle is actually more favorable to us; for, if heat were a form, as they hold, fire would act as fire and not as hot, for it would act through the proper form of fire. Therefore Aristotle means that fire does not act precisely as fire, i.e., not through its form immediately, but precisely as hot, instrumentally.

[17] To the third [7], I reply: not everything prior can be conserved without the subsequent, but only that which is prior simply; the forms of the elements, however, are not prior to qualities simply, but only in the genus of efficient cause, since they do indeed effect them; yet in the genus of material cause qualities are prior because they are dispositions necessary for the form, and so the form cannot exist without the qualities.

133   [T] Fourth Question.   Do the Forms of the Elements
            Undergo Intension and Remission?

[1] From the tractate on alteration, on the
matter of the intension and remission of forms, I
presuppose what it means for a form to undergo intension and remission [N3-8]. I presuppose, moreover, that we are speaking at present only of the
forms of elements, and concerning these we inquire
whether, in whatever way their qualities undergo
intension and remission, their forms undergo intension in this way also.

[2] The first opinion is that of Averroës,
third *De caelo*, comment 67; Nifo and Paul of Venice at the end of the first *De generatione*; Zimara,
proposition 20; Taiapetra, book 2, tract 4; Jandun,
eighth *Metaphysics*, question 5; Achillini, book 2
of *De elementis*, article 3; Contarenus, book 3; and
Alexander, eighth *Metaphysics*, text 10. All of
these say that the substantial forms of the elements undergo intension and remission. To these
can be added Scotus, eighth *Metaphysics*, question
3, whom Antonius Andreas follows, eleventh *Metaphysics*, question 1; Pavesius in the book *De accretione*; and John Canonicus, fifth *Physics*, question
1, who hold the same for any substantial form that
is educed from the potency of matter, so as to ex-
clude the rational soul.

[3] Concerning the way in which forms undergo
intension and remission, however, they do not a-
gree. Contarenus says that the forms of the elements are not introduced successively with the intension of the quality but that an alteration of
the qualities takes place up to a certain degree,
after which the form of the compound follows and
under which the forms of the elements cannot exist
as integral; and, when the form of the compound
comes, then the forms of the elements immediately

192

begin to break down. A second way is Achillini's,
who seems to say that the form of an element is
introduced in an instant according to some minimal
part, after the proper disposition has been made;
afterwards, however, it undergoes intension and remission successively. Others, third, generally
say that the forms of the elements undergo intension and remission successively along with the intension and remission of the qualities.

[4] The second opinion is that of others who
deny that forms undergo intension and remission.
This is Avicenna's in the first *Sufficientia*, chapters 10 and 11, and in the First of the First, doctrine 3, chapter 1; Averroës, however, opposes him.
The same is the opinion of St. Thomas in the opusculum *De mixtione*, in the second *Sentences*, distinction 15, and in the First Part, question 76,
article 4, and there also Cajetan; Capreolus in
the second *Sentences*, distinction 15, question 1,
conclusion 2, and in the solutions to the arguments
against it; Soncinas in the eighth *Metaphysics*,
question 25 and question 26, the tenth *Metaphysics*,   134
question 27, and elsewhere; Gregory in the second
Sentences, distinction 15, question 1; Ockham,
Quodlibet 3, question 4; Marsilius, first *De generatione*, question 22; Themistius, second *De anima*,
text 4; and Philoponus, second *De generatione*, comment 33. These, however, say only this, that the
forms of the elements do not remain actual in the
compound, but from this the other conclusion follows. Moreover, the same opinion is defended by
Durandus in the first *Sentences*, distinction 17,
question 6, Henry, *Quodlibet* 3, question 2, Nobilius, in chapter 3, Buccaferrus in text 18, many of
the commentators on the first *Microtechni*, comment
15, Hervaeus in the tract *De unitate formarum*,
Giles in the first *De generatione*, question 18,
Albert on the first *Techni*, chapter 25, and Javelli,
eighth *Metaphysics*, question 5.

[5] This second, true opinion is proved by the
following arguments. First, from Aristotle in the
chapter on substance; substance does not admit of
more or less; therefore [the substantial forms of
the elements do not undergo intension and remission.] Nor is this to be understood, as Scotus
holds, of substance according to quiddity, i.e.,
genus and difference. For in this way not even
qualities would admit of more and less, and yet

Aristotle holds in the *Categories* that they do admit of more and less; therefore [this is true of
substance generally].

[6] Nor is it to be understood of forms other
than the forms of the elements, for, says Averroës,
the latter are intermediate substances and so it is
not exceptional that they admit of more and less.
To the contrary, however: this is gratuitously as-
serted, since Aristotle is speaking universally
and, in the third *De caelo*, text 1 and elsewhere,
he enumerates the elements among the principal substances.

[7] Confirmation: because it would follow that
the elements admit of more and less, and thus it
should be said that one fire is more fire than another. Proof of the inference: for more and less
are said of composites that take on more or less
of a form; but a composite of fire is fire; therefore, if one fire had more of the form than another
it would be more fire than the other.

[8] Second confirmation: because, since the
quiddity of a thing is constituted by its form,
the form cannot admit of more and less without the
quiddity also admitting of more and less; this is
contrary to Aristotle, eighth *Metaphysics*, text 10,
who states that a quiddity is like a number; in
fact this could not even be said of the quiddity
of a quality.

[9] Third confirmation: because Averroës's
basic position that the forms of the elements are
intermediate between substance and accident is not
true, nor is it pertinent. For if the sense is
that they do not have the true formality of substance but are something intermediate between substance and accident, this is false, since there
cannot be any real being between substance and accident, for to subsist and to inhere divide being
as contradictories. If, on the other hand, the
sense is that the forms of the elements are less
noble than other substances, that indeed is true
but it is not pertinent, since on this account
135   they do not lose the formality and conditions of
substance and so cannot participate in the conditions of accidents.

[10] Confirmation: because it would then fol-

low that the forms of compounds, being less perfect than the forms of living things, would admit
of more and less.

[11] Second: it would follow that the change
to substance would be continuous, contrary to Aristotle.

[12] Third: if the forms of elements undergo
intension in the compound, they should undergo intension outside the compound also; but this is absurd; therefore [they do not undergo intension].
Proof of the major: because, when fire acts on water, the form of water undergoes intension for the
same reason as when it acts in a compound, and so
in this action the form of water undergoes remission, since it is the contrary of the form of fire;
therefore the same thing would happen outside the
compound, since the same argument applies in both
places. Proof of the minor: because no one admits
this, and because boiling water would have a most
remiss form of water and a most intense form of air,
since all of the dispositions of air are there present; yet this is false, for the water returns to
its initial state by itself. Also, since it would
follow that the boiling water would be a perfect
compound, as it would have all four qualities. For,
since fire acts through dryness, it would introduce
some dryness also; as a consequence, according to
those who say that something of the form accompan-
ies each part of the quality, all four qualities
would be there and so it would be truly a compound.

[13] Fourth: it would follow that an element
cannot reduce itself to its former state, because
a remiss form cannot produce itself or intensify
itself -- for nothing intensifies itself, nor does
anything act except insofar as it is in act -- and
because it cannot produce its quality more intensely, since it is remiss, and so only a remiss quality would result.

[14] The followers of the first opinion object, first: Aristotle says in the sixth *Physics*
that whatever undergoes change is partly in the
terminus a quo and partly in the *terminus ad quem*;
so, if the elements undergo change they are partly
in the *terminus a quo* and partly in the *terminus
ad quem*; therefore they are generated and corrupted
successively.

[15] Second: the primary qualities are the proper attributes of the elements; thus, when a proper attribute is changed, the form will be varied.

[16] Third: a more perfect operation indicates a more perfect form; therefore, since greater activity results from greater heat, this is a sign that there is more form there.

[17] Fourth: when water is generated by fire, the form of fire must corrupt before the entire latitude of heat is corrupted. Therefore, either first: there is a maximum heat under which the form of fire can exist and under more than this it cannot; but that is absurd, for the more intense the heat the more compatible it is with the form.

136

[18] Or, second: there is a maximum heat under which it cannot exist and under anything greater it can; and then I ask concerning that maximum heat under which it cannot exist whether it is below the mean latitude of heat, e.g., three degrees, or the mean itself, four, or above the mean, five. Not the first and the second: for, if the perfect form of fire according to substance could remain to the point where the entire mean or practically the entire mean of its heat were corrupted, fire would be cold and not light, which seems absurd. Not the third: for if the form of fire cannot remain under a degree that is slightly above the mean, then the form of water will remain; and, as a consequence, the form of water would be educed from matter standing under a greater latitude of heat than of cold, for the degree of cold must then be three.

[19] Or, third: there must be a minimum heat under which the form of fire can exist and under less than which it cannot; and this is not so, for then there would be a last instant of fire, contrary to Aristotle in the sixth *Physics*. For, if heat is continuously diminished, one will come to an instant at which this minimal heat exists, and so it would be true to say: the form of fire exists now but immediately afterwards it will not.

[20] Or finally, fourth: there is a minimum heat under which the form of fire cannot remain and under less than which it can; and this is not the case, since it would be absurd; therefore [the form

of fire undergoes remission with the decrease of heat].

[21] Since, as a consequence, it is impossible to assign a terminus in which the integral and perfect form ceases to exist, one must say that it undergoes corruption successively with the succession of the heat. ...

[U] [Fifth Question. On the Number and Quantity
of the Elements]

[0] [We inquire, first, concerning the number
of the elements. It should be noted that the number of the elements is not so evident as to be accepted without demonstration, for while earth and
water are themselves quite evident, it is not apparent that they are elements. Also noteworthy is
the fact that the number of the elements is not infinite, for elements are principles of natural bodies, and it has been shown in the first *Physics*
that such principles cannot be infinite in number.
Among various opinions on this matter three are
noteworthy: first is that of certain ancients, who
held for only one; second is that of Cardanus, who
denied that fire is an element but admitted the
other three, viz, air, water, and earth; and third,
the common position of all peripatetics, that there
are four elements, viz, fire, air, water, and earth.
The last position is true and may be proved by various arguments. The first is taken from the second
De caelo, text 28, which argues from the motions of
simple bodies that there must be one that is light-
est and hottest, viz, fire; another that is heaviest and coldest, viz, earth; and two intermediates
that share these qualities partly with their contraries, viz, air and water. The second reason is
similar to this and is in the third *De caelo*. There
are two extreme natural places in the universe, absolutely up and absolutely down, and to these correspond fire and earth; likewise there are two intermediate places, one more up than down, and to
this corresponds air, the other more down than up,
and to this corresponds water.]

[1] The third reason is in the second *De generatione*, text 49. A compound contains earth, as is
obvious from experience in view of its gravity, and
this should be present because it gives consistency;

198

water too should be present since it gives continuity and thickening; but corresponding to these two there ought to be two more contrary elements that break them down; therefore [there must be four elements].

[2] You say: it suffices to have something that breaks down the first two elements, i.e., something that by reason of humidity breaks down the dryness of earth, by reason of heat, the coldness of water. To the contrary: first, as is obvious from experience, the heat of water is not at all active and so it cannot break down the coldness of the two, i.e., of water and earth, especially since there is more of them in the compound than there is of air. Moreover, we see by experience   137
that air is quickly cooled by earth and water when the sun is absent, and so it cannot break them down. Again, because it is obvious from experience that compounds do not come into being unless there is much dry exhalation, for this is the way in which metals are made, etc.; therefore, apart from air, fire should be present also. Nor can you say that the heat of the sun suffices, for this is sometimes absent, and on this account the compound must have some natural heat.

[3] The fourth reason is a certain congruence that Aristotle notes in the first of the *Meteors*: from the fact that we perceive water and earth with the senses, he infers that the two other elements must be required to fill up the rest [of the universe]. Another congruence is noteworthy: so that there might be four humors in animals. Again, in the same book: earth is related to bone; water, to fluids of flesh and of moist parts; air, to blood; fire, to vital spirits. Finally: because in the resolution of a compound the parts that are separated out are proportional to the four elements.

[4] The difficulties that are urged on the part of fire will be solved when I treat of the elements in particular.

[5] But you object, first: why are there not also some elements that have these remiss qualities, so that, just as there are those that have four intense qualities, there will be others that have remiss qualities. I reply, first: these elements must not be determined by the fact that they have

such qualities either intensely or remissly, but
by the fact that they have them simply, with the
result that there will be a certain latitude in
them within which the elements can be conserved.
Yet a pair of qualities is proper to each one, as
I have said. Thus, even if each should be determined by these qualities, in totality they would
not be distinct from those that were determined by
the same qualities when remiss, for otherwise an
infinite number of elements could come into being.
Again: because, since qualities whether remiss or
intense are of the same nature, the elements themselves would be of the same species. Finally:
since the remission of their qualities is brought
about naturally by the admixture of a contrary, it
would follow that the elements would appropriate
contraries for themselves.

[6] Second objection: just as each element
appropriates for itself one quality that is intense, another remiss -- e.g., fire: intense heat,
remiss dryness -- why are there not four other elements, one of which, for example, would appropriate
for itself intense dryness and remiss heat? I reply: even if bodies of this kind were to be found,
they would not be different from the others. Therefore, even if it is said that fire is more hot than
dry, one need not say that a remiss dryness is proper to fire, or that hotness is more proper to fire
138   than dryness; or that it is more apparent by reason
of operation, or in some other way, as I shall point
out; or, that, if the dryness is remiss, this is
from the nature of the thing, because dryness is
dulled, so to speak, by heat.

[7] We inquire, second, concerning the size
and shape of the elements. Aristotle in the third
De caelo, 47, and in the first of the *Meteors*,
first summary, chapter 3, followed by the *Doctores
Parisienses*, establishes a tenfold ratio in the
size of the elements, i.e., water is ten times larger than air, and so on for each. Truly, however,
whether this is understood of the extensive magnitude of their mass or of the magnitude and portion
of their matter, I will show elsewhere by mathematical demonstrations that it is false. On this account Aristotle is to be understood either as meaning that this ratio ought to follow from the nature
of the thing, since he speaks as a physicist -- for
it seems fitting that the elements composing the

universe should have equal portions of matter, and,
since one exceeds another in rareness, the excess
ought to follow some ratio, which can be conveniently assigned as tenfold. Or it might be said that,
since the whole world was not yet known to the ancients, he could have erred on its shape, particularly that of the earth -- which is matter for the
mathematicians, who prove that it is round, as we
shall explain.

[8] Concerning all these matters in general,
Aristotle proves in the third *De caelo*, 66 and 67,
that the elements of themselves do not require any
particular shape, for, since elements are for compounds and compounds require different shapes, elements should be able to assume all shapes; moreover, if they must take on different shapes some of
them would be straight, and so, on this basis, a
vacuum would result, since only a circle can fill
all of place. Add to this that the elements are
homogeneous bodies and are divisible into parts
that subsist *per se*, in each of which the nature
of the element is found; therefore, in themselves
they do not require a particular shape, although
extrinsically they take on a completely circular
shape from the surroundings, especially the fluid
elements such as fire, air, and in a certain way,
water.

[9] We inquire, third, whether elements and
other natural things have any termini of largeness
and smallness. Although we are treating here of
the elements, nonetheless while treating them we
shall extend the same inquiry to all other natural
things, i.e., living and non-living compounds.
For what we ask in general is: whether each natural thing has some terminus of quantity in largeness
such that, when it comes to this, if it exceeds the
terminus through some addition of quantity, the   139
thing can no longer exist or be conserved under the
said larger terminus -- and this will be called the
terminus of largeness; or, on the other hand,
whether the same thing has any terminus of quantity
in smallness, in such a way that, if something be
subtracted from it, the thing can no longer be conserved under this smaller terminus -- and this is
called the terminus of smallness.

[10] Note, first, the explanation of these
four terms: *maximum quod sic, minimum quod sic,*

maximum quod non, and *minimum quod non.* The first
two of these are positive and intrinsic affirma-
tives, whereas the last two are said to be negative and extrinsic; again, the first and the fourth
are termini of largeness, the second and third are
termini of smallness. The *maximum quod sic* is the
maximum quantity that a thing can attain or under
which it can exist, and under a larger it cannot,
so that it can indeed attain that terminus but not
go beyond it. The *minimum quod sic* is the quantity
that a thing can attain and under which it can exist, but under a lesser it cannot. The *maximum
quod non* is the quantity that, by reason of smallness, a thing cannot attain or under which it cannot exist, but under anything larger it can, provided it does not exceed the magnitude of the *maximum quod sic.* The *minimum quod non* is the quantity
that a thing, by reason of size, cannot attain or
under which it cannot exist, but under anything
smaller it can, provided it does not exceed the
minimum quod sic.

[11] On this account we can raise two inquir-
ies concerning each thing: first, whether it has
these maximum and minimum termini; second, granted
that it has, whether they are intrinsic or extrinsic, or, what is the same, affirmative or negative.
For one and the same thing cannot have either terminus, i.e., intrinsic and extrinsic, under the
same respect, e.g., in size. For, since these termini are indivisible, if they should belong to one
thing there would be two immediate indivisibiles,
and this implies a contradiction. Wherefore, if a
thing has an intrinsic terminus of largeness it
cannot have an extrinsic terminus of the same, for
the foregoing reasons, but this does not preclude
that it have an extrinsic terminus with respect to
smallness.

[12] Note, second: one can inquire whether
there is a maximum or a minimum in various things,
such as in quality with respect to intension and
remission, i.e., whether there is any maximum intensity that the quality cannot exceed, or, alternatively, whether there is a minimum, smaller than
which cannot exist. The same can be asked propor-
tionally of a power of acting, of potency or impo-
140   tency, of weight, of perfection, and finally of continuous and permanent quantity; for, concerning
discrete quantity it is certain that there is a

minimum terminus, i.e., unity, but not a maximum,
because numbers can be multiplied to infinity.
Concerning successive entities it is also certain
that there is no maximum, for, since their essence
consists in succession, they can always increase
to infinity; nor is there a minimum either, since
it is of the nature of the successive that, whatever part has been assigned, there can always be
found a smaller, to infinity. Again, permanent
quantity can be considered in three ways. First:
in itself and mathematically, i.e., according to
extension; and so it can be increased and divided
to infinity, third *Physics*, 71. Second: as it is
in physical matter, abstracting from any determined form; and so, from the third *Physics*, 68, it
can be divided to infinity, but not increased.
Third: as it is in matter which is already informed by some determined substantial form, and it is
only of this third way that we are now inquiring,
i.e., whether natural entities have certain termini of largeness and smallness such that, if anything be added or subtracted, such entities can no
longer exist or be conserved.

[13] Note, third: the formality and difference
of extrinsic and intrinsic termini consist in this,
that the intrinsic is that which a natural thing
can attain and beyond which it cannot, such that
the terminus is truly in it and is something of it,
though indivisible. The extrinsic, on the other
hand, is that which is outside the thing and to
which the thing cannot attain, but short of which
it can attain immediately. Thus, for example, the
terminus of a line is a point that is outside the
line, since there is no line, or nothing in a line,
that is not divisible, and so the terminating point
is extrinsic to the line. However, if an intrinsic
terminus is sought in the same line, which is, for
example, seven palms long, since the line cannot
have an indivisible terminus, a divisible one must
be given; this will be the seventh palm, to which
the line truly and intrinsically attains, and it is
something existing in the line.

[14] You say: why do philosophers labor so
much over this, that, granted that a thing must
have some terminus, they inquire whether it is extrinsic or intrinsic? I reply: for two reasons
principally. [a] First: on account of the ceasing
to be and the beginning of change or motion in these

things. For things which have intrinsic termini
begin and cease to be through positive termini,
i.e., through a first *esse* and through a last *esse;*
those on the other hand that are extrinsic, through
a last *non-esse* and through a first *non-esse.*
Since therefore it is especially the task of the
natural philosopher to know how each natural thing

141   begins and ceases to be, he should inquire whether
it has extrinsic or intrinsic termini. [b] Second: because, since, as I shall point out [49],
living things must have termini, and nature in
their generation does not tend to the uncertain
and indeterminate, at the introduction of their
forms some fixed terminus must be assigned to them,
and this can only be affirmative and intrinsic,
since the extrinsic, consisting as it does in a
negation, which is particularly indeterminate, cannot be fixed and determinate.

[15] Note, fourth: concerning natural things
we can inquire whether they have a terminus in two
ways. First, simply and absolutely: whether anything exists that is the largest of all and anything that is the smallest of all. And in this way
it is certain, *de facto,* that there is an outermost
heaven which, since it contains everything within
it, will also be the largest of all things; it is
also certain that there is some other thing so
small that *de facto* there is nothing smaller, although perhaps there are others that are equal to
it. The reason for both is because, if there always were something larger and larger or smaller
and smaller, one would proceed to infinity. Concerning this first way of speaking of termini simply, since it does not pertain to the present question, nothing further will be said.

[16] Second therefore, one can inquire of the
terminus of a natural thing as it belongs to such
and such a species of being: that is, whether a
thing, as it belongs to such a species, has a terminus of largeness and of smallness, and this in
two ways. First, in itself, without any order to
another: that is, whether such a thing, as it belongs to such a species, of itself requires some
terminus under which it can be conserved. Second,
in comparison with other things of the same species: that is, whether there exists in any species,
whether this be the lowest species or one subal-
terned, any individual that is the largest or the

smallest of all things of that species. Our question, however, concerns the first way alone.

[17] Concerning the second, only the following
need be noted. First: if there is an individual
that is the largest in any one species such that
there is no larger or even nothing equal to it,
such an individual is said to have a positive terminus of largeness, since it is positively larger
than all individuals of the same species. So also,
if there is a smallest such that there is nothing
smaller or equal to it, it would be said to have a
positive terminus of smallness. If, however, in
the same species there were an individual such that
there were nothing larger but there were something
equal, or such that there were nothing smaller although there were something equal, then this would
be said to have a negative terminus of largeness
or of smallness, since there is nothing larger or
smaller than it; but it would not be the largest   142
or the smallest positively, since there is something its equal.

[18] Note, second: these two terms positive
and negative are taken here in a different way than
above in the first notation [10], where we distinguished intrinsic and extrinsic termini and called
the former positive or affirmative, the latter negative. For in the present note we are taking the
terms positive and negative relatively, in order to
another, as explained previously; there they were
taken absolutely and in themselves. For this reason these terms, taken relatively, abstract from
their being intrinsic or extrinsic termini, and so
one and the same terminus, absolutely taken, could
be positive in the way explained in the first notation and, relatively taken, it could be negative
in the way explained here. For example, any living
thing will have an intrinsic and positive terminus,
absolutely, of its largeness; yet this terminus
will be negative, relatively, when compared to
other living things, for, although perhaps there
might be nothing larger, there would be something
equal to it. For this reason when reading different authors one should be careful to note the meaning they assign to positive and negative termini;
whether relatively, or absolutely and considered in
themselves.

[19] Note, third: this same distinction of

positive and negative termini, taken relatively, can be accomodated not only to the largeness and smallness of things of the same species, but also in the first mode of comparison given at the beginning of this fourth notation [15], i.e., as one thing simply and in general would be compared in largeness and smallness with any other thing, also simply and in general, abstracting from the fact that it may be of the same species. However, since that mode, as I said, does not pertain to the present question, nothing will be said of it in this comparison.

[20] Note, fourth: our question is principally concerned with the termini of largeness and smallness absolutely and in themselves, not relatively. Concerning relatives it is only necessary to know that those that have a terminus in the same species can be such that, *de facto*, their termini of largeness or of smallness are positive or also negative; i.e., there can be an animal that is largest of all, such that there is neither a larger nor an equal, and so it will be a positive terminus relatively; and there can be an animal such that, although there might not be any larger, there could be something equal, and so its terminus will be negative relatively. The same can be said concerning smallness. Concerning this relative comparison, however, nothing more need be said.

143   [21] Note, fifth: the addition or subtraction of quantity is either found in living things and is said to be augmentation and diminution, and this is proper to the living and is effected by the soul through the force of natural heat; or it is found in the non-living, and this comes about in three ways. First: intrinsically, through rarefaction and condensation, and in this way water when heated rarefies and becomes larger, or air condenses and becomes smaller, and similarly with others. Second: extrinsically, through addition alone, as when one adds earth to earth, etc. Third: through generation, as when wood is added to fire, for from this is generated new fire that, added to the old, augments it. Therefore our question concerns termini of largeness and smallness, whether in living or in other things, whether this be addition or diminution in the first, second, or third way.

[22] Note, sixth: we can inquire whether a

natural thing has a terminus of largeness and
smallness in two ways: first, in itself without an
order to anything outside it, such as an ambience
or a contrary; second, in order to something extrinsic that is ambient or contrary. In this second way it is certain that in elements, for example,
there is a maximum, since, by reason of the impeding surrounding heaven, they cannot increase further; and in this way there is a minimum also, for,
if fire is divided, one will finally come to a fire
that is so small that, by reason of a surrounding
contrary, it can no longer be conserved. Our question, however, concerns the first mode, i.e., setting aside all extrinsic considerations. And so
when it is said that an element or anything else
can increase to infinity, this means as far as in
it lies, if matter could increase to infinity; for
then it would not be impossible that it increase
in itself and by reason of form, though by reason
of something extrinsic, since matter is in itself
finite, it could not increase to infinity.

[23] Note, seventh: either we speak of the
maximum and minimum of a part existing in its
whole, and under this formality it is certain that
there is no minimum because, having assigned any
part in the whole, we can always assign a smaller
in it, since each part will be quantified and divisible to infinity, and if it is homogeneous the
full definition of the form is conserved throughout. With regard to the maximum, the same argument may be given concerning the whole. Or we may
speak of the maximum and the minimum of a part
that is subsistent *per se* outside the whole, and
so we may ask whether there can be a minimal fire,
for example, existing *per se* and separated from
others, such that, if it were divided, one would
finally come to a fire than which nothing smaller
can subsist *per se*, excluding extrinsic considerations.

[24] Note, eighth: this entire question can be   144
reduced to the following -- whether each natural
thing, subsisting *per se*, as it belongs to such and
such a species, absolutely and in itself, excluding
all extrinsic considerations, has any terminus of
largeness and smallness, whether in rarity and density, whether in any other extension that comes
about through true augmentation and diminution,
through addition and subtraction, or through genera-

tion and corruption, in the way already explained
in the fifth notation [21]; and finally, granted
that any thing has a terminus, whether this is intrinsic or extrinsic. Of course, if we are speaking of natural heterogeneous things, such as the
living, it is certain that they have termini both
of largeness and of smallness; the only controvert-
ed point is whether these are extrinsic or intrinsic. If, on the other hand, we are speaking of
homogeneous things, then both are called into question, whether they have termini, and, if they have,
whether these are extrinsic or intrinsic. In this
matter there are four opinions.

　　　[25] The first opinion is that of those saying that all natural things, elements excepted,
have intrinsic termini of largeness and smallness;
elements, on the other hand, have an intrinsic terminus of smallness but none of largeness: so St.
Thomas in the first *Physics*, texts 36, 38, *De generatione*, text 41, and the First Part, question 7,
article 3; Capreolus, in the second *Sentences*, distinction 19; Soto, in the first *Physics*, question
4; and all Thomists. First proof: from the authority of Aristotle, first *Physics*, 36, where he states
this, and in text 38 offers an argument against the
ancients that, if there is no maximum and minimum,
is pointless. For so he concludes against Anaxagoras: if anything can be separated from anything
else, there is no minimum; but all natural things
have a minimum; therefore [the antecedent is not
true]. Nor can you say that Aristotle supposes
this so as to oppose Anaxagoras: for Simplicius
notes here, in his comment 34, that Anaxagoras denied a minimum -- which seems probable, since he
thought that anything can be separated from anything
else. Moreover, Aristotle in the second *De anima*,
41, teaches that every thing constituted by nature
has a fixed terminus of largeness and smallness.

　　　[26] Second: from the argument of Aristotle
in the first *Physics*, 36. If the homogeneous parts
of an animal have no terminus of largeness and
smallness, the animal will have none either; but
this is false; therefore [such parts have these
termini]. The minor is obvious. Proof of the inference: for, if there can be flesh of any size and
bone, nerves, and arteries of any size, there can
be a head of any size also. Confirmation: if there
can be homogeneous parts of any size whatever,

there is no reason why, if God puts them all together, there cannot be a man of any quantity what-   145
soever.

[27] Third: things that are from nature are
determinate.

[28] Fourth: we see that things are corrupted
by attrition, by breaking, etc.; but this would not
be so unless there were a minimum; therefore [there
is a minimum].

[29] Fifth: if there were no minimum, not even
in homogeneous things, it would follow that there
is no minimum in sight; but this is absurd; therefore [there is a minimum in homogeneous things].
The major is apparent, for if there is no minimum
fire, for example, since fire conserves light,
there would be no minimum visible object; therefore, there would be no sight either. The minor is
Aristotle's in the book *De sensu et sensili*, chapter 6, and it is proved by reason: for, the smaller
something visible is, the stronger must be the power that perceives it; therefore, if there were no
visible minimum, there would be no maximum seeing
power, and so the power would increase to infinity.

[30] The second opinion is Averroës's, in all
the places cited above from Aristotle and, moreover,
in the sixth *Physics*, 32 and 91, in the eighth
Physics, 62, in the seventh *Physics*, 2, in the third
De caelo, 9, and elsewhere; again, Themistius, in
the first *Physics*, texts 36 and 37; Jandun, in the
first *Physics*, question 16; and Zimara, in the solution of contradiction 29, on text 41 of the second
De anima; these all say that any thing whatever,
elements included, has termini of largeness and
smallness, but they do not state whether these are
intrinsic or extrinsic.

[31] The third opinion is Paul of Venice's,
in the first *Physics*, 38, maintaining that things
that have termini have extrinsic termini both with
regard to largeness and with regard to smallness,
for otherwise it would follow that substance would
cease to exist through its ultimate *esse*, which is
absurd. Proof of the inference: for, if the largest horse were to swell up under beatings, during
the entire time of the swelling, which begins in
time, the form of horse would no longer exist lest

there be a horse larger than the largest; and nonetheless it existed at the instant before the swelling began; therefore, if largeness has an intrinsic terminus, the horse would cease to exist
through its ultimate *esse*. He proves the same
concerning the minimum: if the minimum water is
condensed. . .

[32] The fourth opinion is Scotus's in the
second *Sentences*, distinction 2, question 9, Ockham's in the second, question 8, and Pererius's,
book 10, chapter 23; these say that all heterogeneous things, such as living things and some compounds, have intrinsic termini of largeness and
smallness, but that homogeneous things, such as
elements and some homogeneous compounds, have neither a maximum nor a minimum in any way.

[33] I say, first: it seems certain, whatever
others may think, that no things have maxima and
minima in relation to God -- not in the sense that
they can go to infinity, for concerning this elsewhere -- but only God can, by his absolute power,
increase and diminish all created things forever
and ever. The proof of this for living things:
these require quantity, as something extrinsic,
for their operation and conservation; but God can
supply for the concursus of any extrinsic cause;
therefore [living things have no maxima and minima
in relation to God].

[34] Concerning qualities, on the other hand,
Scotus and Durandus in the third *Sentences*, distinction 13, Richard and Giles in the first *Sentences*, distinction 17, Henry, *Quodlibet* 5, question 22, Cajetan, on the Third Part, question 7 and
question 10, article 4, and on the Second Part of
the Second, question 24, article 7, speaking of the
quality of grace, deny that a quality can be increased to infinity intensively. For, since qualities other than grace are created and limited, the
properties of the essence must have a fixed limit,
granted intrinsic, in intension. Capreolus, however, in the third *Sentences*, distinction 13, question 1, and in the first *Sentences*, distinction 17,
question 4, Almainus and Gregory, same place, Ockham, same place and in the third *Sentences*, distinction 13, question 7, and Soto, in the first
Physics, question 4, article 2 -- where he shows
that this is the opinion of St. Thomas in *De veri-*

146

tate, question 29, article 3, and that if, in the
Third Part, question 7, article 12, he seems to say
the contrary, this should be understood of ordinary
law -- these all hold that, although quality of itself has a fixed terminus in intension, nonetheless
it can be increased by absolute power. And this
argument can be given: because qualities are not so
intrinsically the instruments of forms that they
essentially include the latitude owed to the form
itself. Bonaventure and Cartarius are in agreement
with this opinion.

[35] And so I say, first: no quality of itself,
abstracting from an order to a subject or an agent,
has a fixed terminus in intension, and yet it does
not tend to infinity simply -- for this is incompatible with a created nature -- but to infinity
syncategorematically. For this reason I say, second: the same quality, so considered, can by God's
power always increase or decrease continually without a terminus. The reason: because a quality, as
a quality, in itself and abstracting from the subject, does not itself require a fixed terminus.
Add to this also that the opinion of Capreolus is
very probable.

[36] You object, first: an intension is a certain perfection or intrinsic mode of an essence,
not in the sense that it is essential but that it
intimately perfects the essence, and in this it
differs from extension, which perfects a quality
only extrinsically; but the essence of a quality
is finite, and thus so is the intension. Confirmation: all other intrinsic modes that follow on a
determinate essence are limited, and so the same
is to be said of intension.

[37] The nominalists reply, first, by denying
the inference, and they cite instances in grace,
charity, and the light of glory; for, although
these have finite, indeed created essences, nonetheless they can be increased to infinity, as is
apparent, they say, in the infinite grace of
Christ. Nor can you say that these qualities are
infinite by reason of an infinite subject, i.e.,
God, for this does not prevent their essence from
being finite. If, therefore, intrinsic modes have
a terminus by reason of a determinate essence, the
same should be said of supernatural qualities.
Confirmation: there is no inconsistency in God's

being able to produce more and more bodies to infinity that are hot to eight degrees; nor is it
inconsistent that God place all of these different
heats in the same body, with the result that they
lose their proper termini and become undivided,
since they are of the same nature; therefore [God
can increase a quality to infinity]. Add to this
again: if from the fact that the essence of a quality is finite and determinate it is licit to infer that any intrinsic mode of such an essence has
a terminus, by the same reasoning I may infer that
any intrinsic mode of a quality can consist in
something indivisible, because the essence of the
quality, from which it flows, consists in something
indivisible.

[38] I reply, second: intension does not perfect an essence from within, nor is it an intrinsic mode of the essence of the quality as such,
but of an essence existing in several integral
parts that have the same nature and contribute to
the integrity of the one quality; and since such
parts are indeterminate in their genus, and can be
larger and larger, more and more, or smaller and
fewer to infinity, the intensity of the quality, of
its nature, does not have a fixed terminus.

[39] I reply, third: intension is called an
intrinsic mode of quality, not that it is anything
immediately consequent on or affecting the essence,
but solely from the fact that it does not inhere
in it by means of any other accident that is really
distinct, as extension does. For quality would
never have parts outside of parts if there were not
quantity, and this is an entity really distinct
from quality, but it has intension from the mere
union of its integral parts existing in the same
part of the subject, and so, if the quality alone
were to exist *per se*, it could, by divine power,
still retain its intension. From this, however,
it is not correct to infer that it has a terminus.

[40] To the confirmation [36], I reply, first,
by denying the antecedent. Again: existence is an
intrinsic mode of essence; and subsistence, of substance; and yet existences and subsistences are
many and indeterminate, whereas essence is one. I
148   reply, second: if the antecedent is true, it is true
only in the modes that follow on the essence as
such, not in the modes that follow on the essence

as it is found in parts of the same nature, as I
have said [38].

[41] You object, second: intension seems to
be more intrinsic to quality than disposition is
to substantial form, and though there is nothing
to prevent a form being produced through the power
of God without a disposition, a quality cannot be
produced without an intension; therefore [inten-
sion is more intrinsic to quality].

[42] I reply: intension is more intrinsic to
quality in this sense, that it is really the same,
re ipsa, as the essence of the quality; the dispositions of a substantial form, on the other hand,
are really distinct from it. This is how it also
happens that through the divine power substantial
forms may be produced and conserved without a disposition, whereas qualities cannot be produced without an intension, for qualities, of their nature,
must be acquired through motion or change, and
this, being successive, has no first part; therefore there cannot be a minimum in the intension of
the quality either. This is also confirmed in
quantity, which, without doubt, cannot exist without extension. Yet from this, for the reasons already given, it is not licit to infer that there
is a minimum or a maximum in quality, just as it
is not valid to reason as follows: quantity cannot
be produced without an extension, but a substantial
form can be produced without its dispositions
through divine power; therefore, to the extent that
a form has a terminus of dispositions of its nature,
so does quantity have a terminus in extension.

[43] You object, third, from Scotus: if quality is not of its nature intensively finite, it follows that there can be a quality that is infinite
in intension and perfection.

[44] I reply: those who admit an actual infinite through the power of God concede the inference,
but those who deny it say that this implies only
that there can be an infinite in the syncategore-
matic sense. And if you should say, let God make
everything he can, and that will be infinite, I reply: this implies that he actually and simultaneously make a whole that is infinite syncategorematically.

[45] You object, fourth: at least it seems incompatible to have a greater and greater intension on the part of a subject that is determinate.

[46] I reply, first: a quality can in any event be intensified when separated from its subject by divine power. Second: granted that this is not true of the passive potency of a natural subject, which is finite, yet it can be true of the passive obediential potency of the same subject, which is just as great as God's active potency. Third: there is no incompatibility in God's making a subject that is more and more capacious to infinity. Fourth: Gabriel adds, perhaps an incorruptible subject, such as primary matter, does not of itself require a quality with a fixed intension, but it has a natural potency to every such quality.

149

[47] I say, second: all living things and heterogeneous compounds, as, for example, the magnet, have a determinate terminus of largeness and smallness. The opinion is common, and it is expressly that of Aristotle in the first *Physics,* 36, in the second *De anima,* 41, in the fourth *De generatione animalium,* chapter 4, and in the seventh *Politics,* chapter 4, where he proves this. For instruments, he says, that are too large are of no use even to the largest living thing, and in fact, they are worthless; but the body is the instrument of the soul, second *De anima,* 37; therefore such a living thing would exist to no purpose, for it could neither operate nor be conserved, since it requires operations for its conservation. Proof of the major: it is obvious from experience that things that are too large can be conserved only with great difficulty; so Aristotle notes in the seventh *Politics* that cities that are too large are extremely difficult to govern. Moreover, even among artifacts instruments that are extremely large are moved with difficulty even by the greatest force, and then at the slowest rate. The same is apparent with smallness: for, if the instruments of the soul [i.e., the organs of living things] were extremely small, they would exist to no purpose, for a man, for example, could not grasp anything with his hands or hold it, etc.; therefore [heterogeneous things have definite termini].

[48] Moreover, the very augmentation through

which the quantity of living things is acquired is
determined, since it is a natural motion; yet nature does not tend to infinity, but acts for an
end; again, growth proceeds from an augmentative
power, and this must be determined. Finally, we
see that living things are always produced, conserved, and increased within a fixed terminus of
quantity; this therefore is a sign that it is natural and cannot be done otherwise; for it is commonly agreed that what has never happened cannot
come to happen.

[49] I say, third: these termini of living
things, *per se* and by way of generation, are intrinsic, since they arise from the determination
of the form; and this form, since it is especially
determinate, requires a quantity having termini
that are especially determinate, and only intrinsic termini are of this kind, as I have said above
[14b]. Confirmation: as I have touched on above
[14a], for example, if the smallest terminus of
quantity and of size were extrinsic, the thing
would begin to exist through the first *non-esse*,
and this is false in the case of living things.
For, when the minimum has already been attained,
if this were intrinsic to the thing to be generated it would be true to say that now the thing is
not and immediately afterward it will be; and so
it would begin to exist through the first *non-esse*.
For the explanation of the major, I say that each   150
form of a living thing has fixed termini of largeness and smallness to which it can attain and beyond which it cannot, and these are called intrinsic termini. Note here that I do not say that
these forms necessarily require such a quantity,
for example in largeness, that they cannot exist
under a smaller provided it does not exceed the
minimum; or so small, that they cannot be conserved under a larger provided it does not exceed the
maximum. Nor is this essential to the notion of
an intrinsic terminus, but only that they require
such an amount to which they can attain and beyond
which they cannot, granted that they can vary within the maximum and minimum for different dispositions.

[50] You say: if nature and form are determinate, they require every determination in any way
whatever, and not merely the one we have posited.
I reply that this is not necessary. For the only

determination that is required is that there be no
process to the indefinite or to infinity in largeness and smallness, since for something to be too
large or too small would harm it and impede it; on
the other hand, to require that there be determination in every way whatever would be more opposed to
nature, which delights in variety so that some
things may be larger, others smaller, but always
within certain limits. Again, I do not hold that
in the way of generation the living thing always
begins to inform a minimal part; rather, it will
generally inform some larger part at the same time.
But this makes little difference.

[51] You object: if the first reason is valid,
that there must be some intrinsic terminus, since
this arises from the demands of the form, which,
being determined, requires a determined quantity
[49], the same would be true of any other thing,
as of the elements, since they also have a determined form; nonetheless, as will appear presently,
this is false, and so that reason proves nothing.
I reply: each form determines its own conditions,
but in order to its end and not otherwise; for the
elements, in order to their end, should not have a
determined quantity so that they can accept any determination whatever that may be necessary for con-
stituting a compound, and on this account they cannot be determined to quantity by their forms. But
this is not so in living things, as is obvious.

[52] I say, fourth: these same termini of living things, *per accidens* and in the way of corruption, are extrinsic. For corruption, coming about
per accidens, does not require such determination;
and, moreover, because something substantial would
cease to exist through its last *esse*, and this is
false. The proof, from an example of Paul of Venice: for, if the largest horse were to begin to
151   swell up and be altered, and if the terminus of
largeness in corruption were intrinsic to it, since
alteration begins in time it would be true to say
that now the animal exists, and immediately afterward, throughout the entire time of alteration,
that it does not; and so it would cease to exist
through its last *esse*. But in truth, if the terminus is extrinsic, at the beginning of alteration
it would be true to say that now the animal does
not exist and that immediately previously it did;
thus it would cease to exist through its first

non-esse, which is true.

[53] This alone I shall add: perhaps it is
not necessary that the horse die as soon as the alteration and swelling occur, for possibly it could
live a little while longer; then it would make no
difference that it should be larger than the largest, for, since the terminus is extrinsic in the
way of corruption and *per accidens,* there is no
incompatibility that this take place. And through
this the reply to the argument of Paul of Venice
[52] is obvious: for it proves only that there must
be an extrinsic terminus of corruption, which I
willingly concede.

[54] You raise the doubt: since the same form
is involved in generation and corruption, why are
intrinsic termini required in the former and extrinsic in the latter? I reply, first: because less is
required for conservation and corruption than for
generation, as is apparent by induction from the
study of natural things.

[55] Second: because it is one thing that a
substance act from within and by virtue of its form,
another, that it be acted upon by an extrinsic
agent. For thus it happens that, while the living
thing through the action of its proper form cannot
extend itself beyond its body of determined quantity, it can be made to extend to larger dimensions
from without, though against its proper nature;
just as, even though a substance may require a
large body or one of such and such a quantity to
exist in a perfect state, it can be impeded and
still exist under a smaller quantity, though imper-
fectly.

[56] Third: since the generation of a thing is
per se and primarily intended by nature, and so the
dispositions requisite in the way of generation are
determined by nature itself, the thing is terminated intrinsically in the way of generation. Corruption, on the other hand, is not *per se* and primarily intended but follows *per accidens* on the generation of something else; and so it happens that an
extrinsic terminus suffices in the way of corruption. And this will be true of living things.

[57] I say, fifth: following the common opinion, elements have termini of largeness and small-

ness with respect to rarity and density. This is
required on the part of compounds, because earth,
if it were not dense at least to a certain terminus, would not yield consistency, and fire, if it
were not rare, would not penetrate, etc.; experience also shows that elements require a certain
density and rarity, that they reduce themselves to
this, and that without it they can neither operate
nor be conserved. So it happens that air or vapor,
152   when condensed too much, turns into water, and air,
when rarefied too much, turns into fire, etc. Finally, if variation of this kind were undetermined,
nothing would prevent fire getting as dense as
earth, and earth as rare as fire -- which is not
the case, among other reasons because lightness and
heat are the concomitants of rarity, and gravity
and cold, of density, and so the lightness and hotness that are found in fire cannot exist in earth,
unless one is to call earth fire.

[58] I say, sixth: these termini are intrinsic
in the way of generation, extrinsic in the way of
corruption. This is proved no differently than it
has been proved in the third [49] and fourth [52]
conclusions concerning living things.

[59] I say, seventh: elements and homogeneous
compounds of themselves have no termini of largeness or smallness, either extrinsic or intrinsic.
Proof: first, from Aristotle in the book *De sensu*,
chapter 6, where he says that something hot can be
divided to infinity and, in chapter 3 -- what a-
mounts to the same thing -- that homogeneous things
cannot be divided down to a minimum. For, since
the form of water, for example, is the same in all
its parts and is itself extended through the extension of quantity, no minimum of water can be assigned, any more than a minimum of quantity. For the
nature of water does not require a fixed quantity
but can exist in any, at least by existing in other
parts, and the same argument holds if each particle
however small you wish, be separated; therefore
[there is no minimum of water]. Proof of the minor:
let that part be separated and withdrawn from its
contrary; then it will certainly subsist -- since
there will be nothing to corrupt it, just as if it
were put in a vacuum, and since the part is prior
to the whole and so can exist without the whole,
and again since it is a substance and therefore
subsists.

[60] You say: if the minimum air is divided in a vacuum it will be converted into earth, and so it will cease to exist because the surroundings corrupt it. To the contrary, first: what is the efficient agent that produces the form of earth? Again: granted that the form of earth requires less quantity than air, nonetheless it requires more matter under such minimal quantity, and so what is less than the minimum of air is also less than the minimum of earth. Finally: I take an element that requires a minimum quantity, and with that I will formulate the same argument.

[61] Second: no matter how heavy a thing be posited, something that is more or less heavy can be found, from the third *De caelo*, chapter 9.

[62] Third: take any minimum fire and let air act on the middle part and water on another part; then something will be produced, and this will necessarily be less than the minimum, if there is a minimum. Confirmation: if water alone acts on that minimum fire, it is certain that, since the whole cannot corrupt at once, the part that is closer will corrupt first and so the more remote part will remain; therefore what was first taken was not the minimum.

153

[63] Fourth: there is no reason why a minimum should be assigned to the elements; therefore [they have no minimum]. Proof of the antecedent: not by reason of the compound, since the more an element is divided the better it will enter into combination; nor by reason of any operation that comes about through primary qualities, since these do not require a determinate quantity for their operation; nor by reason of its augmentative power, since augmentation comes about through addition from without; therefore [there is no reason for a minimum].

[64] These arguments prove that there is no minimum. Much easier is it to prove that there is no maximum, especially since this is denied by no one except Cajetan, on the First Part, question 7, article 3. For Aristotle says, second *De anima*, chapter 41, that fire can increase to infinity. And this is obvious: for, if straw is added to the maximum fire, it will certainly increase; for to say that the straw is not going to burn, or, if it does burn, that in such an event the fire would

turn into air, seems plainly ridiculous. And so
much for substances; now, concerning qualities.

[65] I say, eighth: although, as I noted in
the first conclusion [35], it is not impossible for
a quality as such to be more and more intensifiable
through God's power so as not to have a terminus
of largeness, nonetheless it does have, indirectly
and naturally, a maximum in intension. The proof:
because qualities naturally must come to be from
forms that are not able to produce any quality
whatever, but something determinate, for example,
heat of eight degrees; so indirectly, by reason of
the agent, they have a fixed terminus in the order
of size. This, however, is not an ultimate degree
different in nature from the others, but rather
the total determinate intension that the form can
produce, and no larger -- for example, a total heat
of eight degrees is the maximum terminus of heat,
i.e., the *minimum quod non*.

[66] I say, ninth: in the intension of quality
there is no minimum naturally. For the forms producing a quality are not determined to produce so
much and no less; rather, in view of their producing successively, a minimum cannot be produced on
account of the contrary, and, whatever amount is
designated, something smaller can always be found,
just as in time and in motion.

[67] You object, first: in illumination some
type of quality is produced in an instant through
its first *esse*, and so it has a terminus; thus the
same can be said of others. I reply, first: we
are speaking of qualities that involve a resistance; but these, being acquired through continuous
motion, do not admit of a first minimum part acquired, just as there is no first part or first *mutatum
esse* in motion. So also light, when acquired *per
accidens*, continuously and successively, through
the agent's getting closer, does not admit of a
minimum. Even when produced in an instant, through
its first *esse*, the entity of illumination that
first takes on *esse* by its nature is not a minimum,
and so there can be something smaller and smaller
in the order of intension, as is obvious from experience -- for much illumination and little illumination are both produced in an instant, through
their first *esse*.

154

[68] You object, second: the same reasoning applies to largeness as to smallness; therefore, if a quality naturally has a maximum it will have a minimum also. I reply: *de facto* a quality natural- ly has a maximum, not that it is determined of its nature, for this is false, as I maintained in the first conclusion [35], because it has been ordain- ed by the Author of Nature to serve a determinate substantial form and to add to the perfection of a determinate universe; thus, just as of its nature it is not determined in augmentation, so not in di- minution. Likewise quantity, in relation to the universe, is determinate in size, and yet it does not have a minimum of its nature. But quality *de facto* does have a maximum and not a minimum, since a regress to infinity with the maximum would be im- proper for the substantial form and for the uni- verse, whereas there would be nothing improper in the order of smallness -- indeed this seems neces- sary for there to be continuous motion in which there is no first *mutatum esse*. Add to this that it is not proper to infer that because there is a maximum there must be a minimum also, for a person can carry a thousand pounds and not more, and yet he can always carry less and less, to infinity.

[69] You object, third: acts of the intellect and of the will have a minimum, and for this reason habits that are produced through them will have a minimum; but these are qualities, therefore [quali- ties have a minimum]. I reply by denying the an- tecedent. Second: I admit the antecedent but deny the inference, since these acts are free and per- formed without resistance, whence intension and succession arise, and so the case is not the same as with other qualities. Add to this, third: even if we admit that this is true of actions, it is not true of habits.

[70] You object, fourth: let a hot agent be applied, for example, in an instant; then the mini- mum heat will necessarily result. I reply: although the application be made in an instant, nonetheless on account of the resistance of the contrary no quality will be produced at that instant, but only in the time following; such a resistance is always found naturally in motion, for there is no action without a contrary. And again: even though some minimum particle could be introduced at one time, one may not infer from this that a quality of its

155

nature requires a minimum terminus.

[71] I say, tenth: powers have an intrinsic *maximum quod sic* but not a minimum. For example, a carrying power has a maximum weight it can carry and a larger that it cannot, from the first *De caelo*, 116, but not a minimum; for no matter how small a weight be designated, a smaller can always be found, and the power will be able to carry that. Indeed the measure of termini is taken one way in powers, another way in qualities. In the latter it is determined by degrees, for we say that the maximum heat is eight degrees, whereas in powers we determine the maximum from the object, for we say that the maximum carrying power is, for example, a thousand pounds. The reason is that the magnitude of the object and the intensity of degree of the power are mutually connected, since a power that has the greater degree can affect the greater object; yet, in view of the fact that the measure must be more known, and the object is more known than the intensity of the power, we determine the power from the object rather than vice versa.

[72] You object: it seems that a power's maximum would better be determined from a minimum object than from a maximum, for the maximum visual power is the one that sees the smallest thing visible. I reply: although the smallest thing visible is minimal on the part of the thing, it is maximal by reason of visibility, for to apprehend it a more intense power is required.

[73] Concerning lack of power or impotency, on the other hand, Aristotle and Averroës maintain, first *De caelo*, 116, that it is determined by a minimum with respect to smallness; so they say, for example, that the minimum carrying impotency is one that cannot carry the smallest particle, e.g., one dram, beyond what the maximum power can carry. Thus, [if the maximum power can carry a thousand pounds,] the minimum impotency would be one that cannot carry one dram beyond a thousand pounds.

[74] But this seems to be false. For the terminus of a maximum power, as I stated, is intrinsic and indivisible, and so whatever lies beyond it must be divisible, for otherwise two indivisibles would be together; but a minimum impotency can ef-

fect nothing beyond the maximum power, and thus it
cannot be determined by a minimum in any way, since
there is no minimum that it cannot attain. For example, let the maximum power be one that can carry
a thousand pounds; then the minimum impotency is
one that can carry nothing beyond a thousand pounds;
but beyond a thousand pounds there is no indivisible
but only something divisible to infinity, of which
one cannot take a minimum part; therefore there is
no minimum by which the minimum impotency can be   156
ascertained.

[75] I reply: an impotency is a privation and
for this reason it cannot have intrinsic termini,
but must be terminated extrinsically by the termini
of the power to which it is conjoined; as a result
the minimum impotency that is conjoined to a maximum power has the same terminus as the maximum power, but this is intrinsic to the power and extrinsic to the impotency. When therefore the maximum
power is one that can carry a thousand pounds, the
minimum impotency will be one that can carry nothing beyond a thousand pounds. For Aristotle, in
determining impotency through a minimum, must be
understood in relation to us, with respect to whom
there is a minimum quantity; for, in relation to
us, the minimum impotency is one that, beyond a
thousand pounds, cannot carry even a dram.

[76] Therefore, to the first argument of the
first opinion [25], I reply: Aristotle says that
similar things have a minimum when arguing *ad hominem* against Anaxagoras. For although, as I said
[25], it seems probable from Simplicius that Anaxagoras denied a minimum, nonetheless Anaxagoras
was defending two incompatible assertions. In the
first he said that the first principles of all
things are certain similar parts, and because of
this, minimal; and from their mixing each thing is
thought to be, and is named from, the species of
which it contains the greater number of parts --
for Simplicius attributes this to him, first *Physics*, comment 34. In the second he held that anything can be separated out of anything; nor did he
advert to the fact that the second assertion is inconsistent with the first, for, if anything can be
separated out of anything, one will never arrive
at a minimum. Therefore Aristotle, so as to use
the second assertion against Anaxagoras, supposes
the first *ad hominem*. In fact, in a text of the

second *De anima* he speaks of living things, and
indeed states there that fire does not have a terminus of largeness.

[77] To the second [26], I deny the inference:
for, although parts may be as large as one likes,
nonetheless a living thing cannot be as large as
one likes. The reason for the disparity is that
similar parts do not need a determinate quantity
for their operation, whereas living things do. But
this argument concludes demonstratively against the
ancients who denied a substantial form, for which
reason they were not able formally to distinguish
a whole from its parts, and on this account they
could not say that the whole required anything except by reason of its parts. If therefore the
parts do not require a determinate quantity, they
could not say why the whole does. Yet those who
posit a substantial form can assign a reason for
the disparity.

157

[78] To the third [27], I reply: if this proposition means that all accidents and all conditions
in each natural thing are determined from the nature of that thing, the proposition is completely
false. For matter is a natural thing and yet it
is indeterminate, and the same for the elements.
Confirmation: for, according to almost everyone,
homogeneous things such as the elements do not have
a determinate maximum terminus of largeness. If,
on the other hand, the sense is that whatever belongs to a thing naturally always belongs to it in
the same determinate manner, this is true. For,
since nature does not change, whatever it does, it
does always. Moreover, since the elements of their
nature have an indeterminate quantity, they always
will have an indeterminate quantity.

[79] To the fourth [28], I reply: things that
are cut are corrupted by virtue of their surroundings; things that are crushed, on the other hand,
are corrupted either because they rarefy or because
they are cut. For we are speaking of elements in
their proper nature, according as they can subsist
and operate in any quantity, no matter how small.

[80] To the fifth [29], I reply by denying
that it follows that if there were no minimum there
would be no sensible minimum. For a greater power
is required for perceiving a smaller thing; there-

fore even though, if we divide fire, something lucid of its nature would remain, nonetheless this
would not be perceived by any sense, since there
is no sense so powerful that it could perceive such
an object.

[V] SECOND DISPUTATION. ON THE QUALITIES OF THE
ELEMENTS

First Question. On the Number of Primary Qualities

[1] Note, first: Aristotle from text 7 onwards
makes use of the following method to investigate
the number of primary qualities. Elements, he
says, being primary bodies, should be constituted
through primary qualities; yet elements are not
bodies of any kind whatever, but sensible bodies;
therefore they should be constituted through primary sensible qualities alone. Besides, among sensible qualities the first are those that are touchable, since they are sensed by the primary sense,
touch, which is presupposed to all the senses and
itself supposes no other; for this reason the qualities should be touchable. Again, since elements
must mutually interact they should be constituted
through primary touchable qualities that are active
and passive. Moreover, there are seven contrarie-
ties of touchable qualities, viz, hot and cold, wet
and dry, heavy and light, hard and soft, moist and
arrid, rough and smooth, coarse and fine; of these
seven Aristotle proves that the first two alone are
proper to the elements from the fact that they a-
lone are primary, since all the others are reduced
to these two. For this reason he concludes that
they alone, i.e., hotness, coldness, wetness, and
dryness, are the primary sensible qualities that
are touchable and active and passive in a mutual
way.

[2] You object, first: Aristotle, in the first
Physics, 10 and 56, says that in each genus there
is one primary contrariety, so why does he enumer-
ate two here? I reply: in each genus there is only
one privative contrariety, i.e., that between the
quality and its privation, and it is of this alone

158

226

that Aristotle is speaking here, not of contrary
contrariety, which can be manifold.

[3] You object, second: Aristotle seems to be
too brief, for he omits one touchable contrariety,
i.e., rare and dense. I reply: first, these are
not qualities, as I shall prove elsewhere; moreover, they are not active.

[4] Note, second: for qualities to be said to
be primary, in the meaning of primacy that Aristotle intends here, all these conditions are required: (1) that they be sensible; (2) that they
be touchable; (3) that they be contrary and as a
consequence active and passive, such that they act
and react with an action that is truly alterative
and corruptive, so that they can be the cause of
substantial mutation and of mixture; (4) that they
be universal, i.e., found in all transmutations;
(5) that all others come to be from them; and (6)
that they not presuppose others with the same conditions and come to be from them, for then they
would not be primary. And from the foregoing it
is apparent, if we run through the individual conditions, that each and every one of the four qualities we have enumerated is primary, nor is any of
them prior to the others by a priority of genus --
although one may be prior to another in nobility,
as heat to cold, cold to wetness, and, lowest of
all, dryness.

[5] Nor can one object that wetness and dryness, from the fourth *Meteors*, are sometimes produced from hot and cold, from which it would seem
to follow that the first two are not primary. For   159
that is *per accidens*, as will be more apparent in
question 3 [X3-9] -- since dryness comes to be *per
se* from dryness, and wetness from wetness.

[6] You object: one thing is primary in each
genus, and so there will be only one primary in
the genus of quality. I reply: these qualities
are not said to be primary within the essence of
the genus, the way in which one thing is the most
perfect in the genus; rather they are said to be
primary based on a comparison with other qualities
in the order of causality, and because none of
these four is dependent on the others when caus-
ing.

[7] Note, third; the foregoing conditions ex-
clude all other qualities that, though prior to
these for some reason such as nobility, time, etc.,
are still not primary in the sense of which Aristotle speaks. And so, first, light is excluded,
for, though prior in nobility and time to these
qualities, being proper to the heavens, an incorruptible body, yet it is not a touchable quality,
nor does it act with reaction, not having a contrary; for the same reason hardness, perspicuity,
and figure, not being active, are also excluded.
Second are excluded influences, if such things exist, for, though primary in nobility and time and
also in generation, since they produce these four,
nonetheless they are neither sensible nor active,
especially by an action that alters, by way of reaction, since they lack a contrary. The same judgment holds for virtual qualities, understood of
compounds, such as stones, herbs, etc.

[8] You object, first: gravity and levity
seem prior to alterative qualities, [a] since Aristotle treats of the former before the latter in
the third and fourth *De caelo*, and [b] since, from
the eighth *Physics*, local motion is prior to alteration. I reply that motive qualities are subsequent to alterative, for the former are produced
by the latter. And to the first argument [a], I
reply that Aristotle treats of the former first because in the books *De caelo* he is treating of the
elements, and so he has to treat of the motive
qualities by which elements are brought to their
proper places. To the second [b], I reply, first:
local motion is said to be prior only by reason of
the motion of the heavens, and this is not brought
about by motive qualities but by intelligences.
Second: even if local motion is prior to alteration
in things here below, where nothing alters or is
altered except through proximity, nonetheless I deny the inference: because, even though he treats
the motive before the alterative, still the alterative first produce the motive, just as the substantial form first produces accidents and yet accidents act first, before the substantial form is generated.

160   [9] You object, second: motion is not a primary quality. I reply, first: motion does not act
with [the requisite] reaction. Second: motion
causes heat *per accidens*, as Albert teaches in the

twelfth *Metaphysics,* chapter 8, since it tears a-
part and separates, and rarity, itself a disposition to heat, follows from this.

[10] You object, third: sound is a quality
and nonetheless it is not produced from these four
qualities; therefore [they are not primary]. I
reply that sound is a secondary quality, not that
it comes to be from the mixing of primary qualities but that, in some way, it arises from them in
that it presupposes bodies having these qualities.

[W] Second Question. Are All Four Qualities Positive, or Are Some Privative?

[1] The first opinion was that of certain ancients, from Plutarch in the book *De primo frigido,*
who maintained that coldness is the privation of
heat. Cardanus follows their opinion in the second book of *De subtilitate,* and he also affirms
the same of dryness, which he regards as the privation of wetness.

[2] The first proof: from Aristotle in the
second *De caelo,* 18, first *De generatione,* 18, second *De generatione,* 32, twelfth *Metaphysics,* 22,
and elsewhere -- in these places he refers to cold
as a privation.

[3] Second: the rigor of tertian fevers comes
about not through the advent of some cold material
but merely through the absence of heat, and the
same can be said of many other things that are seen
to get cold merely from the absence of heat, e.g.,
when an animal dies, when vapors ascend to the intermediate region of the atmosphere, etc.

[4] Third: Aristotle teaches in the book *De
longitudine et brevitate vitae* that all operations
come about through heat; but if coldness were a
real quality it would produce some effect; therefore [coldness is merely privative]. Confirmation:
because physicians say that coldness does not enter
into the work of nature, and Aristotle, in the
fourth *Meteors,* says that cold is the enemy of nature; on this account we also see that the warmer
places, such as the southern regions, abound in the
number and nobility of their compounds.

[5] The second opinion is that of certain
physicians who, for the reasons given, posit a twofold coldness, one real, that of the elements, the

other privative, that coming into existence when
heat goes away.

[6] The third opinion is that of others saying   161
that all of these are real and positive qualities,
but that wetness and dryness are not qualities but
substances, i.e., that wetness is a fluid substance
whereas dryness is a solid substance. Their proof:
because nothing can be made wet except through the
reception of a humid substance, such as vapors,
etc., and nothing can be made dry except through
the extraction of a humid substance.

[7] Confirmation: because wetness cannot be
separated from water without destroying the water;
therefore it is not its accident.

[8] The fourth and true opinion is that of
Aristotle and of all the peripatetics, text 8 of
the second *De generatione,* fourth *Meteors,* and
elsewhere, saying that all four qualities are true,
real, and positive; this opinion is best urged by
Scaliger, against Cardanus, exercises 18, 19, 22,
and by Plutarch. The basis: otherwise true action
and passion would be impossible, for these do not
occur except with true and positive contrariety;
also, otherwise the introduction of heat and of
wetness would come about instantaneously, since
succession arises by reason of resistance, which
comes to be from a positive contrary -- so that,
if there were only a privative contrary there would
be no succession, as is apparent with light; and,
if coldness and dryness are not positive, earth
would have no qualities and air and fire one only,
and from this it would follow that earth could never be corrupted by a contrary.

[9] I say, first: cold is truly a positive
and real quality. The proof: for positive effects
there must be a positive cause, and many effects of
cold are positive; therefore [cold is a positive
and real quality]. Proof of the minor: because
cold acts on plants and on the extremities of animals, by numbing them, and on water, by freezing
it; because gravity and density follow from coldness, etc.; and finally, because cold corrupts the
heat that is its contrary, as is obvious. If cold
is applied to a thing that is apt to conserve heat
by itself, such as animal flesh, it will certainly
freeze it, and the more effectively the colder it

is; this then is a sign that cold is something
positive, for a privation is not active nor does
it admit of more and less. The result is confirmed by experience, in reactions where cold dulls
the power of heat.

[10] I say, second: dryness is a positive
quality. Proof of this, first: from its effect on
wetness in reactions, and from the production of
compounds that require dryness. Second: Cardanus's
argument, in particular, that dryness is not a
positive quality is because in such cases we see
that moisture is produced only with the greatest
difficulty, and this can arise for no other reason,
162   he says, than that dryness be a privation, and
there can be no regress from privation to possession; but this argument is worthless; therefore
[dryness is a positive quality]. The proof: because, according to him, heat would be produced
with the greatest difficulty for the same reason,
since cold is its privation; and because the difficulty, indeed, the natural impossibility, of a
transition from privation to possession is to the
same possession numerically, not specifically, as
is apparent with light, which returns the same in
species; and finally, because there is another
cause of this difficulty, namely, that moisture is
only slightly active.

[11] I say, third: although sometimes humec-
tation comes about through the entry of a humid
substance and drying through the forcing out of
the same, as will be more apparent from the following, nonetheless wetness is not a fluid substance,
nor is dryness a solid substance, nor are humecta-
tion and desiccation always brought about in the
aforesaid manner.

[12] The proof, first: just as substance of
itself is not hot or cold, so it cannot be of itself humid or fluid, for substance of itself abstracts from all such quality; if, therefore, there
is a fluid substance, it will certainly be such
through a quality joined to it. Confirmation: because to speak of a fluid substance is to speak of
a substance that has something apart from its con-
cept of substance, and this is what we call wetness. Second confirmation: fluidity cannot be understood without motion and quantity; but substance
abstracts from these; therefore, when people speak

of a fluid substance they do not mean a substance
alone, but a substance with an accident, i.e., with
wetness.

[13] Second: humidity comes into being without
the introduction of a fluid substance and dryness
without the extraction of the same; therefore wetness and dryness are not substances. Proof of the
antecedent: since a metal has all the conditions of
dryness and a predominance of earth, it is dry;
following Galen, the same is true of pitch, which
is dry; also of liquefiable stones, etc.; and yet
through the action of fire alone all these become
fluid when melted; therefore [wetness is not caused by a fluid substance]. Again, when a south wind
blows, salt enclosed in a vessel gets moist, and
this is not through the entrance of a humid substance. The same is proved of dryness, since ice
comes from water through sudden freezing, as Pliny
teaches in book 37, chapter 2, and yet it comes to
be from a thing that is clearly humid, and is itself dry; on this account, although some moisture
might be pressed out, nonetheless what remained
would also be plainly humid. Add to this that
there is no pressing out, for freezing does not
press out but retains, i.e., it condenses the
parts. The same can be said of the generation of
rock, and of the little water that, when thrown into a furnace, becomes dry as soon as the fire acts
on it; yet there is no humid substance there.

[14] From the foregoing is apparent the reply
to the basis for the third opinion [6]. To the
confirmation [7], I reply, first: by denying the   163
inference, for there are certain accidents that,
though common, are inseparable. Second: wetness
can be separated from water, for ice is dry, not
wet, from the second *De generatione*, 15. Third:
to establish that wetness is an accident it is not
necessary to separate it from water; it suffices
to separate it from anything without corrupting
that thing, and this is apparent with metal, pitch,
etc. Finally I add: since wetness is lost through
the inefficacy of dryness, it is never separated
from water unless it has already suffered considerably from heat or compression or otherwise, and on
this account corrupts.

[15] To the first argument of the first opinion [2], I reply: from the same texts and particu-

larly from the second *De caelo*, 18, it is known
that coldness is the positive contrary of heat,
for Aristotle says that when one contrary is found
in the universe the other must be there also. Yet
he refers to cold as a privation, because, as he
himself teaches in the third *Physics*, 5, the more
imperfect contrary should be called a privation,
and, in the tenth *Metaphysics*, 16, he states that
all contrariety is privation, for otherwise gravity would be merely privation; again, because in the
second *De caelo* he calls gravity a privation;
again, in the third *Physics*, 5, and the tenth *Metaphysics*, 7, he speaks of black as the privation of
white, though it is obvious that black is something
positive.

[16] To the second [3], I reply: the rigor of
fevers comes either from a cold humor or from the
recession of warm vapors; positive cold comes into
being in the external members because these members are cold *per se*, being watery and earthly,
and on this account they get cold when the vapors
recede, just as water does when fire recedes. The
same thing happens in death, for then the warm
spirits disappear with the departure of the soul,
and so the earthly body, cold of itself, and the
watery humors, cold of themselves, reduce themselves to their proper positive coldness. And the
same is to be said of the earth and vapors.

[17] To the third [4], I reply: this axiom of
physicians and the saying of Aristotle are to be
understood particularly of the operations of living
things, whose life consists mainly in a temperate
heat. Add also, however, that we do not deny that
heat has more effects than cold in things generally:
for this is also the reason why more and nobler compounds are generated in the warmer regions. Still
it is not to be denied that yet other bodies which
are cold of their nature are generated by cold rather than by heat.

[1] Note, first: Aristotle, in the second *De generatione*, text 8, says that all four qualities are active, and yet in the same place he refers to two as passive, i.e., wetness and dryness; and he teaches the same in the fourth *Meteors*, at the beginning. Moreover he defines heat and cold through aggregation and segregation, which is a type of action, whereas he defines wetness and dryness through their being terminated with ease or with difficulty, which is a type of reception. Indeed, in the same place, fourth *Meteors*, he teaches that heat and cold humidify and dry out; and in the same place, comment 35 according to the division of Averroës, he teaches that heat and cold solidify and make things be compressed; but the solidified and the compressed are dry, from text 15 of the second *De generatione*. Confirmation of the same from experience: we see that a hot fire and a cold wind dry clothing; likewise fire, when melting fat, for example, renders it moist; on this account, since dryness and wetness come into being from hot and cold, here seems an evident sign that only the two former are active whereas the other two are passive. For this reason Aristotle seems neither to speak the truth nor to be consistent.

[2] Note, second: for Aristotle's sayings to be true and consistent, three things should be understood: (1) how heat and cold humidify and dry out; (2) whether wetness and dryness have any proper action; and (3) what Aristotle means when he says that two qualities are active and two passive.

[3] Note, third: if heat and cold were to humidify and to dry out *per se* and not *per accidens*, certainly wet and dry would then be merely passive qualities, for this would leave no action proper to them. The reason: because one effect *per se* can

have only a single cause *per se;* for this reason
one must say that heat and cold humidify and dry
out only *per accidens.* And from this it should be
sufficiently obvious why we see that wetness and
dryness sometimes go with heat and not with cold;
sometimes, on the other hand, with cold and not
with heat. For wetness is found with hot air and
with cold water, although it cannot exist with hot
fire and with cold air; on the other hand, dryness
goes with the latter and cannot be with the former;
this then is a sign that wetness and dryness do not
165   arise *per se* from hot or from cold, for if they did
they would always be together; therefore they must
arise from qualities other than wetness and dryness.

[4] You say: heat can produce both wetness
and dryness, but it is impeded by the substantial
form to which it is united, so that sometimes it
produces the former and not the latter. But, to
the contrary: first, substantial forms are not directly active so as to produce anything whatever;
again, because we see that no form can prevent an
accident that is in the same matter from producing
its effect, for otherwise water would prevent heat
from heating it, or, when hot, would prevent it
from heating other things.

[5] Nor can you say that it would not be pre-
vented for the reason given, but merely from the
fact of its being joined to the substantial form
it would be determined to produce this quality rather than that. To the contrary: for from the fact
of being conjoined a quality acquires only a relation; but a real relation cannot make the nature
of the quality such that, if it were apt of itself
to produce something, it would not produce it.
Confirmation: for the same heat-fire, as is noted
in Aristotle, fourth *Meteors,* second summary, chapter 3, sometimes dries out, as is apparent with
mud, and sometimes moistens, as in the melting of
wax; therefore it cannot be a *per se* cause that always produces a similar effect, nor can it be impeded by a form to which it is conjoined.

[6] You say: the heavens produce effects that
are completely diverse. I reply: the heavens are
a universal and equivocal cause, whereas hot or
cold are not. Thus one must conclude that hot and
cold do not humidify and dry out *per se* but *per ac-*

cidens. Now, concerning the manner in which this
is done:

[7] Note, fourth: by way of example, heat
dries out *per accidens,* first, because heating produces a type of form that requires dryness, as
when heat produces fire; second, because it rarefies humid substances, and from such rarefaction
the evaporation of humidity follows, with the result that only the dry part remains -- thus the
sun dries out clothes, fruit, etc.; third, because
it makes things be compressed, but compressed
things are dry, therefore [it dries them]; fourth:
because it conduces to dryness, as I shall note
below, following Albert [15].

[8] For the same reason heat humidifies,
first, because it produces a form that requires
wetness, as, for example, the form of air coming
from the substance of fruit; second, by inducing
wetness into a dry object through diffusion, as
when it draws oil through clothing; third, by dissolving and liquefying, for, from Aristotle,
fourth *Meteors,* summary 2, chapter 3, things that
are made solid by heat are dissolved by cold, and
vice versa; fourth, by aiding the action of wetness, as I shall explain below [15].   166

[9] Cold also dries out *per accidens,* first,
because when freezing it produces a form that requires dryness, such as the form of earth; second,
because when pressing parts together it forces out
the wet substance and makes it evaporate, and so
cold dries out mud; third, by solidifying. And in
similar ways it humidifies.

[10] Note, fifth: wetness and dryness have a
kind of proper action when humidifying and drying
out, and, as a result, they are not purely passive
qualities -- so Galen, in the first book *De causis
symptomatum,* and commonly all physicians and peripatetics. First proof: on the authority of Aristotle, text 8; also, in text 24 he states that any
element can be changed into any other, and that the
transition is easier *inter symbola;* and yet some
elements differ only in a passive quality, as air
and fire in wetness; therefore they should act and
react with one another on the basis of this quality. Second: elements should mutually react in a
compound on the basis of all qualities, for other-

wise two contrary qualities would remain at the
maximum in the same part of the matter, contrary
to everyone; therefore wetness and dryness must
also be active. Third: when a south wind blows or
rain is impending, salt liquefies from the humidity of the air whether the air is cold or hot; this
then is a sign that it arises from humidity, for
whether the same air is hot or cold it always liquefies salt. Again, earth is corrupted in water
by the action of wetness alone; so ice dissolves
in water whether the water is hot or cold, therefore from wetness alone. Fourth: dryness also
acts, as is apparent, since bodies that are left
close to the sea are dry from the dry exhalation
that comes from the sea; the same thing happens to
those that are left in places where there is a
great quantity of salt. Again, we see that salt
dries out well but heats little; therefore dryness
acts without heat.

[11] You object: wet hands, for example, no
matter how long they are set on a dry thing, as on
marble, are never dried out; whereas, on the other
hand, they are dried out by heat immediately; therefore [dryness has no proper action]. I reply,
first: they are dried out by heat *per accidens*,
and indeed the more quickly the more vehement the
action is; second, even the hand is dried out a
little by the dryness of the marble, but its action
is not perceived since the dryness acts only slightly, if not helped by heat.

[12] Here it is to be noted: although dryness
and wetness dry out and humidify *per se*, cold and
heat do so only *per accidens;* and yet wetness and
167   dryness act very slowly and weakly, whereas heat and
cold act quite intensely and quickly. For moist
clothing, under the sun or with a north wind, dries
out most quickly, whereas over the driest marble it
scarcely ever will dry out; again, heat, in melting,
immediately makes a metal liquid, and yet a metal,
even when remaining in water for the longest time,
will hardly ever turn liquid.

[13] Hence it happens, first, that the wetting
and drying out that takes place in a compound, coming about, as it must, most intensely and most
quickly, is brought about particularly by heat and
cold, and only in a slight way by wetness and dryness, and then when helped by heat, as I shall hold

below, following Albert [15]. It is also apparent,
second, why Aristotle, in the fourth *Meteors* at the
beginning, attributes wetting and drying to heat
and cold: because these are effected more quickly
and more intensely by heat and cold than by wetness
and dryness, and by them only when helped by heat;
and because, when in that book he treats of compounds, he treats only of the dryness and wetness
that are found in compounds, in which case they
come to be exclusively from heat and cold.

[14] Note, sixth: so as to make clear what
Aristotle himself means when he states that two
qualities are passive, passion here is to be understood as corruption; others hold here for termina-
tive passion, for a subject is said to undergo passion subjectively even when it does not corrupt.
Thus Marsilius, in the second *De generatione*, says
that heat and cold are to be called active qualities and the others passive, first, because their
action is most known to the senses, whereas that
of the others is least known; second, because the
former act most and resist least, whereas with the
latter the converse happens. But his second argument is unsatisfactory, since resisting is not a
passion but a non-passion; hence what he asserts
about the activity and resistance of qualities is
also false, as will become apparent in the following question [Y].

[15] On this account I assign the following
reasons for these statements of Aristotle. The
first is that heat and cold are said to be active
and wet and dry passive because the former act very
forcefully, in such wise that, when the latter are
compared to them, they seem hardly to act at all.
Second: because heat and cold bring about the effects of wetness and dryness more quickly and more
intensely than do wetness and dryness alone. The
third reason is that given by Philoponus, second
De generatione on text 8, St. Thomas, Averroës in
the beginning of the fourth *Meteors*, and Pomponatius in the same place, third doubt, and Albert,
the same place, first treatise, chapter 2: namely,
that Aristotle said this not absolutely but only
with regard to compounds, wherein heat and cold act
most effectively and wetness and dryness receive
most effectively, though the former also receive a
little and the latter act, as Albert and Buccaferrus have correctly noted. Yet they add that wet-

ness and dryness act only with the aid of the other
two, and particularly with heat; since wetness,
for example, does not act in a compound *per se*,
except insofar as previously, by virtue of the
heat, a humid vapor is raised that can be mixed
with the humidifying body; then, in virtue of the
same heat, the body will be opened up so that the
vapor can penetrate it and moisten it. Thus heat
is said to aid the action of wetness, and in a similar way it aids the action of dryness also. So
that this third reason may be better understood:

[16] Note, first: these four qualities have
two kinds of effects, some primary, as that of fire
to heat, of wetness to moisten, etc., others secondary, as that of heat to aggregate the homogeneous
and separate the heterogeneous, of cold to aggregate everything, of wetness to be bounded readily
by a foreign boundary, and of dryness to be bounded
by something foreign with difficulty. Moreover, the
primary effects of all qualities are true actions,
as I have proved [W9-13], as are also the secondary
effects of heat and of cold. But the secondary effects of wetness and of dryness are receptions,
which a wet and dry body receives more than do the
wetness and dryness, for the body is receptive as
"that which" (*quod*) is bounded, wetness and dryness,
as that "by which" (*quo*).

[17] Note, second: wetness and dryness are
conducive to what is proper and principal in a compound, precisely as it is a compound, through their
secondary effects and, as a consequence, by receiving. For two things are found in a compound: first,
there is the mutual fracturing of all elements and
qualities, but this is not proper to a compound,
although it takes place there, for it is found also
in the interaction of elements that takes place
outside the compound; second, there is boundedness,
and this consists in the fact that dryness mixed
with wetness takes on a unity of parts and a simple
terminability that it lacks of itself; similarly,
that wetness mixed with dryness takes on a consistency that it likewise lacks of itself. But such
boundedness is brought about by heat dividing, ma-
turing, segregating the heterogeneous, aggregating
the homogeneous, and so forth, and again by coldness hardening and tempering the heat. Wetness
and dryness, on the other hand, are receptive of
this boundedness, dryness by consistency, wetness

168

by its ability to be bounded readily. Thus it is
apparent that wetness and dryness are conducive to
what is proper to a compound through their secondary effects, and therefore, by receiving.

[18] Note, third: even if mixing were to consist only in fracturing, one should nonetheless
hold that heat and cold are active whereas the
others are passive. For such fracturing is brought
about by heat most of all. First: because heat is   169
more active than the other qualities, and so it
fractures the more. Second: because heat, as I
have said [15], aids wetness and dryness in their
actions, and without heat's assistance they can do
hardly anything. Third: because, as I have also
said [15], even drying out and wetting are done
more quickly and more intensely by heat than by
wetness or dryness. Fourth: because in the compound there is greater fracturing of heat and of
cold than of wetness and of dryness, for there is
a kind of difformity in the intension of accidents
within the compound, so that some parts are thick-
er, others finer; and this dissimilarity arises
particularly in the parts that are wet and dry.
For heat and cold, acting as they do very strongly,
are immediately refractive to each other and a-
chieve their results almost equally in all parts
of the matter. The parts that are wet and dry, on
the other hand, can never be so refractive that
some wetness and dryness does not still remain.

[19] This result is also made probable by the
following considerations: because wetness and dryness, as I shall explain in the following question
[Y10-25], resist very well, and for this reason
they fracture each other only with the greatest difficulty. Again: because we observe in wood and in
flesh that this diversity occurs particularly in
the parts that are wet and dry; for the fibers are
drier, while the fluid that fills the spaces between them is wetter; what therefore occurs in
flesh, where this diversity is more evident, occurs
also in things where it is more hidden. And finally: because, as I have said [18], wet things and
dry things quite frequently undergo mixing according to their minimal parts rather than by fracturing each other, so that humidifying is often
brought about through the entrance of a humid substance and drying out through the ejection of the
same. Since, therefore, it is obvious from these

considerations that fracturing comes about less
through wetness and dryness than through heat and
cold, it is obvious that what we concluded in this
fourth argument is also true, that fracturing is
brought about mainly by heat [18]. After heat,
cold is most effective in fracturing, for the same
reasons we have given for heat.

[20] On this account I conclude that Aristotle
refers to heat and cold as active qualities and
the others as passive because, by reason of their
primary effects, the former act more and the latter practically not at all, and the latter's effects are brought about by the former; and because
Aristotle wished to explain qualities through their
secondary effects, not through their primary, not
only since secondary effects are more known, particularly in wetness -- and this argument is also
valid outside the compound -- but also since he
explained them in relation to the compound, where,
if we consider the main point, they are particularly productive through secondary effects.

170   [21] You object: Aristotle, in the fourth *Meteors* at the beginning, says that dryness and wetness are receptive in all things, not only in compounds but also in themselves, i.e., when outside
the compound; therefore what we said is not to be
understood as only in the compound, as I held in
the third reason [15]. I reply, first: with regard to the effects of the secondaries, of which
Aristotle there treats both within the compound
and without, two can be said to be active, two passive, for the reasons given; nonetheless, because
he is treating of compounds throughout the fourth
book, this ought especially to be understood of
the things with which he is concerned in that book,
i.e., of compounds. Second: the "in themselves"
should be taken to mean that some are active, some
receptive, not only in elements but also in themselves, i.e., by reason of themselves, when separated from the elements, as happens in compounds.

[Y] Fourth Question. How Are Primary Qualities
        Involved in Activity and Resistance?

    [1] The first problem is: what is resistance?
Vallesius, in the first *Controversiarum*, chapter 5,
and others say that resistance is action and that
to resist is somehow to act. The proof, first:
[a] augmentation comes about from the addition of
similars; but resistance is augmented by an increase of action; therefore [resistance is action].
Second: [b] from the continuation of action on a
contrary there results greater resistance in the
agent and the contrary is more weakened; therefore
[resistance increases with action]. Third: [c] a
resistive power is active, and so to resist is to
act. Proof of the antecedent: a resistive power
is not passive, because a passive potency disposes
a subject to receive, whereas a resistive power
impedes reception; therefore it is active.

    [2] I say, first: resistance is not action
formally, because a stone resists a hand pressing
on it and yet there is no action; because the
least heat resists the greatest coldness -- for
otherwise alteration would take place in an instant -- and nonetheless heat does not react on
cold; because the medium resists in local motion
and yet it does not react *per se*; and finally, because bodies here below resist the action of the
heavens and nonetheless do not react on them.

    [3] I say, second: resistance is not recep-
tion. For, when iron is pressed it does not receive, though it resists; again, the heavens would
resist something pressing them, and nonetheless
they would not be receptive. Add to this: to resist is proper to a thing as it is in act, to receive, as it is in potency.

    [4] I say, third: resistance is permanence in   171

                        243

a proper state against a contrary action. I say
"against a contrary action," for resistance, while
not an action, nonetheless connotes the action of
the contrary that it impedes. I say "is permanence in a proper state," because I do not differentiate resistance from the thing's very existence
whereby it endures; indeed resistance formally bespeaks this permanence of a thing in its state and
connotes the impeding of a contrary action. This
is against Pomponatius, in the second section of
De reactione, chapter 3, who holds that resistance
formally bespeaks the impeding of a contrary action, while connoting the action of the contrary
and permanence in its proper state; but he is
wrong, for resistance is something positive, whereas such impeding is the negation of action.

[5] From this it follows, first, that resistance differs from the permanence of a thing in its
state or from its conservation considered in itself, which bespeak only a permanence of existence
received from an agent; resistance connotes the impeding of the contrary action, whereas permanence
abstracts from this.

[6] It follows, second, that resistance formally pertains to the category of the thing resisting, just as does existence itself, for intrinsic
modes pertain to the same category as does the
thing; on the other hand the same resistance, by
reason of the thing connoted, pertains to the category of action, for the connoted impeding is a certain privation or negation of action, and priva-
tions are reduced to the category of their corresponding possession.

[7] It follows, third, that three factors can
be found in any resistance. The first is what it
formally connotes, and this is permanence in a
proper state; the second is what it implies conno-
tatively, and this is the impeded action of the
contrary; the third is the cause of such permanence, i.e., the cause that makes the thing perse-
vere in its state easily and resist the contrary
action. And this cause can be manifold, e.g., the
act of resisting, as when an animal by its own powers guards itself through appropriate action; or
weight and hardness, as in a stone; or the binding
of matter by which the action of a contrary is
slowed down, etc. Indeed, in the resistance of

qualities the two prior factors are obvious whereas
the third is somewhat hidden, for it is not apparent by what property wetness is able to resist to
such a degree that it is not dried out. Yet, since
in animals and in many other things, like stones,
etc., such a cause is always observed, it must be
held that even qualities and similar things have a
certain natural property by which they more or less
resist a contrary; and this is said to be the cause
of resistance, and can be reduced to power or impo-   172
tency.

[8] From this is apparent the error of Nobili
who, in the first *De generatione*, doubt 11 in chapter 7, distinguishes a twofold resistance: one in
animals, which would consist in a certain effort
that is a kind of action; another in other things,
which he reduces to an impotency for receiving;
here, as you can see, he takes the extrinsic cause
of resistance for resistance formally, when they
should be differentiated. Add to this that a natural power or impotency is always present in a
thing, whereas the thing is not always resisting,
but only when the action of the contrary is present.

[9] To the first argument [1a], I reply: resistance increases from an increase of action not
per se and formally, but after the manner of a consequence or causally, i.e., because the cause of
resistance is increased; for example, when heating,
which is the cause of resistance, is increased, the
heat becomes more perfect and is conservative of
itself. To the second [1b], I reply: through the
continued action on the contrary only the power of
the contrary agent is properly diminished; then
afterward follows the permanence of the thing in
existence, and this is resistance formally. To
the third [1c], I reply: properly and formally resistance is neither action nor passion but is reducible to the category of the thing resisting, as
I have said [6]; and if sometimes an action or passion intervenes, that will be merely the cause of
the resistance, as I have said [7].

[10] The second problem is how primary qualities are related to activity and resistance. Concerning this matter read the Calculator in the
treatise *De reactione*, Heytesbury in the sophism
An aliquid fiat, Marlianus in his introductory *De*

reactione, Buccaferrus on the second *De generatione* in the question *De reactione*, Thiene in the treatise *De reactione*, Pomponatius at chapter 13, and the fourth *Meteors*, doubts 4 and 9.

[11] Note, first: since comparisons are properly made between things of the same species and not between things of different kind, it also results that we can properly compare such qualities among themselves in activity and resistance only by comparing the activity of one with the activity of the other, and similarly the resistance of one with that of the other, for this alone is comparison in the proper sense. In an improper way, however, we can compare activity with resistance even though they are of a different kind, and this in two ways: first, absolutely; second, not absolutely but in its kind, by seeing which of them is closer to the highest and most perfect of its kind. For example, the heavens can be compared with a fly even though they are of a different kind, in two ways: first, absolutely, by inquiring which of these is more perfect, and in this way it is certain that the fly, being an animal, is more perfect absolutely than the inanimate heavens; second, not absolutely, and in this way the heavens are more perfect than the fly, because, in the genus of simple body, the heavens are closer to the highest degree of perfection since they are the most perfect simple body; on the other hand the fly, in the genus of animal, is farthest away from the highest perfection of animal. So in either way we can also improperly compare resistance with the activity of a quality; and each of these two ways can further be divided into two additional ways.

173

[12] From this one may gather that these four qualities can generally be compared five ways in activity and resistance: first, if we ask which of them is more active and which more resistive; second, if we inquire absolutely whether the activity of one is greater than the activity of the other absolutely; third, also absolutely, whether the activity of one is greater than the resistance of the same; fourth, not absolutely but in its kind, i.e., whether the activity of one in its kind is greater than the resistance of the same in its kind in the way explained; fifth and finally, not absolutely but in its kind, whether the activity of one is closer to the maximum in the genus of activity than

the resistance of the contrary to the maximum in
the genus of resistance. And of all these comparisons only the first is proper, while the remaining four are improper.

[13] Note, second: intension and remission
are understood in different ways in quality, in
activity, and in resistance. For the maximum intensity of a quality is to have eight degrees, and
the more it departs from eight the less intense it
is. But the maximum action is one that takes place
in an instant; for other actions, from the sixth
Physics, 16 and 23, the greater is that which introduces more of the form in the shorter time. The
maximum resistance, on the other hand, is that
which has received nothing over the entire time;
but for other resistances, the greater is that
which receives nothing over the longer time. Thus
a large action requires little time and much form
introduced, for this is closer to the maximum action, whereas a large resistance requires much time
and little of the contrary form, for this is closer
to the maximum resistance.

[14] From this it follows that the maximum
resistance can sometimes be separated from the minimum action, for example, when wood resists water
for ten years, not becoming moist, and finally gets
soft. Here, as we see, there is maximum resistance, for the wood receives little over a long
time, and minimum action, for the water effects   174
little over a long time; and yet this minimum action overcomes such maximum resistance. Nor is this
to be marveled at: for a minimum action is not said
to be minimum because it is smaller than the resistance absolutely; indeed it is larger, since it
overcomes the aforesaid resistance; rather it is
said to be minimum in its kind, because it is farthest away from the maximum action. Indeed, if it
were the maximum action in its kind, it would not
be overcoming a maximum resistance, but a minimum,
for it would overcome that in the shortest time.

[15] And from this one has the solution to
the following objection: if a small action overcomes a large resistance and a large action a small
resistance, then more is accomplished through a
small action than through a large. The objection
is solved, I say, because the inference is not valid. For to overcome a large resistance is not to

act much, but little, for it is to act so weakly
that the thing acted upon can resist over a longer
time; on the other hand, to overcome a small resistance is to act much, for it is to act so
strongly that the thing acted upon cannot resist
over a long period. And for this reason more is
always accomplished through a large action than
through a small.

[16] Note, third: if the comparison is made
in the first way posited in the first notation
[12], then I say, first, that qualities have the
following order in activity: other things being
equal, the most active of all is heat, then cold,
after that wetness, finally dryness. I say "other
things being equal," i.e., if it is understood
that these qualities are equally intense and with
circumstances that are otherwise equal, in a shorter time heat will introduce more of the form than
cold, and so on. Proof of the conclusion: both
from experience, since we see that fire acts more
quickly than anything cold, indeed in certain materials that are somewhat more disposed it seems
that fire acts in an instant, as on straw, etc.,
whereas nothing cold, not even the coldest, acts
with equal speed in any matter however well disposed; and since we see that a hand can be held in
snow without any injury, whereas it cannot be held
in fire for even the shortest period of time; and
finally, since fire penetrates extremely well, it
fractures with greatest force, and so on, and we
do not see this happen with a cold body.

[17] Proof that hot and cold are more active
than wet and dry: because the former are called
absolutely active by Aristotle, the others passive; and because experience shows that heat and
cold effect more in a shorter time than wet and
dry. Finally, that wetness is more active than
dryness is apparent to the senses: for humid air
moistens things placed in it more readily than
earth dries them out; and anything moistens in water more quickly than it dries out in earth.

[18] Add to this that by its action the humid
175 rarefies and dissolves, whereas the dry compresses;
but dissolving disposes a subject to change, while
compressing impedes this. And note that I am
speaking of the moistening and drying that come
about from wetness and dryness; for it can happen

that drying be done more quickly than wetting if
the drying be done by fire, because then the fire,
by rarefying, draws out the humid parts, as is apparent in moist garments placed close to a fire.
And this is the reason why physicians say that it
is more difficult for a body to become moist than
to dry out, for they mean by this the moistening
and the drying out that are done by fire, through
the entrance and departure of a humid substance.
For it is certain that a humid substance enters
more easily than it departs.

[19] I say, second: qualities follow the same
order in resistance, viz, hotness is more resistive than coldness, the latter more than wetness,
and in last place, dryness. The proof: if heat
introduces its entire latitude in a quarter of an
hour, cold, being less active, cannot produce it
in less than one hour; but, since as much of one
quality is lost as is produced of the contrary, it
follows that all of the cold is lost in one quarter hour whereas the heat takes one hour; and, as
a consequence, cold resists heat only for a quarter of an hour, whereas heat resists cold for an
hour; hence the result is that cold is exceeded in
resistance, just as in activity. And the same argument can be made concerning the other two qualities.

[20] You object: things heated grow cold more
readily than things cooled become heated; therefore [heat does not resist more than cold]. I reply: things heated grow cold more readily *per accidens*, because of the evaporation of the warm vapors, which, because of their fineness, disappear
more easily.

[21] Against this conclusion is the argument
of those who grant the first conclusion [16]: they
maintain that the resistance of dryness is the maximum, after that, wetness, then cold, and finally
heat, and yet they hold that the action of each is
greater than its own resistance. But, to the contrary: from this it would follow that the latitude
of the greatest resistance would be less than the
latitude of the greatest activity, which is absurd.
Proof of the inference: for the latitude of the
greatest activity in heat, for example, is eight
degrees; therefore in dryness, which, even according to them, is least active of all, it will be,

for example, four degrees; but the greatest resistance *per se* is in dryness, and, at the same time,
the activity of this same dryness is greater than
its own resistance; therefore the latitude of the
greatest resistance is less than four degrees.

[22] Note, fourth: if comparison is made in
the second way [12], then I say absolutely that the
action of any quality is greater than the resistance of the contrary, because whatever quality
acts on another, it will always overcome the latter
even though this take the longest time. And this
is most noticeable in the activity of heat and
wetness against the resistance of cold and dryness;
for the former are more active than the latter,
and consequently, from the third notation [19],
the latter are less resistive. Concerning the action of cold and dryness against the resistance of
heat and wetness, on the other hand, this seems to
offer more difficulty, for the cold and dryness,
from what has been said, are less active than heat
and wetness. Yet the conclusion is still true,
i.e., with regard to their action absolutely, for
then they are in the ratio of greater inequality,
i.e., for example, five or six degrees of cold or
dryness act on three or four degrees of hotness or
wetness, so that the action can take place, since
the resistance of the latter is always greater.
And although these resist for a very long time,
nonetheless they are overcome eventually. So, absolutely, the action of the former is said to be
greater than the resistance of the latter.

[23] You object: above, in the third notation
[19], we claimed that the action and resistance of
heat are greater than those of cold; similarly,
that the action and resistance of wetness are
greater than the action and resistance of dryness;
so there is a contradiction if we say here that
the action of any quality whatever overcomes the
resistance of the contrary.

[24] I reply: there is no contradiction. For
here we are speaking absolutely, and we say absolutely that the action of any quality whatever
overcomes the resistance of the contrary provided
the action is effected in the proper ratio; but
with this it stands that the activity and resistance of heat in its kind, of which we were speaking in the third notation [19], is greater because

176

it is closer to the maximum, since heat and wetness introduce their latitude in a shorter time
than coldness and dryness introduce theirs. But
in the present case we are not saying that the
action is greater in its kind, but absolutely, because it overcomes the contrary resistance eventually. And this, far from being opposed to what
was said in the third notation, in fact greatly
favors it: for to say that the action of cold and
dryness over a very long time finally overcomes
the resistance of heat and wetness is to say that
the action of cold and dryness is least in its
kind, i.e., in its approach to the maximum, and
the resistance of heat and of wetness is greatest
in their kind. But a maximum resistance in its
kind cannot be overcome except by a minimum action
in its kind. And this is made clear by the example
of one army that resists another over a very long
time but is finally conquered; for then we would
say that the activity of the conqueror is little
and the resistance of the conquered great; at the
same time we would also say, absolutely, when the
former army has been conquered, that its resistance   177
was less than the activity of the conqueror. The
same can be illustrated by the example of the
marble and the falling drops that wear a hole in
it.

     [25] Note, fifth: if comparison is made in the
third way [12], I say that this is impossible.
For, if the resistance of one quality is compared
with its own action, it ought to be compared in a
way different from these two: first, by seeing. . .

Commentary and Notes

Commentary

[INTRODUCTORY TREATISE]

There is no general title to this "Treatise"
in Galileo's manuscript, which begins simply with
the first question. Some of the Jesuit *reportationes* insert the heading *Proemium* or *Exordium*, or
otherwise indicate that it is introductory to the
study of the books being commented on. This treatise and the two following, viz, the Treatise on the
Universe and the Treatise on the Heavens, constitute Galileo's exposition of Aristotle's *De caelo
et mundo*. There is no comparable introduction to
his exposition of the *De generatione et corruptione*.

*　　*　　*

A. Galileo's treatment here is closest to Rugerius's, where agreement can be found for all
paragraphs except 12, 17, and 18; the agreement
with Vitelleschi is less extensive, being restrict-
ed to only 12 of the 21 paragraphs, although for
pars. 20 and 21 Galileo is closer to Vitelleschi
than he is to Rugerius.[35] Less extensive still are
the similarities to De Gregoriis and to Jones, but
these are sufficient to be at least noted. Menu
has no treatment of this question, nor does Pererius in his lectures on the *De caelo*. The content
agrees generally with Jacobus Zabarella, *De naturalis scientiae constitutione*, Venice 1586, especi-

253

ally pars. 3, 7, 11, 14, 15, & 17. Pars. 1, 13,
14, & 19 indicate that the author taught logic as
well as natural philosophy, and this would not be
the case generally with professors at the Univer-
sities of Pisa or of Padua (Zabarella was an exception in this regard), but it would be true of
practically all professors at the Collegio Romano.[36]

A1. Marginal rubric: "First opinion."
    First sentence: Rugerius notes that the teach-
ing here derives from Galen and he thinks that the
reference is to Antonius Genua; he also cites Pererius, *De communibus*, lib. 2, cap. 2.
    Last sentence: this indicates that Galileo had
already written (or perhaps only planned to write)
a commentary on the *Physics*; the precise title giv-
en, "On the subject of the whole of the *Physics*,"
Latin, *De obiecto totius physicae* (15.8), is found
only in Jones's notes on the *Physics*. See the comment at I39; also N6 and O9.

A2. Marginal rubric: "Second opinion." These rub-
rics continue throughout the manuscript, up to K63
inclusive; they are printed in the margins of the
National Edition. In what follows no further note
will be made of marginal notations unless their
significance is more than rubrical.

A3. First sentence, "Syrianus Magnus": reading *magnus* for Favaro's *magis* (16.1); some sixteenth-century authors refer to Syrianus Magnus, but the Magnus is generally omitted in the Jesuit notes.

A4. First sentence, "subject," and second sentence,
"subject of the whole of the *Physics*": here Galileo
obviously copied from the wrong line, first writing
obiectum totius physicae at 16.5, then crossing out
the *totius physicae*, and correctly writing the entire expression again at 16.6. Vitelleschi alone
has the expression *obiectum totius physicae* in this
context.

A6. The reference is to the exposition of the *De
caelo* by Augustinus Niphus, which names Averroës
in place of Albertus; see his *In quattuor libros
de celo et mundo expositio*, Naples 1517, fol. 1r.
See also the comment on B3.

A8. Second sentence, "the elements are not considered," and third sentence, "the elements are know-

able *per se*": here Galileo again copied from the
wrong line, first writing *elementa sunt per se sci-
bilia* at 17.10, then crossing out *sunt per se sci-
bilia,* and correctly writing the entire expression
again at 17.11. The thought is contained in Vitelleschi and Rugerius, but neither has this precise
expression.

A10. The last two sentences are Galileo's marginal
insert.

A13. The first sentence implies that Galileo had
composed a commentary on Aristotle's *Posterior
Analytics.* Rugerius establishes the point in his
Logic notes: *de singularibus non potest esse sci-
entia;* to the translator's knowledge it is not made
in MS Gal. 27 (see Preface).

A14. Fifth sentence, "category": reading *praedicamento* for Favaro's *praedicato* (18.29). The "us"
in this same sentence could include Zabarella; see
his *De naturalis scientiae constitutione,* pp. 28
ff. & 46.

A15. First sentence: note Galileo's use of "motive
qualities" (*qualitates motivae,* 19.6 & 11) and
"motive force" (*vis motrix,* 19.8), concepts discussed more fully in his early notes *De motu.*

A17. Galileo discusses the content of the first
sentence in his logic notes, MS Gal. 27, fol. 84;
it is also mentioned in the *reportatio* of Jones's
logic course.[37]

A19. First sentence, "category": reading *praedicamento* for Favaro's *praedicato* (20.7). This sentence is an indication that Galileo had commented
on the portion of the logic course dealing with
the categories; see K157 and N7, with their comments.

*   *   *

B. Again Rugerius's treatment is the most similar to Galileo's, although for only five of the
question's nine paragraphs, viz, 1, 3, 4, 6, & 8;
Vitelleschi shows agreement for only two paragraphs,
1 & 8. There is no discussion of this subject in
Menu or other earlier writers.

B1. The reference is to Bernardus Antonius Mirandulanus, *Eversionis singularis certaminis liber*,
Basel 1562?, whose opinion is discussed by Vitelleschi in his *Physics* course and by Rugerius in
his *De caelo*.

B3. This statement occurs in Nifo's exposition of
the *De caelo*, but naming Averroës in place of Albertus Magnus (Naples 1517 ed., fol. 1r).

B4. The last sentence is inserted by Galileo as a
marginal note; reference to this text is made by
Rugerius, but the latter does not give the quotation itself. Galileo cites the opening words of
Aristotle's *Meteorology* (338a20); the Latin text
is approximately that contained in the Junta editions of Aristotle's *Opera* of 1550-1552 and 1562,
but there are some variations. For details, compare Favaro's reading (21.16-20) with the *Opera*,
1562 ed., Vol. 5, fol. 400ra. Since this is Galileo's marginal insertion, it may provide a clue
to the Latin translation of Aristotle he himself
used. See the comments at I27, I28, K17, and K52.

B5. The argument is in Nifo's exposition of the
De caelo (Naples 1517, fol. 1r).

*   *   *

TREATISE ON THE UNIVERSE

Galileo's title for this treatise is *Tractatio prima de mundo* (22.6); Menu gives *Tractatus
primus de mundo*, and Vitelleschi, *De mundo tractatio prima*. Rugerius does not use the term "treatise," but Galileo's content is roughly duplicated
in the second question of his *Prima disputatio de
universo*, entitled *An mundus et motus sit aeternus*.

*   *   *

C. Practically all of this question, pars. 1-
8, agrees almost verbatim with Menu's exposition,
although arranged somewhat differently; equivalent
materials for pars. 2-7 & 9 are to be found in Rugerius; pars. 3-6 are based on book 15 of Perer-

ius's *De communibus;* and pars. 3-6 & 9 have equivalent counterparts in Vitelleschi. There are
some parallels with the notes of De Gregoriis and
the lectures of Pererius, but these are too early
to be significant for dating purposes.

C1. Menu explains that the sensible universe that
is "small" refers to man; he also indicates that
Galen is the source of the information about Pythagoras.

C3. Menu does not list Porphyry and Proclus, but
these names are in Pererius, *De communibus,* p.
492B.

C4. Here Menu cites only Aristotle, Alexander,
Theophrastus, Plutarch, St. Basil, Clement of Alexandria, and Eusebius, and adds to this "all peripatetics with the exception of Simplicius." All
of the authors cited, however, are to be found in
Pererius, *De communibus,* p. 495B-C, with the exception of Apicus (cf. Pererius's Atticus), Seleucus (cf. Pererius's Severus), and Theophilactus
(cf. Pererius's Theodoretus). For Pleto Pererius
gives Plheto; Galileo writes this as Fleto here
(23.20), but later, in J1, as Pleto (63.22).

C6. Vitelleschi names Domingo de Soto as such an
objector.

C9. Note Galileo's explicit reference to Pererius,
although this obviously is not Galileo's only
source; similar references are found in Vitelleschi
and Rugerius, the latter acknowledging that the
citations in C4 are all from Pererius's work.

*   *   *

D. All paragraphs of this question except the
last follow Menu's exposition almost verbatim; the
contents of pars. 5 & 7 are found in Vitelleschi,
and those of pars. 1, 2, 5, & 6 in Rugerius. Again
parallels can be found in Pererius and De Gregoriis, but these are too early and fragmentary to be
noteworthy.

D5. Last sentence: the material following "Lateran
Council" is not in Menu; but see the comment below
at D8.

D6. First sentence: Rugerius identifies Macrobius as the source of this conjecture.

D8. This paragraph does not occur in any known *reportatio*.

First sentence, "Sixtus of Siena": the reference is to Sixtus Senensis, *Bibliotheca sancta*, Venice 1566; none of Galileo's figures, however, agree with the calculations recorded by Sixtus. The epochs given by Galileo are about the same as those of Benedictus Pererius in his commentaries on Daniel and Genesis, viz, *Commentariorum in Danielem prophetam libri sexdecim*, Rome 1587, and *Prior tomus commentariorum et disputationum in Genesim*, Rome 1589.[38]

Second sentence, "5748 years ago": apparently Galileo first wrote 50 in Arabic numerals, then wrote the Latin for "five thousand four and eighty" in longhand, then inserted the equivalent of "seven hundred" after the "five thousand," and finally crossed out the Latin for "four and eighty" and corrected it in the margin to read "eight and forty." None of the other figures on this folio (10r) are changed in any way.

The apparent date of composition of this paragraph, from its last line, would appear to be A.D. 1580, since it was written 1510 years after the destruction of Jerusalem, which occurred in A.D. 70. However, Favaro, assuming that the birth of Christ took place in A.D. 0 (rather than in 4 B.C.), added the last two figures, 1510 and 74, to get A.D. 1584 for the date of composition. The translator thinks that the 1580 date is more likely, on the conjecture that the original on which this paragraph is based, like the first seven paragraphs, was written by Menu. The *reportatio* of Menu's lectures that the translator has used was begun in 1577 and finished in 1579; however, Menu taught this course again in 1580-1581, and he might well have made additions at that time to his previous notes, thus giving the chronology to 1580 (and, incidentally, adding to D5). If this was the case, Galileo's corrections of the figures noted above might be interpreted as an initial attempt, on his part, to revise Menu's calculations to agree with the time of his own writing, then giving up on the attempt and simply copying the figures given by Menu. This would leave the actual time of Galileo's composition undetermined. An alternative possibility, consistent with the *circa*

1590 mentioned in the Introduction, would be that
Galileo did try to revise the calculations and yet
made an error of one digit, getting 1580 rather
than the 1590 he intended.[39]

*   *   *

   E. The content of all these paragraphs is in
Menu; some paragraphs are so similar as to suggest
copying, whereas others are more abbreviated than
Galileo's and the order of treatment is different.
Vitelleschi has similar content for pars. 1-7,
9-11, & 14-16. Franciscus Bonamicus discusses the
same subject matter in book 10 of his *De motu libri
decem*, Florence 1591, pp. 921-928, but his mode of
treatment has nothing in common with Galileo's.
Rugerius does not treat this question at all, and
De Gregoriis and Pererius mention it only in passing.

E2. Fifth sentence, "question 47": reading 47 for
Favaro's 43. Both Menu and Vitelleschi cite this
as 47.

E7. Last sentence,"as he himself states elsewhere":
the reference is to the First Part, question 25,
article 5, reply to the first objection, where
Aquinas speaks of God's "ordained power" (*potentia
ordinata*). Menu, however, has Galileo's terminology (*naturali. . .ordinaria*, 29.17), noting that
Cajetan uses the expression "natural power" whereas
others employ the expression "ordinary power."

E8. Last sentence, "question 25": reading 25 for
Favaro's 21. Menu also has 25 in this context.

E10. Menu does not make this distinction explicit,
whereas Vitelleschi does.

E12. The analogy of the musical instrument is not
in Menu.

E17. Last sentece, "and place": this emendation is
found in Menu (*suis temporibus et locis*).

*   *   *

F. The first eighteen paragraphs are very
similar to the text of Pererius's *De communibus*,
pp. 505-511, although the material is arranged differently; the similarity in some places is strik-
ing enough to suggest copying. Pars. 19-27 are
not found in Pererius, however, though the content
of pars. 19 & 22-26 is found in Vitelleschi, and
that of pars. 19-21, 23, & 25-26 in Rugerius.
Vitelleschi duplicates some of the material in
Pererius (pars. 1-2, 9-11, 15-16, & 18) and Rugerius likewise (pars. 5-8, 11-18). In some instances
Galileo's expressions are closer to these authors'
than to Pererius's; indeed, Vitelleschi's exposition of pars. 1, 11, 15, & 18 is close enough to
Galileo's to suggest copying. Menu has very little
on this question, showing parallels only with pars.
1, 2, 11, & 18. A few passages in Toletus's commentary on the *Physics* also show similarities to
Galileo's expression, viz, in pars. 11, 15, & 21.

F1. This is Pererius's "third opinion," and he does
not include Ferrariensis and John Canonicus among
its adherents, nor does he cite the *De potentia* of
Aquinas. Like Galileo, Vitelleschi gives this as
the "first opinion," and he has all the material
missing from Pererius. Menu has it as a "second
opinion," does not include Aquinas and Ferrariensis
among its adherents, but does add John Canonicus to
Pererius's list.
    Second sentence, "Ferrariensis": the reference
here is to Franciscus Sylvester de Ferrara, *In libros physicorum*, Venice 1573.
    Third sentence, "question 3": reading 3 for
Favaro's 13 (32.10-11); Vitelleschi also has 3 in
this context.

F6. First sentence, "because even if God": this
passage again suggests copying, for after having
written *quia etiam si Deus* (33.6), Galileo repeated exactly this expression on the next line and
then crossed it out. These words occur in neither
Pererius nor Rugerius.

F11. This is Pererius's and Vitelleschi's "second
opinion" also, whereas it is Menu's "fourth opinion." Pererius does not mention the "moderns" (*recentiores*, 34.11), but Vitelleschi does and includes Soto in their number. Rugerius mentions
Soto but not the moderns.

F14. Second sentence, "intelligence": where Galileo has *intelligentia* (34.24-25) Pererius has *angelus;* like Galileo, Rugerius phrases the argument
in terms of intelligences.

F15. This is Pererius's "first opinion," and he
does not include Bonaventure, Marsilius, and Burley among its followers; Menu lists it as his
"first opinion" also, and adds the names of Bonaventure and Burley, but puts Aureoli in place of
Marsilius. For Vitelleschi, as for Galileo, this
is the "third opinion," and it is ascribed to Marsilius and others besides, including Albertus,
Canonicus, Halensis, and William of Paris. Rugerius names only Philoponus, Bonaventure, Henry, and
Marsilius, but it is noteworthy that he adds Toletus to the list.

F17. Second sentence, "because it is true to say":
another evidence of copying. After having written
*quia de eo quod producitur verum est dicere pro-
ducitur* (35.18-19), Galileo repeated the *verum
est dicere producitur,* and then crossed it out.
This phrase does not occur in either Pererius or
Rugerius.

F18. Pererius attributes his "fourth opinion" to
Scotus and to himself, having included Aquinas in
his third opinion along with the nominalists (see
the comment on F1); moreover, he does not mention
the *Doctores Parisieneses* here or elsewhere. Vitelleschi, on the other hand, gives this position as a
subdivision of his "first opinion," and specifically names the *Parisienses* along with Scotus, Aquinas, and various Thomists; he further names Pererius as a general source at the beginning of his
treatment.[40] Rugerius similarly mentions Pererius and the *Doctores Parisienses* as a general reference, along with Aquilinus and Zabarella. Menu
lists six opinions in all, viz, those of (1) Bonaventure, etc., (2) Ockham and other nominalists,
(3) Scotus, (4) Durandus, (5) certain Thomists,
and (6) Thomas himself; he does not cite the *Parisienses.*

F19. See D7; in this and the remaining two conclusions there is material agreement with Vitelleschi
and Rugerius. Pererius gives four propositions
following his listing of opinions, but these all
differ from Galileo's three conclusions.

F20. Note that this is a medical argument; Rugerius gives a related line of reasoning and attributes it to Hippocrates.

F21. Second sentence, "difference 9": reading 9 for
Favaro's 4 (36.18). This citation of the Conciliator, Petrus de Abano, is found in Toletus's commentary on the *Physics* and in Rugerius's notes on
the *De caelo*. Toletus has other references also,
but differs from Galileo in citing book 7 of Pliny
and book 7 of Crinitus, whereas Galileo references
book 6 of each (36.14 & 19). The latter reference
is to Petrus Crinitus, *De honesta disciplina*, Lyons
1554.

F22. "6748 years ago": Galileo does not give all
numerals, but writes part of this out in Latin,
viz, *sex mille septingentos et 48 annos*. Note
that this does not agree with the total of 5748
given in D8, for a mistake of one digit has been
made. See the comment at D8 above. Vitelleschi
gives the general argument without illustrating it
in terms of the number of years thought to have e-
lapsed since creation.

F23. This conclusion and its supporting argument
are in Vitelleschi and Rugerius.

F24. This conclusion is also Vitelleschi's, but it
is not held by Pererius or Rugerius.

*   *   *

TREATISE ON THE HEAVENS

Galileo entitles this the *Tractatio de caelo*
(38.1). Titles are missing in Menu and Vitelleschi,
but these should be the same as Galileo's; Rugerius
captions his treatise *Secunda disputatio de corpore
coelesti*. All three Jesuits treat only of Galileo's
last four questions, i.e., I through L, in these
treatises. Earlier *reportationes*, such as those of
Pererius and De Gregoriis, discuss the matter of
the first two questions, i.e., G and H. Pererius
does this in the second part of his *Tractatus de
caelo* under the titles *De numero orbium* and *De ordine orbium* respectively; the first part of this
tractate is devoted to materials similar to Gali-

leo's K and L. De Gregoriis enumerates among his
questions on the first book of *De caelo* those
equivalent to Galileo's G and H, viz, *De numero
orbium caelestium* and *De ordine orbium caelestium*.
Neither Pererius nor De Gregoriis, however, discuss
G and H at any length; Galileo's exposition, on the
other hand, is detailed in its astronomy, following
closely the material contained in Clavius's commentary on the *Sphaera* of Sacrobosco.

*   *   *

     G. The entire contents of this question are
sufficiently similar to Clavius's *In sphaeram Ioannis de Sacrobosco*, 2d ed., Rome 1581, pp. 42-62,
to suggest almost verbatim copying. Pars. 1, 13,
17, 25, & 29 offer evidence that the first edition
of 1570 was not used; the copyist, however, could
have used the later edition of Rome 1585, which
was printed from the same type as the 1581 edition.
Difficulties for holding that Galileo himself was
the copyist are posed by pars. 1, 13, & 17.[41]

G1. First sentence: "Chrysostom" is not mentioned
by Clavius, but he is cited by De Gregoriis in his
question on the number of the heavens.
     Second sentence, "we raise our eyes": the
words *attolimus oculos* (38.7) are in the 1581 edition of Clavius but not in the 1570 edition, which
reads *intuemur* at this place.

G4. First sentence: reading *Arsatilis* for Favaro's
Arsatiris (38.27).
     Fourth sentence, "After 170 years. . .Agrias":
reading 170 for Favaro's 120 (39.6) and *Agrias* for
Favaro's *Agrippa* (39.6).
     The above corrected readings are in Clavius,
pp. 43-44.

G7. This paragraph follows G4 in the manuscript,
but Galileo has inserted a note in the margin reading: "This doubt should be placed at the end of the
fourth opinion," i.e., after G5-6.

G10. Last sentence, "successively the same orientations": the Latin, *eosdem aspectus successive*, was
first written after *respectu* (41.18), then crossed
out and written in its proper place (41.19), as in

Clavius, p. 46.

G13. Third sentence, "But this. . .at one time" is in the 1581 edition of Clavius, p. 56, not in the 1570 edition.

Fourth sentence: "23760" is written by Galileo as "237°60"; the correct number is clearly printed in Clavius, p. 56.

G14. Last sentence, "according to the mathematicians" is not in either edition of Clavius.

G17. First sentence: where Galileo has "15" seconds, Clavius reads "16," p. 57.

Second sentence: this is Galileo's only explicit reference to Clavius; actually it is a partial quote, for Clavius continues, "as is supposed in the Roman Calendar" (*ut in Calendario Romano supponitur*).

Last sentence: this material is in Clavius's 1581 edition, not in that of 1570. Note the reference to Copernicus, who is cited more fully *infra* at H1.

G20. Not in either edition of Clavius.

G21. Second sentence: "as the mathematicians abundantly demonstrate" is not in either edition of Clavius.

G25. Second sentence: this is in Clavius's 1581 edition, not in his 1571 edition.

G27. Second sentence: "By the mathematicians" is not in either edition of Clavius.

G28. Last sentence: reading "17" for Favaro's "12" (45.27); Clavius also has 17.

G29. Fourth sentence: "just as the parallels. . . same points" is in Clavius's 1581 edition, not in that of 1570.

*   *   *

H. The entire contents of this question, like the preceding, are copied or adapted from Clavius, *In sphaeram Ioannis de Sacrobosco*, Rome 1581, pp.

63-71, 135-144. Clavius's title, however, is *De ordine sphaerarum caelestium*, whereas Galileo's is *De ordine orbium caelestium*; the latter duplicates the title in De Gregoriis's lectures. Indications that the 1581 edition was used and not that of 1570 are found in pars. 21, 27, & 31; a difficulty for holding that Galileo himself was the copyist is posed by par. 12. See also the comment below at J24.

H1. Note Galileo's reference to Copernicus's *De revolutionibus orbium caelestium*, Nuremberg 1543; Galileo cites this in the singular, i.e., *De revolutione orbium caelestium* (47.34), whereas Clavius speaks of it only as "the work on the celestial revolutions" (*in opere de revolutionibus caelestibus*). Galileo's use of "orb," "heaven," and "globe" in this paragraph follows Clavius's exactly. See also G17 and its comment.

H3. The arguments begun here and continuing through H13 are much abbreviated from Clavius, pp. 135-144.

H11. The last sentence is in neither edition of Clavius.

H12. Last sentence: for the three appearances of *dioptra* (49.31, 49.34, & 50.2) Galileo transcribes the word as *dioctra*, although it is clearly printed in Clavius as *dioptra*.

H19. In the parentheses: "For me" is not in Clavius.
     Last sentence: "as the mathematicians clearly prove" is not in Clavius.

H21. The last sentence is in Clavius's 1581 edition, not in his 1570 edition.

H23. Second sentence: Clavius has no explicit reference to "mathematicians," stating simply "as is explained in Theories of the Planets" (*ut in Theoricis planetarum explicatur*, p. 69).

H27. Second sentence: this is in the 1581 edition, not in that of 1570.

H28. Last sentence: the classical citation is from Clavius, p. 69, who gives also the second verse of the couplet, "Or lower, the earth; safest go on the middle course" (*Inferius terras, medio tutissi-*

mus ibis, Ovid, *Metamorphoses*, II, 136-137).

H31. In his 1570 edition Clavius gives five references to Euclid (from books 5, 6, & 12) for the
geometrical reasoning given here; these references
do not appear in the 1581 edition.

*   *   *

I. The matters discussed in this question
have identifiable counterparts in Menu, Vitelleschi, and Rugerius, with the exception of pars. 15,
24-25, 34, 36, & 41.   Menu shows the most extensive
agreement, in 35 of the 47 paragraphs, Vitelleschi
in 28 paragraphs, and Rugerius in only 18.   Some of
the topics treated, viz, pars. 7-12, are found in
Bonamicus, *De motu libri decem*, pp. 893-898, but
these are not in discernible agreement with Galileo's text.

I1. First sentence, "simple bodies": since Galileo
has already maintained in A1 that the heavens are
a simple body, the sense of simple here must be
that of elemental.   The material in this and the
next two paragraphs is very similar to that in
Menu, though arranged in a slightly different sequence.
    Third sentence, "as its properties": Latin,
quae sunt proprietates illius.   The words *quae sunt
proprietates ignis* are in Menu's notes, and Galileo
probably here misread *illius* for *ignis*.   To be correct the argument should read: "because light and
heat are found in the heavens as properties of fire,
also the perspicuity that is proper to air," etc.

I2. The line of reasoning in this paragraph is further elaborated in paragraphs I7, I38, and J16.

I9. Second sentence, "Plato puts this as follows
in the *Timaeus*": this is not a direct quote, but
rather a paraphrase of the argument in 31B-C.

I10. First sentence: "Ficino" is inserted in the
margin by Galileo.   The authorities referenced here
are approximately the same as those given by Menu,
Vitelleschi, and Rugerius, but none of these cites
Philoponus's refutation of Proclus in as much detail as does Galileo.

I11. Last sentence, "has been embraced": for this
Galileo's Latin is somewhat peculiar, *complexi
sunt* (57.21); here Menu has *sequuti sunt* and Vitelleschi, *sequuntur*.

I12. Second sentence, "text 5": Galileo omitted
the "5" in writing this, but the number is in Vitelleschi and in Rugerius.
    Last sentence, "that a different motion": Gal-
ileo wrote *diversum motum* (57.34), then wrote it
again, and then crossed out the repetition. These
words are not in Menu, Vitelleschi, or Rugerius.

I21. "as will be proved in its place": possibly a
reference to the material missing from M0 and M1.

I27. The Latin text of Aristotle (298a28-33) is
that given in the Junta edition of Aristotle's
Opera, Venice 1562, Vol. 5, fol. 172v.

I28. The Latin text of Aristotle (1028b9-13) is
the translation of Cardinal Bessarion, as given in
the Junta edition of the *Opera*, Venice 1562, Vol.
8, fol. 155r. Note that when writing "such as the
heavens," Latin, *ut caelum*, Galileo left out the
ut (59.34), and it had to be supplied by Favaro.
The omission is rather odd in view of the subsequent discussion of this quotation in I31-34.

I38. First sentence, "nothing violent. . .can be
perpetual": Latin, *nullum violentum. . .possit esse
perpetuum* (61.24-25). In place of *violentum* Galileo first wrote *perpetuum*, then crossed it out and
wrote *violentum* over it; the expression is in Menu.
    Second sentence: see the further elaboration
in J16.

I39. First sentence, "of active qualities, since
many of these are compatible": Galileo inserted
the Latin for this into the text as a marginal
note. The matter inserted is in Menu.
    Last sentence: note the indication that Gali-
leo has already written a commentary on the *Physics*.
Menu makes all of these points in his analysis of
local motion in that commentary. See the comment
on A1.

*   *   *

J. The contents of all these paragraphs are
duplicated collectively in the notes of Menu, Vitelleschi, and Rugerius, with the exception of
pars. 15, 26, & 29. The greatest number of corresponding paragraphs is found in Vitelleschi, with
25; Menu and Rugerius have 17 apiece, though not
the same 17. Stylistic features in several cases
align Galileo more with Menu than with Vitelleschi.

J1. Second sentence, "by the kindness": Latin, *be-
nignitate* (63.18); Menu has *beneficio* in this context, Rugerius, *potestate*.
    Third and fourth sentences: none of the Jesuit
notes has as extensive a citation of authors as
has Galileo; see the comment above at C4.

J6. Second sentence, "nearly all the Church Fathers": Latin, *omnes fere sancti patres* (64.18).
Here a possible sign of copying: Galileo first
wrote *sphaerae sa...*, then crossed these words out
and rewrote correctly *fere sancti*. In this context
Menu has *multi sanctorum patrum*, Vitelleschi, *multi
patres*, and Rugerius, *fere sequuntur antiqui patres*.

J7. "in the second Epistle," Latin, *in secunda
Epistola*: a possible sign of copying. In writing
this Galileo repeated the *secunda*, then crossed
out the repetition. The term occurs here in Menu
and Vitelleschi.

J13. See the comment at J18.

J16. This paragraph explains the statements made
earlier in pars. I2, I7, and I38.

J18. Galileo's position here, taken in conjunction
with J13, is similar to that of Menu, who writes:
"It seems more probable and according to truth that
the heavens are incorruptible by nature, although
the contrary does not lack its probability because
of the authority of its proponents and the Church
Fathers."[42] Vitelleschi gives only a single conclusion to this question, and without qualification:
"The heavens are incorruptible by their nature."[43]
Rugerius, on the other hand, gives a more nuanced
response, in three propositions: (1) "It is not yet
completely improbable that the heavens be generable
and corruptible through mutual transformation with
lower bodies"[44]; (2) "Much more probable is it that
the heavens are generable and corruptible, but only

through substantial transformation with other celestial parts"[45]; and (3) "It is most probable. . . that the heavens are ingenerable and incorruptible, though this cannot be positively demonstrated."[46] See the comment at J24.

J24. First sentence, "over all preceding centuries": note that Galileo makes no mention of any novas observed throughout history, including that of 1572; in this his exposition is similar to Menu's. Vitelleschi, however, explicitly raises this problem as an objection to his own position (see the comment at J18), and goes on to discuss the nova of 1572 in particular, referring to Clavius's commentary on the *Sphaera* of Sacrobosco for fuller details. Vitelleschi's answer is that the nova was not a comet, that it was truly situated in the firmament, that it was not produced by exhalations, that its appearances cannot be saved by an epicycle, and that it was not generated from celestial matter. The only remaining possibility, for him, is that it was created *de novo* by God, just as was the star that guided the Magi, as a portent of something not yet known to man. Rugerius also raises the problem and gives a reply similar to Vitelleschi's; he is explicit in upholding the validity of mathematical demonstrations to establish the positions of the stars. Clavius has a full discussion of the nova of 1572 in the 1581 edition, pp. 191-195. The question naturally suggests itself as to why, if Galileo used this edition of Clavius to compose G and H, he chose to state this sentence so simplistically and unequivocally.

J28. First sentence, "because": a possible indication of copying. At the *quia* here (68.22), Galileo first wrote *tum quia*, an expression that occurs three times in the previous sentence (60.18, 20, 20-21), then crossed out the *tum*.

J31. First sentence, "alteration is twofold": for more details, see M0.

J36. Last sentence, "as will be proved in its place": see K27-28 and 116-117; also K5. Alternatively, this may be an indication that the treatment of motive powers and resistances in local motion, usually discussed at the end of the *Physics*, will be postponed until the end of the *De caelo*

commentary. Vitelleschi and Rugerius follow this
procedure, and Galileo himself takes up the general problem in the *De motu antiquiora*, a composition he possibly already had in mind. See the comment on U7.

*   *   *

K. This, the longest of Galileo's physical
questions, treats a problem on which the Jesuits
of the Collegio Romano were internally divided.
Galileo's exposition is more detailed than any of
the *reportationes* available, but in all essentials
it follows Menu, in whom one can find correspondences for 109 out of the 183 paragraphs that make
up the question. Vitelleschi and Rugerius show
considerably less extensive agreement, on only 34
and 29 paragraphs respectively, and they come to
conclusions different from Galileo's and from each
other's. Some of the material in Pererius's *De
communibus*, pp. 179-183, resembles Galileo's, but
in nothing like the detail given here.

K9. All of the authorities cited are to be found
in the Jesuit notes, with the exception of John of
Bacon, Lychetus, Antonius Andreas, and Marsilius;
the Jesuits, on the other hand, include more Averroists, e.g., Achillini, Pavesius, Taiapetra, and
Zabarella. See the comment at K38. The Lychetus
whom Galileo cites here is Franciscus Lychetus, *In
sententiarum libros Scoti*, Venice 1520.
     A possible sign of copying: Galileo wrote *Zi-
mara, propositione, propositione* (72.16), then
crossed out the first *propositione;* this citation
is given by Menu.

K13. First sentence, "136": Galileo first wrote
"196," then crossed this out and wrote "136" above
it. The figure as corrected is found in Menu and
in Pererius, *De communibus*, p. 182.
     End of second sentence, "34": Galileo first
wrote "83," then crossed this out and wrote "34"
above it. For this Menu has "31" and Pererius,
"43" (*De communibus*, p. 181).

K17. The text cited from Aristotle (298b3-4) is
similar to that given in the Junta edition of his
Opera, 1562, Vol. 5, fol. 172v, but it is not ex-

actly the same.

K38. The citations here are all found collectively in Menu, Vitelleschi, and Rugerius, with the exception of Philoponus, Simplicius, Rabbi Moses, and Achillini.

    Fourth sentence, "Thomists": Latin, *Tomistae* (76.31). The Cajetan referred to is Thomas de Vio Caietanus, *In summam theologicam*, Lyons 1562. Soncinas is Paulus Soncinas, *Acutissime questiones metaphysicales*, Venice 1505, and the reference is to question 7, reading 7 for Favaro's 3 (76.33). Ferrariensis is Franciscus Sylvester de Ferrara, *In summam contra gentiles*, Paris 1552; the chapter referred to in this commentary is incorrect -- it should be 20 rather than 30. The Jesuits augment Galileo's list of Thomists to include Dominic of Flanders, Herveus Natalis, and Amadeus Meygretus.[47]

    Fifth sentence, "Achillini": Galileo first wrote *Aquilinus*, then crossed out the *Aqui* and wrote *Achil* above it. It is noteworthy that Menu cites Aquilinus in this place; also, the fact that the name Achillinus occurs later down on this folio (77.16) could have led Galileo to believe that Aquilinus was a mistake, and to go back and make the change. According to Rugerius, Achillini held the opposite opinion; see the comment at K9 and also that at L13. The Scaliger referred to here is Julius Caesar Scaliger, *Exercitationes de subtilitate. . .ad Cardanum*, Paris 1557; on Mirandulanus, see the comment at B1.

K52. The text cited from Aristotle (335a28-30) is similar to that found in the Junta 1562 edition of his *Opera*, Vol. 5, fol. 383b, but it is not exactly the same.

K57. First sentence: Galileo's position here is directly opposed to that of Vitelleschi, whose conclusion to this question reads simply: "The heavens are a simple body lacking all composition from matter and form."[48] See K93 and its accompanying comment.

K58. First sentence, "those opposed": Latin, *adversarii* (79.28). This could include Jesuits such as Vitelleschi.

K63. The last marginal rubric to be found in the manuscript of the physical questions occurs at this paragraph. See the comment at A2.

K75-76. See the comment at K58. Vitelleschi took
the adversary position on these matters.

K93. First sentence: this position is similar to
Menu's, and less so to Rugerius's, both of whom
make allowances for opposed views such as Vitelleschi's. Thus Menu presents his teaching under
three conclusions: (1) "It is probable, and especially according to Aristotle, that the heavens are
a corporeal substance that is completely simple
and lacking matter and form"[49]; (2) "It seems more
probable, and especially according to the truth,
that the heavens are composed of matter and form"[50];
and (3) "The matter of the heavens is different in
kind from that of inferior bodies."[51] Rugerius, on
the other hand, has three preliminary propositions
in which he states Aristotle's teaching, admits
that it is impossible to demonstrate that there is
matter and form in the heavens, and further admits
that it is impossible to demonstrate that there is
not. He then presents his three conclusions, which
favor Vitelleschi more than Galileo and Menu: (1)
"It is not improbable that the heavens are composed
of a matter the same in kind as that of inferiors"[52]; (2) "It is more probable that they are composed of matter different in kind from that of inferiors"[53]; and (3) "It seems most probable to me
that the heavens are not composed of matter and
form."[54]
      Last sentence, "some immovables, such as the
earth": note that Galileo is here maintaining the
earth's immobility, as he does in his *Trattato della
Sfera*; see *Opere* 2:223-224.

K95. See J13, J18, and K93, with their comments.

K96. First sentence, "nature will make a thing simple rather than composite": Latin, *natura faciat
rem simplicem, non compositam* (86.15-16). Note
that Galileo uses a similar argument in the *Two New
Sciences* to justify his definition of naturally ac-
celerated motion; see *Opere* 8:197.

K109. This paragraph was added by Galileo in the
margin of the manuscript, with an asterisk indicat-
ing the place in the manuscript where the reply will
be found, viz, at K117.

K116. Second sentence, "more below": there is some brief treatment of this subject in K117, but the reference could be to the fuller discussion of motive powers and resistances mentioned previously; see the comment at J36.

K130. First sentence: Galileo's position here agrees with Menu's, and is compatible with Rugerius's "more probable" opinion. It is opposed, however, to Vitelleschi's, which rules out all composition from matter and form. See the comments at K57 and K93.

K143. Second sentence: altering Favaro's punctuation of the Latin text by inserting a comma after *corrumpi* (94.27).

K157. Fourth and fifth sentences, "category" and "On the Categories": reading *praedicamento* for Favaro's *praedicato* (96.27) and *praedicamentis* for his *praedicatis* (96.28). See the comment at A19.

K159. Third sentence: Menu takes essentially the same position, though he sides more explicitly with Cajetan than does Galileo. Neither Vitelleschi nor Rugerius discusses this query.

K165. First sentence, "concerning the matter of corruption": Latin, *in materia de corruptione* (98.30). This expression indicates that Galileo had already dealt with the subject of corruption, usually a part of the course on the *De generatione*. Compare this Latin construction with that of Q16, *in materia de mixtione,* and of T1, *in materia de intensione et remissione formarum,* as discussed in the comment at T1.

K170. Galileo's position here is the same as that taken by Menu. Rugerius denies that there is a different kind of matter in each sphere.
    Third sentence, "tenth *Metaphysics*": this is an erroneous reference; it should read "twelfth *Metaphysics*." See K38, where Galileo correctly locates Soncinas's discussion of this problem.

K181. Second sentence, "from what is to be said concerning the influence of the heavens": see V7 and its comment.

K183. Third sentence: another sign of copying. The Latin of the manuscript was written in the following sequence: *responsio patet ex si*[*t*] *valida quod patet ex eo quod minor et maior densitas non mutat.* Then the first *patet ex* was crossed out, and the first *quod* also, and finally the words *in elementis* were inserted between the *densitas* and the *non*.

*   *   *

L. The matters treated in this question bear resemblances to the lecture notes of Pererius, Menu, Vitelleschi, and Rugerius. Of the 41 paragraphs, 32 have counterparts in Vitelleschi, 24 in Rugerius, 23 in Menu, and 13 in Pererius; when these sources are considered collectively, only pars. 18 & 37-38 remain unaccounted for. Galileo's conclusions are closest to those formulated by Vitelleschi. There continue to be stylistic similarities with Menu, but par. 29 shows a departure from Menu's teaching and the adoption of a position similar to those of Vitelleschi and Rugerius.

L1. This transition paragraph is not found in the four Jesuits noted above, but it has a counterpart in the lectures of Stephanus del Bufalo on the *De caelo*, who begins this question with the words: *Vidimus coelum compositum ex materia et forma; vidimus quae sit materia, nunc de forma.*

L2. Vitelleschi cites all of these authorities with the exception of Philolaus the Pythagorean; none of the other Jesuits is so complete.

L3. Menu attributes this opinion also to Plutarch; Vitelleschi, also to Philoponus and Pavesius.

L4. Vitelleschi and Rugerius include Scaliger here along with Avicenna.

L6. All the Jesuit notes are in agreement with this conclusion.

L7. All *reportationes* are again in agreement, but Menu's statement is closer to Galileo's than is Vitelleschi's or Rugerius's.

L9. First sentence, "with respect to the first part": Galileo here wrote *secundam partem*, apparently forgetting the order of treatment indicated in the second sentence of L7.

L10. Menu does not have this paragraph; neither Vitelleschi nor Rugerius, both of whom have its equivalent, mentions Timaeus's *De natura et anima mundi*. For Damascene Favaro reads Galileo's hand as *Damasus* (105.15); the reading should be *Damascenus*.

L11. First sentence, "in the order of final causality": Latin, *finaliter*, which is Favaro's substitution for the word Galileo actually wrote here, viz, *inaniter*. In this context Menu also has *finaliter*. The citation of authorities mentioned in this paragraph is found only in Menu.

L13. The Renaissance authorities cited here are Alexander Achillinus, *De orbibus*, Bologna 1498 and later editions; Mirandulanus, as in B1; and Hieronymus Balduinus, *Quaesita logica et naturalia*, Venice 1563. Vitelleschi gives only these names, along with Pomponatius; Menu has Aquilinus in place of Achillinus, and he also references St. Thomas, Ferrariensis, and St. Bonaventure. See the comment at K38.

L24. Galileo's citation here of St. Thomas's First Part is incorrect; it should be question 70, article 3, as given by Vitelleschi and Rugerius. In this context Menu gives question 60, article 3, and *De spiritualibus creaturis*, article 6, the last figure a possible source of Galileo's error.

L25. Both Vitelleschi and Rugerius state the equivalent proposition: "The heavens are not informed by an intellective soul distinct from an intelligence."[55]

L27. Note Galileo's expression, "to physics or to animastics," Latin, *ad physicum vel ad animasticum* (108.6-7). For *animasticum* Vitelleschi here has *metaphysicum*. Galileo's term possibly derives from Pererius's statement in his 1566 lectures on the *De caelo*: ". . .a physico debet considerari vel ergo in libris De caelo, vel in De anima, sed neutro in loco tractatur. . ."

L29. Galileo's teaching here seems different from Menu's, who states his conclusion in three parts: (1) "The form of the heavens is not any kind of rational or intellective soul"[56]; (2) "Intelligences are not forms informing the heavens, either according to Aristotle or according to the truth";[57] and (3) "The heaven or the intelligence according to Aristotle is an assisting form and a heaven seems to be said to be animated analogically or by way of similitude. I say 'according to Aristotle' because according to the truth I believe it more probable that they are neither informing nor assisting forms."[58] Vitelleschi's conclusion, by contrast, is equivalent to Galileo's: "The intelligence that moves a heaven is not a form informing and giving it existence, but only assisting it in its motion."[59] Rugerius's shows less complete agreement: "The intelligence that is a mover of the heavens is not a form informing it, for which reason it does not confer existence (*esse*) as does a formal cause."[60]

L30. Vitelleschi alone has the same references as Galileo.

L32. First sentence, "Those opposed reply": Latin, *Respondent adversarii*. This expression is common in Vitelleschi and Rugerius.

L41. This paragraph concludes at the end of the last line of folio 54v. Following this there are two folios containing drawings and calculations that are unrelated to the text, and then a folio containing a discussion relating to Aristotle's *De generatione et corruptione*. Favaro's edition suggests that the question is incomplete at 110.33. This need not be the case, however, for the exposition of the question up to this point is consistent and integral, leaving no difficulties yet to be solved. The Jesuit *reportationes*, of course, frequently include additional questions on the *De caelo*, and in view of the possibility of their inclusion, Galileo's treatment of the *De caelo* may be seen as incomplete.

*   *   *

[TRACTATE ON ALTERATION]

There is no title for this tractate in Galileo's manuscript; it begins with a brief fragment concluding an introductory question on alteration, then has a longer question on intension and remission, and ends with a short question on the parts or degrees of qualities. The matter treated indicates that this is no longer an exposition of Aristotle's *De caelo et mundo*, for it relates to questions arising from the *De generatione et corruptione*. The fact that the fragment of the introductory question is only six lines long and begins at the top of the recto side of a folio is a good sign that other folios from this manuscript have been lost. The title, *Tractatus de alteratione*, is reconstructed by the translator from the indication in T1. Galileo uses *Tractatio* in his exposition of the *De caelo* and *Tractatus* in that of the *De generatione;* to preserve the nuance the first is translated as treatise, the second as tractate.

*   *   *

M. The surviving fragment of this question is too brief to permit an identification of sources. All of the Jesuit *reportationes* from Pererius through Del Bufalo treat of alteration at some length. Galileo's two sentences show better agreement, however, with the later *reportationes*, i.e., those of Rugerius and Del Bufalo, than with those of Pererius, Menu, and Vitelleschi.

M0. This paragraph has been reconstructed by the translator from materials in Menu, Rugerius, and Del Bufalo. Menu gives three meanings for alteration, whereas Rugerius and Del Bufalo give four; only the latter's four, however, fit into the division implied by M2.
Third sentence, "alterations are. . .perfective or corruptive": see above at J31.

M1. The first three sentences and the beginning of the fourth, all enclosed in square brackets, are supplied by the translator. The three conclusions are likely antecedents of the fourth conclusion

given in M2. In the missing folios it is probable
that each conclusion was given fuller and independent treatment, and was preceded by definitions
and distinctions similar to those sketched in M0.

M2. The essentials of this paragraph, together
with the reference to Aristotle, are found in Menu;
more extensive expositions are in Rugerius and Del
Bufalo.

*   *   *

N. The matter covered in this question is
treated in various *reportationes*, with the sole
exception of pars. 8, 22, & 25. Vitelleschi shows
the greatest agreement, with correspondences for
25 of the 32 paragraphs; after him come Rugerius
with 20, Pererius with 10, and Menu with 8. There
is a lacuna in the manuscript at the end of par.
17, and it is probable that a conclusion is missing
from Galileo's exposition; see the comments at N9
and N17.

N1. Last clause, "to understand action": it is
perhaps significant that Menu treats action immediately after discussing intension and remission,
whereas both Vitelleschi and Rugerius follow this
question with treatises on augmentation.

N2. All of the authors cited here are found in
Vitelleschi, and most of them are in Rugerius;
both also include the *Parisienses* among the authorities. Galileo's reference to St. Thomas, first
Sentences, distinction 16, is mistaken; the citation should be to distinction 17, which is given
correctly by all the Jesuit *reportationes*.

N3. Third sentence, "not the qualities but the subjects": see *infra*, O7-8.

N4. Second sentence, "category": reading *praedicamento* for Favaro's *praedicato* (112.25).

N6. Second sentence: an indication that Galileo
had already composed a commentary on the sixth book
of the *Physics*, where the continuity of motion is
discussed. See O9; also A1 and I39.

N7. First sentence: another indication that Galileo is familiar with logic and in particular with the categories. See A19, K157, and N4, with their respective comments.

N9. This obviously states Galileo's first conclusion. Because of the words "nor second" after the semicolon, however, there is also the possibility that two different points are being made here, with the result that this paragraph could count for two conclusions. This is unlikely, as explained in the comment on N17.

N12. Second sentence, "motion is nothing more than a *forma fluens*": these exact words are found in Rugerius. The definition of motion as a *forma fluens* is nominalist in inspiration, but it was adopted by some Thomists such as Herveus Natalis.[61]

N17. This paragraph is written on the verso of a folio and terminates with one third of the page blank; the next folio is blank on both sides, and the text of N18 begins at the top of the verso side of the following folio. Since Galileo begins N18 with "I say, third," and has only one explicit conclusion previous to this, the "I say, first" of N9, it is probable that he left this space blank to be filled in later with a second conclusion. The paragraph in square brackets that follows N17 is the translator's reconstruction of the conclusion Galileo possibly had in mind, based on the *reportatio* of Vitelleschi, although the latter's teachings are expressed in a different series of conclusions. See, however, the comment at N9.

N18. Fourth sentence, "for the first degree of heat . . .to be corrupted": a possible sign of copying. Galileo wrote *corrumpi primus gradus caloris* (116. 4), then repeated the *corrumpi* and crossed it out, perhaps because he had lost his place in the text he was using.

N25. End of first sentence, "seven of heat": there is no space in the manuscript after these words, but the insertion of "in the fire" seems required for sense.

N26. First sentence, "because otherwise. . .to come about": another possible sign of copying. Galileo wrote *quia agens alias nullo modo. . ."* (117.13),

then crossed out the *agens*, perhaps as a meaning-
less interpolation; the term *agens* occurs a few
lines previous, at 117.9.

N28. Second sentence, "Thomists": Latin, *Thomistae*,
as in the notes of Pererius and Rugerius. Previously, at K38, Galileo had written *Tomistae*, the
spelling used by Vitelleschi. Pererius references
Paulus Soncinas in this context and then gives the
opinion of "other Thomists." Vitelleschi has the
most complete enumeration of the members of this
school, viz, Soncinas, Ferrariensis, Javelli, Capreolus, Dominicus de Flandria, Caietanus, Astudil-
lo, and Banesius. See the comment at K38; also
infra at N31.

N31. First sentence: this summarizes the teaching
of Soncinas on the eighth *Metaphysics*, question 22,
already mentioned in N2. See his *Acutissime ques-
tiones metaphysicales*, Venice 1505, fol. 110rb.

*   *   *

0. Portions of this question bear resemblances
to printed texts such as Toletus's commentary on
the *Physics*, fol. 135r, and Bonamicus's *De motu libri decem*, book 8, chapters 21-23, but the best cor-
respondence is with Rugerius's *reportatio*, which
treats all nine paragraphs in much fuller detail.
Lesser agreement is found with Vitelleschi, in sev-
en paragraphs, with Menu in four, and with Pererius in only one.

04. The terminology here, and particularly the expression "uniformly difform" (*uniformiter difformis*, 120.21) is what induced Pierre Duhem to see
the *Doctores Parisienses* as the precursors of Galileo.[62] Menu has a briefer discussion than Galileo's, but Rugerius's is more detailed and mentions
the sources from which the terminology is drawn,
viz, the Calculator (Richard Swineshead), Burleus,
Albertus de Saxonia and the *Doctores Parisienses*,
Franciscus de Meyronnes, Forliviensis, Joannes
Canonicus, and various nominalists and Thomists.[63]

05. Third sentence, "degree-like parts": Latin,
partes graduales (121.3). This expression occurs
in Menu and in Vitelleschi.

O6. Last sentence, "more rooted": Latin, *magis radicari* (121.23). The fuller expression is *radicari in subiecto*, which is found in Pererius and Rugerius.

O9. Another indication that Galileo also had a commentary on Aristotle's *Physics*; see N6 and its comment. About a quarter of a page is left blank after this paragraph, and then the next tractate begins at the top of the verso side of the same folio.

*   *   *

TRACTATE ON THE ELEMENTS

P. This is not a question in the usual sense, but rather an introduction or prologue to the last tractate of the physical questions, entitled *Tractatus de elementis*. The *reportationes* of Pererius and Vitelleschi have very little on this matter, but collectively Menu, Valla, and Rugerius can account for all its paragraphs: Valla has the greatest number of correspondences, with 14 paragraphs; Menu comes next with 13, and Rugerius next with 12. Paragraph 1 is very similar to Menu's treatment, and pars. 9-12 are very similar to Rugerius's, suggesting the possibility that these paragraphs were copied from them or a similar source.

P1. First sentence, "physicians": Latin, *medici*. The authorities cited in this paragraph are all contained in Menu, except for the references to Hippocrates; Valla cites only Galen, Avicenna, Achillini, Gregory of Nyssa, and Cardanus. For Nyssa (122.21) Galileo has *Missenus*, and Valla, *Misenus*. The printed sources referred to by Galileo include Alexander Achillinus, *De elementis*, Bologna 1505; Hieronymus Cardanus, *De subtilitate*, Nuremberg 1550; Jacobus Carpentarius, *Descriptio universae naturae*, Paris 1548; Gaspar Contarenus, *De elementis eorumque mixtione*, Paris 1548; and Franciscus Valleriola, *Commentarium in libros Galeni*, Venice 1548.

P7. The authorities cited here are all mentioned by Rugerius; Menu refers the reader only to the Conciliator (see F21).

P8. Valla cites the same authorities as are given in this paragraph by Galileo; Rugerius has all but St. Thomas, whom he possibly includes with his *et alii.*

P10. Rugerius is more detailed here: he explains that he is treating only the second meaning because he has already treated the first, and he prefers to leave the third and the fourth to the physicians.

P11. Second sentence, "ancients": here Rugerius names "Empedocles, Anaxagoras, Democritus, and others."

Last sentence, "but rather are altered": a possible sign of copying. Galileo wrote *sed sed sint alterata* (124.31), then forgot to cross out the extra *sed.*

P13. First sentence: note the peculiar manner of citing "fourth *Meteors,* summary 2," rather than by chapter or text number. In the manuscript Galileo wrote *quarto Metheororum summa secunda capite,* then crossed out the *capite;* oddly enough, Rugerius's reference to this text is in the same mode, except that it concludes with *capite primo et secundo.* Perhaps these numbers were missing or unclear in the source Galileo was using.

Same sentence, "the Athenian": Latin, *Athenaeum.* Valla has a similar reference to the Athenian in discussing the number of the elements; see *infra* at U0.

P15. Note that from the outline of the tractate (here Galileo uses treatise, *tractatio*) as given, it does not survive in complete form, for Galileo covers only the first two parts of the remainder of the manuscript. The Jesuit *reportationes,* on the other hand, generally cover all four. See also U4.

Last sentence, *an sint:* this is the question of the existence of the elements, which Galileo feels does not require treatment. Both Menu and Valla, by contrast, have explicit treatments of this problem; Rugerius, however, does not.

The last fifth of the folio on which this paragraph is written is blank, and the next question begins at the top of its verso side; the content indicates, however, that the treatment is complete.

*   *   *

Q. Here begins the first major subdivision of
the Tractate on the Elements, inscribed by Galileo
as *Prima pars. De quidditate et substantia elementorum.* Notice that the *Prima pars* is consistent
with the division indicated by Galileo in P15, but
it is not consistent with the inscription over the
second major subdivision of the tractate, which is
Secunda disputatio rather than *Secunda pars* -- see
the title over V1. The confusion could result from
a source such as Valla's, which subdivides the
Tractatus de elementis into *disputationes* and then
into *partes,* with the result that he uses both terms
in close sequence. All seventeen paragraphs of
this question have counterparts in the *reportationes*
from the Collegio Romano, but the closest corres-
pondence is with Valla's, in which parallels can be
found for thirteen paragraphs, with six being so
similar as to suggest copying, viz, 2-6 & 7. The
next best agreement is with Menu, for twelve paragraphs. Rugerius and Pererius also show general
agreement for twelve paragraphs, but without the
detail found in Menu and Valla; the resemblances in
Pererius, in fact, are quite remote. Vitelleschi
treats this material very briefly, and has counterparts for two paragraphs only, viz, 5 & 8.

Q1. This is a transitional paragraph with no clear-
cut counterpart in any of the Jesuit notes.

Q2. "can be defined in two ways": note that Galileo,
having written this, goes on inconsistently to enu-
merate three ways of defining a natural entity. In
his parallel passage, Valla explains that an element can be defined in two ways, metaphysically and
physically, and that in each of these ways there is
the possibility of a further twofold division,
either "in itself" (*secundum se*) or "as related to
another" (*in ordine ad aliud*). Apparently Galileo
interpreted this statement, incorrectly, as a third
way of defining.

Q8. "potentially or actually," adopting Favaro's
emendation of Galileo's text (126.25). Galileo
wrote *inest p⁰ aut actu.* In corresponding passages
Vitelleschi and Rugerius both have *inest aut potentia aut actu,* and Valla has *vel actu vel virtute.*

Rugerius's abbreviation of *potentia (po'a)* suggests a possible source of Galileo's error: he apparently made the *"o"* a superscript, and then forgot to add the *"a"* to it.

Q9. The two loci in Galen are given by Menu, Valla, and Rugerius. For Gregory of Nyssa Galileo wrote *Greg. Misseni;* in corresponding passages Menu has *Greg. Nys.,* Valla has *Greg. Lis.,* and Rugerius, *Greg. Nysseno.* See the comments at P1 and R5.

Q10. The two loci cited from Avicenna are not contained in any one *reportatio;* the first is referenced by Menu and Valla, the second by Rugerius.

Q11. Mention of the Stoics and Laërtius is found only in Rugerius.

Q16. First sentence, "actually or potentially": Latin, *vel actu vel potentia* (127.28-29). This expression is found only in Menu; here Valla and Pererius have *vel actu vel virtute,* and Rugerius notes that he will discuss elsewhere how the bodies are present -- see the comment at Q8.
　　Second sentence, "in treating of compounds": Latin, *in materia de mixtione.* Note the similarity of Latin construction to those remarked in the comments at K165 and T1; also that Galileo apparently planned to have a *Tractatus de mixtis,* which, however, is missing from this manuscript, although it is found in the Jesuit *reportationes.* See also P15 and its comment.

*   *   *

R. Counterparts of this question are to be found only in Pererius, Menu, and Valla; the later *reportationes* do not discuss it. All six of the paragraphs have correspondences in Menu and Valla; for the first four paragraphs and part of the fifth the similarities with Menu are close enough to suggest copying. Pererius touches on matters relating to pars. 5 & 6 only.

R1. Second sentence, "explained elsewhere": Galileo has mentioned Aristotle's distinctive views on the temporal origin of the universe in C5-6, but there is nothing explicit there about the elements. Menu

mentions in this context that there is a controversy as to whether Aristotle thought that elements
depend totally on God in the order of efficient
causality, and that he will discuss this in his
Metaphysics in the question whether eternals (*aeter-
na*) are dependent on God. Valla is more explicit
in noting that it is a serious problem among peripatetics whether, for Aristotle, God is the total
efficient cause of the elements in their initial
production, or whether the heavens also exercise
some efficiency on them; this problem, he says, is
to be treated in the *Tractatus de Deo*.

R2. Second sentence, "some moderns": Latin, *aliqui
recentiores*. This expression is used by Menu also,
without identification. In a slightly different
context Pererius mentions *recentiores* and includes
Achillini among them.

R5. Of the authorities cited here, Pererius and
Menu cite only Empedocles, Democritus, and Plato,
and Valla mentions only the first two. For Nyssa
Galileo wrote *Mixenus*, which is related to his
spelling in P1 and Q9, and possibly derives from
a source such as Valla; see the comments on P1 and
Q9.

R6. In giving the citation of the second *De generatione*, Valla has text 27 where Galileo gives 37.

*   *   *

S. This question occurs in all the Jesuit *reportationes*, and is touched on by Toletus in his
De generatione, fol. 64v. All of Galileo's paragraphs have counterparts in the *reportationes* taken
collectively, but the best correspondences are with
Valla, for 15 paragraphs, and with Vitelleschi, for
12; Pererius treats the matter of 15 of Galileo's
paragraphs, but in a fairly different way, and Rugerius has the matter of only 4. Valla's pars. 9
& 12 are sufficiently similar to Galileo's to suggest copying; the same may be said of Vitelleschi's
pars. 2, 7, & 17.

S1. The reference here is apparently to the commentary on the first book of the *Physics*; see the more
explicit reference in S14.

S2. The citation here is of a printed text, Flaminius Nobilius, *De generatione et interitu*, Lucca 1567; Valla gives the *dubitatio* as *ii* rather than *11*, but Galileo's citation is correct, and this is found in Vitelleschi also.

S3. First sentence, "in the third *De elementis*": reading "3" for Favaro's "7" (129.31). All of the citations in this paragraph are to be found in Valla; Menu omits the reference to Alexander.
    Second sentence, "differences of the elements": Latin, *differentias elementorum*, i.e., the *differentiae* in the sense of species being composed of genus and *differentia*. This expression recurs in Menu, Valla, and Rugerius.

S4. First sentence, "who holds for primary qualities": this is a marginal insert in Galileo's manuscript. All of the authors cited in this paragraph are to be found in Valla; the other *reportationes* are less complete. For Dexippus (130.13-14) Menu has *Leucippus*, Valla has *Desippus*, and Vitelleschi, *Dexippus*.

S7. Phrase enclosed in square brackets: here, immediately following the "therefore" (*ergo*), Galileo wrote *3 arg. si qualitas non est forma elementi*, then crossed it out. This is an apparent repetition of the first part of the first sentence of this paragraph; note, however, that there the argument is given in the plural form (130.27-28), whereas in the clause crossed out it is in the singular, an indication that even if Galileo copied he did not reproduce each time the exact words in his source.

S8. First sentence, expression in square brackets: there is a lacuna of several words in Galileo's manuscript, and the material in square brackets has been inserted by the translator to make sense of the surrounding text. Galileo wrote *formas elementorum esse formas substantiales. . .qualitates nobis occultas*, with the elipsis being an empty space allowing room for about three words. At this place in their *reportationes* Menu has *formas elementorum esse quasdam substantias occultas quae explicantur per qualitates motivas et alterativas*, and Valla has *formas substantiales elementorum esse substantias quasdam occultas quae interdum explicantur per qualitates motivas, interdum per altera-*

tivas. Note that the thought as reconstructed is
consistent with that expressed in the first sentence of S13 and in S15.

Second sentence, "likewise the Conciliator,
difference 13": between *Conciliator* and *differentiae* there is a space in Galileo's manuscript,
leaving room for a word or two. Menu, Valla, and
Rugerius all give this citation, but without any
additional wording. In another context, however,
Rugerius cites an opinion of the *Conciliator in
dilucidario ad differentiam 10;* perhaps Galileo
saw the abbreviation for *in dilucidario* but was
unable to decipher it, and so left a space to be
filled in later.

Second sentence, last phrase, "seventh *De elementis*": an obvious error on Galileo's part, since
there are but five books in this work. Rugerius
cites only the first book.

It should be noted that no one *reportatio*
gives all the authorities cited in this paragraph;
Rugerius is the most complete, lacking only the
reference to Giles, although he cites question 28
of Jandun's *De sensu,* not question 25 as given by
Galileo.

S9. The matter in square brackets at the concluding half of the paragraph: here in Galileo's manuscript there is a lacuna of about a third of a
page at the bottom of the recto side of the folio,
and another two thirds of a page in the upper part
of the verso side of the same folio. Galileo apparently left space to insert additional arguments
at a later date. In Valla's *reportatio* there are
such arguments, and these occupy about the amount
of space left by Galileo. The sentences in square
brackets are the translator's summary of Valla's
teaching, which resembles Galileo's in all partic-
ulars.

S10. Only Valla has a counterpart of this paragraph, and he mentions the Greeks and Dexippus
alone, omitting the remaining citations.

S12. First sentence, "i.e., by reason of gravitation and levitation": an insertion in Galileo's
manuscript, not found in Valla, that disrupts the
parallelism of the sentence structure. Galileo
apparently first intended to preserve the parallelism, for he wrote *in actu secundo, et,* then
crossed out the *et* and inserted the explanatory

phrase, and then continued on with *et sic dicuntur qualitates.*

Second sentence, "in the category": reading *praedicamento* for Favaro's *praedicato* (132.2).

S13. First sentence, "ultimate substantial differences": the Latin for "substantial," *substantialium* (132.8-9), was inserted later by Galileo, apparently to clarify his meaning. See the comment at S8.

Last sentence, "but principles": Galileo's manuscript has another lacuna at this point, about a line in length. He wrote *principia autem instrumentalia,* then crossed out the *instrumentalia,* but did not finish the sentence. The translator has inserted in square brackets words that complete his thought, as also expressed in S16. At the corresponding place Valla writes: *Respondeo qualitates motivas non esse principia principalia motus sed tantum instrumentaria, et ideo non esse naturam.*

S16. Rugerius has a good summary of the thought contained in Galileo's S8, S13, S14, and S16 when he writes: "If, with Aristotle, the Greeks and others sometimes seem so to treat of active and motive qualities as to make of them the essential differences of the elements, the reason is that the differences of things are unknown, and so they wish to explain their natures through qualities that are more known."[64]

*   *   *

T. This question, which treats the intension and remission of substantial forms, is left incomplete by Galileo, possibly because he was at a loss as to how to complete it. It has counterparts in the *reportationes* of Menu, Valla, and Rugerius, but not in its later portions, i.e., in pars. 18-21. The number of parallels are greatest with Valla, in 14 paragraphs, next with Rugerius, in 11, and last with Menu, in 10; yet Menu's exposition corresponding to par. 3 is close enough to Galileo's to suggest copying. Both Valla and Menu, however, disagree with Galileo's position, taking the Averroist side of the controversy rather than the Thomist, as advocated by Galileo in pars. 5 & 9; Rugerius, on the other hand, has essentially the same teaching as Galileo.

T1. First sentence, "From the tractate on alteration, on the matter of the intension and remission
of forms": altering Favaro's punctuation in 133.3-4,
which reads, *Suppono, ex tractatu De alteratione in
materia, De intensione et remissione formarum.* . .
The comma should come after *alteratione* and the second *De* should not be capitalized. Galileo gives
the basis for the translator's reading of *in materia de* in K165 and Q16; see the comments at those
places. Menu mentions that he has treated problems
related to the intension of forms *copiose in Logica,
capite de differentia,* an indication that he has
also composed logic notes, which are not known to
be extant.

T2. All of the authorities cited are found in the
Jesuit *reportationes.* Menu has the most complete
listing, omitting only Alexander; Valla also omits
Alexander, but Rugerius informs us that the reference is to Alexander of Hales. The sixteenth-century printed sources cited by Galileo include Augustinus Niphus, *In libros de generatione,* Venice 1526;
Joannes Jacobus Pavesius, *De accretione,* Venice
1566; and Hieronymus Taiapetra, *Summa divinarum et
naturalium questionum,* Venice 1506.

T4. Of the authorities mentioned here, Rugerius a-
lone gives Avicenna; Valla adds Soto to the Thomist
opinion; none of the *reportationes* studied mentions
Gregory, Ockham, Themistius, Philoponus, Nobilius,
Buccaferreus, Albertus, or Javelli. The sixteenth-
century printed sources referenced by Galileo include Ludovicus Buccaferreus, *In libros de generatione,* Venice 1571, and Chrysostomus Javellus,
Totius. . .*philosophiae compendium,* Venice 1555;
for Nobili, see the comment on S2, also Y8 *infra.*
  Third sentence, "Soncinas": Latin, *Soncinatis.*
Oddly, Galileo wrote this word out in its entirety,
then crossed out the *atis,* leaving only the abbreviation, although he was correct at first writing;
possibly he was not sure of this. Both Menu and
Valla give only the abbreviated form.
  Last sentence, "Javelli, eighth *Metaphysics,*
question 5": this appears to be a miscitation, for
Javelli discusses the intension and remission of
substantial forms in questions 4 and 6, but not in
question 5.[65]

T5. First sentence, "This second, true opinion is proved by the following arguments": Latin, *Probatur haec secunda sententia vera his argumentis*. The *vera* here is one of Galileo's indications of his position on this subject (see also T9). Menu explicitly takes the opposite: "I think it is consonant with the peripatetics that the forms of the elements can be intensified and remitted, but other forms cannot."[66] So also Valla, who reverses the order of the two opinions, giving Aquinas's first and Averroës's last. He writes: "Though the first opinion [the Thomists'] is probable, as is apparent from what has been said, the second seems much more probable: the substantial forms of elements, since they are imperfect substances and must remain actual in a compound, undergo intension and remission, as hold Averroës and other authors of the second opinion."[67] Rugerius, however, defends the opinion presented in this paragraph as true.

Third sentence, "Scotus": Rugerius is the only one who identifies Scotus as the author of this view.

T7. First sentence, "one fire is more fire than another": Galileo wrote the Latin for this correctly, viz, *unus ignis esse magis ignis quam alius*, then crossed out the second *ignis*, thus inexplicably changing the sense. In corresponding passages both Menu and Valla have *unum ignem esse magis ignem quam alium*.

T9. This is a more explicit indication, apart from that in T5, of Galileo's rejection of the Averroist position and his adoption of that of the Thomists. Both Menu and Valla differ from Galileo on the points made in this paragraph. For Menu, "the form of an element is intermediate between perfect substantial forms and accidental forms,"[68] and for Valla "incomplete [and imperfect] substances are true substances."[69]

T17-20. The argumentation here is typical of the nominalist tradition. Valla uses such arguments briefly, in a sentence or two, but otherwise they are not in the *reportationes* that have been analyzed.

T21. This sentence begins the top of the recto side of a folio; the rest of the folio is blank on both sides. The question is obviously incomplete, since,

if Galileo is defending the second opinion, he
should reply to the objections raised in paragraphs
T14-21. The material included by Favaro from
136.26 onward does not pertain to this question,
but is a different topic altogether.

                    *   *   *

        U. The title is missing in Galileo's composi-
tion, which begins on the verso side of a folio
whose recto is blank; that given is adapted from
the *reportatio* of Rugerius, who treats all of the
matters discussed by Galileo under the general title *De numero et quantitate elementorum;* other Jesuits devote entire questions to the particular topics included here, such as *De numero elementorum,
De figura elementorum,* and *De maximo et minimo elementorum.* Some paragraphs of this question bear
resemblances to Toletus's commentary on the *Physics,*
fol. 25, and to Pererius's *De communibus,* pp. 354-
357; fuller correspondences, for 33 paragraphs,
are to be found in the *reportatio* of Pererius's
lectures on the *De generatione.* The best agreement,
however, is with the notes of Valla and Vitelleschi,
where parallels can be found for 44 and 41 paragraphs respectively. Menu and Rugerius supply fewer details, and so have fewer counterparts, in 27
and 23 paragraphs respectively. Taken collectively, these *reportationes* can account for all the
material covered by Galileo, with the exception of
pars. 38-46 & 67-70. Some of Valla's expressions
are sufficiently close to Galileo's to suggest
copying, viz, those in pars. 25, 30-32, & 73-75.

U0. This paragraph is reconstructed by the translator from Valla's question *De numero et distinctione
elementorum,* whose content agrees well with Galileo's subsequent exposition. It is a more abbreviated account, however, than that from which Galileo apparently worked.
        First sentence, "We inquire, first": compare
U7, "We inquire, second," and U9, "We inquire,
third," which indicate that the topics covered in
this question are the number of the elements, their
size and shape, and their termini of largeness and
smallness.
        Second sentence, "the number. . .is not infi-
nite": see the reinforcement of this statement in
U5.

Third sentence, "who denied that fire is an element": see U4. Apparently Galileo's source listed Cardanus's arguments at this point, and thus the reference back to them in U4.

U2. Second sentence, "and so it cannot break down": the Latin for this, *ergo non potest refrangere*, is a marginal insert in Galileo's manuscript.

U4. ". . .when I treat of the elements in particular": Latin, *cum agam de elementis in particulari*. This is an indication that Galileo planned to complete the course in natural philosophy with matters extending into the *Meteorology*; see also P15. At this place Valla similarly has *quando agemus de elementis in particulari*.

U6. First sentence, "one of which": a possible sign of copying. Galileo wrote *quorum unum unum* and apparently forgot to cross out the repetition.

Third sentence, "as I shall point out": a possible reference to the matter discussed in V10 or, more likely, in X2-8.

U7. Second sentence, *Doctores Parisienses*: this reference is given by Valla in the precise form found in Galileo; see X5 and its comment. Menu also cites the *Doctores Parisienses*, but on the first *Meteors*, question 3. An earlier reference by Galileo to the *Doctores Parisienses* is at F18.

Third sentence, "I will show elsewhere": a possible reference to the mathematical demonstrations contained in Galileo's *De motu antiquiora* (*Opere*, 1:345-346), which also include a marginal reference to chapter 3 of the first *Meteors*; if so, this establishes a temporal connection between these notebooks and the *De motu* manuscripts.

Last sentence, "for the mathematicians": Latin, *ad mathematicos*. Both Valla and Rugerius use this expression in the same context; see G14, 21, & 27, and H19 & 23 for Galileo's related expressions.

Same sentence, "as we shall explain": an apparent reference to the treatise on the elements in particular (P15 & U4), where the earth's sphericity was usually explained when discussing *De terra*. Proofs that the earth is round are also given in Clavius's *Sphaera*, pp. 110-117, and in Galileo's own *Trattato della Sfera* (*Opere*, 2:217-220).

U9. Immediately before this paragraph in the manuscript Galileo started to write a heading, *De mag-
ni...*, as though he was beginning a new question,
then crossed it out. Possibly he had in mind *De
magnitudinis et parvitatis terminis*, as suggested
by his words following, *an elementa. . .habeant
aliquos terminos magnitudinis et parvitatis* (138.
29-30). At the corresponding place in his notes
Valla begins with a new heading, which reads: *Pars
quarta. De quantitate elementorum. Quaestio prima.
An dentur maximum et minimum in elementis.* In Pererius's notes there is a related title, *De magni-
tudine et figura elementorum*, though it does not
occur in this context.

U12. Sixth sentence, "and so, from the third *Physics*": Latin, *et sic, ex tertio Physicorum* (140.11).
A possible sign of copying. Galileo first wrote
et sit, then crossed out the *sit* and wrote *sic* after it, possibly having first read *sit* for *sic*;
Menu has a similar expression at this place.

U13. First sentence, "the formality and difference
of extrinsic and intrinsic termini consists in
this": another possible indication of copying.
Galileo wrote *ratio et differentia termini in hoc*,
then crossed out the *in hoc* and went on, *extrinsici
et intrinsici in hoc consistit*, as though he had
skipped over the *extrinsici et intrinsici* in his
first writing.

U20. Second sentence, "an animal": reading *aliquod
animal* for Favaro's *aliquid aliud* (142.31 & 33).

U22. Fourth sentence, "as far as in it lies": Latin, *quantum est ex se* (142.23). Note the similarity, apparently fortuitous, between this expression
and *quantum in se est*, which derives from Lucretius
and was used by both Descartes and Newton in the
statement and explanation of their laws of motion.

U25. The reference to Soto here is to Dominicus So-
tus, *Quaestiones in physicam Aristotelis*, Salamanca
1551 and later editions. Galileo's citation of
authorities parallels that in Valla and Vitelleschi,
except that where Galileo has *Thomistarum* Valla
cites Ferrariensis and Vitelleschi names "Cajetan
and others." Note the peculiar way of citing Aquinas's commentaries on Aristotle, which are usually
given by book and *lectio*; this derives, apparently,

from Valla, Vitelleschi, and Rugerius, all of whom
have the same manner of citation as Galileo. Again,
no book number is given by Galileo for Aquinas's
De generatione, text 41; this citation is not found
in the Jesuit *reportationes,* but in its place Valla
has the second *De anima,* text 41.

Third sentence, "if anything can be separated
from anything else": Latin, *si ex quolibet potest
quodlibet separari* (144.23). Galileo had difficulty with this expression, writing *ex quodlibet potest quodlibet* and having to delete the *"d"* in the
first *quodlibet.* Then, in the next sentence, where
the expression *quodlibet ex quolibet* (144.27) also
occurs, Galileo again wrote *quodlibet ex quodlibet*
and this time had to delete the *"d"* from the second
quodlibet. The expression occurs in Valla in the
same context.

U30. Valla cites all four authorities given by Galileo, and adds to them Achillini and Gaetano da Thiene.

U31. The last sentence is incomplete, has no period, and is followed by a blank space about two
inches long. This sentence is not in Valla, who
otherwise agrees closely with Galileo's exposition
in this paragraph.

U32. Scotus and Ockham are cited here by Menu,
Valla, Vitelleschi, and Rugerius, but Vitelleschi
alone has the reference to Pererius. The occur-
rence of such a citation of Pererius in a Jesuit
reportatio, it should be noted, alerts one to the
possibility that Galileo's references to Pererius,
as in C9 and F18, were not made directly but from
a secondary source.

U33. First sentence, "concerning this elsewhere":
an indication that Galileo either had written or
planned to write a treatise on infinity, probably
as a part of his commentary on the *Physics.*

U34. The Jesuit notes generally lack the list of
authorities cited by Galileo, with the exception
of Vitelleschi, who gives them all, but in place
of Richard has Godfrey, and in place of Almainus
has *Bacconus et alii.* The Almainus referred to is
Jacobus Almainus, who published a commentary on the
Sentences at Paris in 1512.

Third sentence, "Capreolus": the citation to

the third *Sentences,* distinction 17, should be
question 2, not question 4; there are only two
questions in Capreolus's distinction 17.

Same sentence, "Third Part": reading 3 for
Favaro's 13 (146.15).

Last sentence: the reference is to Joannes
Ludovicus Cartarius, *Lectiones super Aristotelis
proemio in libros de physico auditu,* Perugia 1572.

U37. Last sentence, "any intrinsic mode of such an
essence. . .any intrinsic mode of a quality": another possible sign of copying. At the first oc-
currence Galileo wrote *quemcunque modum intrinsecum
qualitatis,* then crossed out the *qualitatis* and
wrote *essentiae* after it (147.13); later he wrote
quemcunque modum intrinsecum qualitatis properly
(147.15), probably having lost his place at the
first writing.

U47. The discussion in this paragraph has some
bearing on a topic treated in the first day of the
dialogues reported in Galileo's *Two New Sciences,
Opere,* 8:50-54, especially p. 54, where Galileo
makes explicit reference to Aristotle's thought on
this subject.

U49. Fourth sentence, "has fixed termini of largeness": another possible sign of copying. Galileo
wrote *habere certos terminos terminos magnitudinis,*
then crossed out the second *terminos,* which apparently he had inadvertently copied a second time.

U55. Second sentence, "just as, even though": yet
another possible indication of copying. Galileo
wrote *sicut etiam res,* then crossed out the *res*
and wrote *licet res* (151.22), apparently having
omitted the *licet* at his first writing.

U68. Last sentence, "a thousand pounds": following
Favaro's emendation of Galileo's manuscript, which
has 100 in place of 1000 (154.24).

U71. Fourth sentence, "a thousand pounds": following Favaro's reading again. Here Galileo wrote
1000, then crossed out one zero to leave the figure
at 100 (155.11).

U73. Last sentence: the clause in square brackets
is required for sense; its counterpart is in Valla,
but Galileo omitted it in his writing.

Same sentence, "a thousand pounds": here Galileo's manuscript has 1000 (155.27). Valla, however, in using the same example, gives the pounds as 100. See the comments at U68, U71, and U75.

U74. For the three occurrences of "a thousand pounds" in this paragraph, Galileo has 1000 each time in his manuscript.

U75. Here again there are three occurrences of "a thousand pounds," but now Galileo writes 100 each time; Valla, whose exposition is close enough to Galileo's to suggest copying, also has 100 in this context.

                    *   *   *

V. This question begins the second part of Galileo's proposed four-part tractate on the elements, i.e., that relating to their qualities and other accidents (see P15). Instead of captioning this *Secunda pars*, consistent with his earlier usage, he titles it *Secunda disputatio*; a possible explanation is given above in the introduction to the commentary on Q. Some expressions in pars. 1, 3, 4, & 6 are similar to those in Toletus's commentary on the *De generatione*, fols. 63r-65v. Eight of the paragraphs have counterparts in the *reportationes*, viz, all except 2 & 6; the best correspondences are with Rugerius and Valla, in 7 and 6 paragraphs respectively. Menu shows counterparts for five paragraphs and a part of a sixth, and Vitelleschi for only four.

V2. Second sentence, "privative contrariety. . . contrary contrariety": Latin, *contrarietatem privativam. . .contrarietate contraria* (158.16-18). To avoid the apparent redundancy of "contrary contrariety," scholastics frequently speak of this as contrary opposition, as between one color and another, and so distinguish it from privative opposition, as between sight and blindness. A related terminology is to contrast a "positive contrary" with a "privative contrary," as Galileo does *infra* in W8.

V3. Second sentence, "as I shall prove elsewhere": possibly in the projected fourth part of the tractate dealing with compounds; see P15. Menu treats

this subject immediately after his section on maxima and minima.

V7. Third sentence, "influences, if such things exist": Latin, *influentiae, si dantur* (159.16-17).
By influences the Jesuits understood powers or qualities other than light and motion whereby the heavenly bodies could act on the sublunary region. In
general they were skeptical about their existence,
but there was no uniform position on them. Valla
denied their existence outright, whereas Vitelleschi
and Rugerius held it as less probable, as can be
seen from the texts cited in the next paragraph.
    Fourth sentence, "virtual qualities": Latin,
de qualitatibus virtualibus (159.20). Valla explains these as follows: "Moreover, there are other
qualities that act by true action and by corruptive
alteration, and of this kind are the virtues of
plants and compounds; since these, however, depend
on the four primaries and act by reason of them,
they are not primary qualities."[71] He goes on to
relate these to influences: "Even if occult virtues
and qualities be admitted, these are not effected
by influences, as some erroneously think, because
influences do not exist; rather they are effected
by a mixture of primary qualities."[72] In a similar
context Vitelleschi writes: "Notwithstanding Aristotle's claim that there are other primary qualities apart from these four, such as the light of
the sun and stars, this is not a tangible quality
nor is it endowed with a proper action inclining
toward generation and corruption; rather it acts
by means of the heat that it contains virtually.
Practically the same is to be said of influences."[73]
Rugerius sums up his reasoning on the matter in a
more nuanced conclusion: "It is not improbable
that the heavens have some influence on inferiors
apart from illuminating and heating, whether they
do this by a virtue of light itself that is hidden
from us, or by qualities other than light; but it
seems to me much more probable, and more consonant
with the right way of philosophizing, to deny any
influence to the heavens other than illuminating
and heating."[74] The position set forth by Galileo
seems more compatible with Vitelleschi's and Rugerius's than with Valla's.

V9. Third sentence, "itself a disposition to heat":
Latin, *quae est dispositio ad calorem*. A possible
sign of copying. Galileo wrote *quae est causa*

calo..., then crossed out *causa calo...* and continued on, *dispositio ad calorem* (160.5); the expression *causat calorem* occurs earlier in the sentence (160.3).

*   *   *

W. This question is found in all the Jesuit
reportationes, and cumulatively they can account
for all of Galileo's material except par. 7. Galileo's exposition is closest to that of Vitelleschi
and Rugerius, both of whom have the counterparts
of 15 paragraphs; after them comes Valla, with correspondences for 14 paragraphs, and then Menu and
Pererius, with 10 and 9 respectively. The contents
corresponding to pars. 1-6 & 8 in Valla, 2 & 3 in
Rugerius, and 4 & 5 in Menu are close enough to
suggest copying.

W1. Second sentence, "privation of wetness": Latin,
privationem humoris (160.16-17). Here and in pars.
6-8 & 10-14 Galileo uses *humor* consistently for
wetness; in this he is in agreement with Vitelleschi, who employs the same term throughout. All the
other Jesuits use *humiditas* to designate this quality in the abstract, and *humidum* to designate it in
the concrete.

W4. Second sentence, "nobility of their compounds":
Latin, *nobilioribus mixtis* (160.28-29). Immediately after *mixtis* Galileo wrote *ut,* then crossed it
out and began a new paragraph. The word *ut,* it
should be noted, occurs in the line above in his
manuscript (160.28), and so this could be an indication of copying.

W6. First sentence, "that of others": Vitelleschi
attributes this opinion to Telesio.

W11. "As will be more apparent from the following":
a possible reference to the next three paragraphs,
or, more likely, to X19, where a mechanism that
can account for this is explained.

W13. Fourth sentence, "as Pliny teaches": the reference to Pliny is found only in Vitelleschi, not
in the other Jesuit authors.

W16. First sentence, altering Favaro's punctuation
by inserting s semicolon after *calidorum* (163.20)
and deleting the colon after *externis* (163.21).

W17. Second sentence, "Add also, however": Latin,
Tamen adde etiam. Here Galileo wrote *at vero* after *tamen,* a sequence that does not make sense,
then crossed out the *at vero* and continued with
the *adde etiam.* Possibly he lost his train of
thought, or was trying different connectives so as
to express himself more clearly.

*   *   *

X. The first paragraph of this question has
counterparts in Toletus's commentary on the *De generatione,* fols. 66r–67r; the remaining paragraphs
of the question, with the exception of 2 & 5, are
to be found in the lecture notes of Menu, Valla,
Vitelleschi, and Rugerius. The closest agreement
is with Vitelleschi, for 15 of the 21 paragraphs;
after him, with Valla, Rugerius, and Menu, in that
order, for 10, 8, and 6 paragraphs respectively.
The contents of pars. 10 & 17 in Vitelleschi, and
of 7–9 & 16 in Rugerius, are sufficiently close to
Galileo's composition to suggest copying.

X3. Fourth sentence, "with cold air": emending Galileo's *cum aqua frigida* (164.31) to read *cum aere
frigido,* for otherwise the argument does not make
sense.

X5. Third sentence: note the peculiar manner of
citing "fourth *Meteors,* second summary, chapter 3."
The same type of citation is found in U7, and there
a counterpart for it is to be found in Valla; see
the comment on U7.

X10. Second sentence, *inter symbola:* a technical
expression that applies to pairs of elements that
have one quality in common, e.g., air, which is hot
and wet, and water, which is cold and wet. By vary-
ing the qualities that are not common, in this case
hot and cold, one element, say air, may be readily
converted into the other, water.
    Fifth sentence, "whether the water is hot or
cold": Latin, *sive aqua calida sit sive frigida.* A
possible sign of copying. Galileo wrote *sive aqua*

sive calida sit sive frigida, then crossed out the
second *sive* as not making sense.

X14. Second sentence: the reference to Marsilius is
given only by Valla and Vitelleschi.

X15. Fourth sentence, "wherein heat and cold act
most effectively and wetness and dryness receive
most effectively": Latin, *in qua calor et frigus
potissimum agunt, humor et siccitas potissimum pa-
tiuntur* (167.32-33). A possible sign of copying.
Galileo started to write *humor* after *potissimum,*
then crossed it out and wrote *agunt* instead; note
the use of *humor,* as pointed out in the comment on
W1. Another indication of copying occurs later in
the same sentence, at "the latter act as. . .cor-
rectly noted": here Galileo wrote *hae agant sed ut
recte notavit* (167.34), then crossed out the *sed*
as not making sense. The term *sed* occurs earlier
in the same sentence, at 167.32.

X16. First sentence: Rugerius attributes this teaching to Angelus Mercenarius.

X19. Second sentence, "occurs also in things where
it is more hidden": Latin, *contingit in aliis in
quibus est occultior* (169.19-20). Yet another indication of copying. Galileo started to write *occultior* after *aliis,* then crossed it out and resum-
ed with *in quibus est occultior.*

*   *   *

Y. The contents of this question are not completely contained in the Jesuit lecture notes, and
much of what is contained in them is not in the
treatment of the qualities of the elements but in
the discussion of action and reaction. Cumulatively the notes of Menu, Valla, Vitelleschi, Rugerius,
and Del Bufalo can account for all but five of the
paragraphs, viz, 9, 21, & 23-25. Vitelleschi has
counterparts for the greatest number of paragraphs,
14, but his positions diverge from Galileo's in
pars. 4 & 19. Valla has correspondences with 9
paragraphs, and Rugerius with 7, although the latter too takes a position different from Galileo's,
in par. 8. Both Menu and Del Bufalo have counterparts for only four paragraphs, but significantly

the latter agrees with Galileo in pars. 4 & 8,
where Vitelleschi and Rugerius diverge from him
respectively.

Y1. Second sentence: Rugerius alone cites Vallesius in this context, and he, like Galileo, spells
the name with only one "l." The work referred to
is Franciscus Vallesius, *Controversiarum medicarum
et philosophicarum libri*, Alcalà 1556 and later
editions.

Y4. First sentence: Vitelleschi rejects this conclusion, attributing it to the moderns (*recentiores*). Del Bufalo, however, in the anonymous manuscript attributed to him by the translator,[75] holds
the same conclusion and states it in terms very
similar to Galileo's.
     Fourth sentence: Rugerius and Del Bufalo alone
mention Pomponatius in this context; the reference
is to Petrus Pomponatius, *De reactione*, Bologna
1514 and later editions.

Y6. First sentence, "by reason of the thing connoted, pertains to the category of action": Latin,
*ratione connotati pertinere ad praedicamentum acti-
onis* (171.19). A possible sign of copying. After
writing *praedicamentum*, Galileo wrote *ratione* again,
then crossed it out and wrote *actionis*, apparently
having lost his place in the source he was working
from.

Y7. Second sentence, "the second": Galileo abbreviated the Latin for this, *secundum*, as *s'm* rather
than as *2um*, apparently confusing the preposition
with the ordinal number, as one might when copying
without grasping the correct sense.

Y8. First sentence, "the error of Nobili": Del Bufalo gives the same reference to Nobili, and the
same evaluation of his views; see the comment at
S2. Rugerius, on the other hand, is favorable to
Nobili and takes a position opposite to Galileo's.
     Same sentence, "when they should be differen-
tiated": Latin, *cum tamen distinguatur* (172.6).
Another indication of copying. After *tamen* Galileo
first wrote *adde*, then crossed it out and wrote
distinguatur; the next sentence then begins with
adde.

Y10. Second sentence: here Galileo writes Heytes-

bury as *Entisberum*, Marliani as *Marmianum*, and
Thiene as *Pienensem*. Rugerius's *reportatio* is the
only one that contains these names, and he too has
some improper spellings, viz, *Mariliani* for Marliani and *Viennensis* for *Thienensis* or Thiene. Rugerius also includes James of Forli, Toletus, and
Zabarella, and identifies the Calculator as *Suis-
set*, or Swineshead.

Y11. Third sentence, "being an animal": for "animal" Galileo inexplicably wrote the abbreviation
for Aristotle. From the second sentence onward
this paragraph is sufficiently similar to Vitelleschi's composition to suggest copying, but in
Vitelleschi's manuscript *animal* is written out,
not abbreviated.

Y19. First sentence, "I say, second": the first
conclusion, "I say, first," has already been given
in the latter part of the first sentence of Y16.
Vitelleschi seems opposed to this second conclusion, for he holds that not all qualities that are
more active are also more resistive.

Y20. First sentence, "things heated grow cold more
readily than things cooled become heated": Latin,
*res calefactae facilius frigefiunt quam frigefactae
calefiant* (175.20-21). Here Galileo apparently got
confused, for after writing up to *quam*, he began to
repeat the *calefactae*, then crossed out the repetition and continued onward with *frigefactae calefiant*.

Y22. Third sentence, "for the cold and dryness":
emending Galileo's *quia humiditas et siccitas*
(176.6) to read *quia frigor et siccitas*, for otherwise the construction is devoid of sense. Check-
ing the manuscript on this, one finds that Galileo
first wrote *quia hae*, i.e., "for the latter," and
then crossed out the *hae* and wrote in the margin,
humiditas et siccitas. In doing so he apparently
made a mistake, confused the "latter" and the "former," and in his attempt to be clear actually wrote
down the wrong pair of qualities.

Y25. This paragraph is incomplete, ending at the
bottom of the verso side of a folio, and thus suggesting that there was more to the original composition, which has since been lost. Following
this folio in MS Gal. 46 there is a blank page con-

taining some numbers, whose verso side has drawings of human figures and calculations.   Then follow ten more folios containing materials pertain-
ing to Galileo's Dialogue on Motion and the Memoranda on Motion; these materials have been translated into English by I. E. Drabkin and are contained in *Mechanics in Sixteenth-Century Italy*
(see note 2), from the first line on p. 340 to the
first four lines on p. 343 ending with "in comparison," and from p. 378 to p. 387.   The presence of
these materials, whose composition has consistently
been dated "around 1590," in this codex, is a con-
firmatory argument for the later dating of its composition, as has been explained in the Introduction.

Notes

1. Bibliotheca Nazionale Centrale, Firenze, Manoscritti Galileiani 46 (henceforth abbreviated as MS Gal. 46), fol. 4r-100v.

2. Apart from the memoranda on motion in MS Gal. 46, these other writings are contained in MS Gal. 71; they have been transcribed by Antonio Favaro and printed in the National Edition of Galileo's works, *Le Opere di Galileo Galilei*, ed. Antonio Favaro, 20 vols. in 21, Florence: G. Barbèra Editore, 1890-1909, reprinted 1968, Vol. 1, pp. 243-419 (henceforth abbreviated as *Opere* 1:243-419). English translations of these compositions are contained in Galileo Galilei, *On Motion* and *On Mechanics*, translated by I. E. Drabkin and Stillman Drake, Madison: The University of Wisconsin Press, 1960, pp. 3-131, and *Mechanics in Sixteenth-Century Italy*, Selections from Tartaglia, Benedetti, Guido Ubaldo, and Galileo, translated and annotated by Stillman Drake and I. E. Drabkin, Madison: The University of Wisconsin Press, 1969, pp. 329-387.

3. Favaro reports this inscription in his Avvertimento, *Opere* 1:9, as "L'esame dell'opera d' Aristotele 'De Caelo' fatto da Galileo circa l'anno 1590."

4. In the introduction to his translation of Galileo's *On Motion*, pp. 3-12, and the Memoranda on Motion, *Mechanics in Sixteenth-Century Italy*, p. 378.

5. See Favaro's Avvertimento, *Opere* 1:9-13;

305

also the commentary, *infra*, on D8.

6. In a paper given in 1967, subsequently published as "The 'Calculatores' in Early Sixteenth-Century Physics," *The British Journal for the History of Science*, 4 (1969), p. 232. This suspicion was further confirmed by the researches reported in his "Galileo and the Thomists," *St. Thomas Aquinas Commemorative Studies 1274-1974*, ed. A. Maurer, 2 vols., Toronto: Pontifical Institute for Mediaeval Studies, 1974, Vol. 2, pp. 293-330. In this article, written in 1971, the translator accepted uncritically Favaro's judgment that the notes contained in MS Gal. 46 were *Juvenilia*, a characterization he now questions, as explained in the Introduction.

7. See A. C. Crombie, "Sources of Galileo's Early Natural Philosophy," in M. L. Righini Bonelli and W. R. Shea, eds., *Reason, Experiment, and Mysticism in the Scientific Revolution*, New York: Science History Publications, 1975, pp. 160-165.

8. These lecture notes are preserved in Vienna at the Oesterreichische Nationalbibliothek; for details, see note 12 *infra*.

9. Additional details of this process of discovery are given in W. A. Wallace, "Galileo and Reasoning *Ex Suppositione:* The Methodology of the *Two New Sciences*, in *Proceedings of the 1974 Biennial Meeting of the Philosophy of Science Association*, ed. R. S. Cohen et al., Synthese Library 101, Boston Studies in the Philosophy of Science 32, Dordrecht-Boston: D. Reidel Publishing Co., 1976, pp. 79-104; "Galileo Galilei and the *Doctores Parisienses*," forthcoming in *New Perspectives on Galileo*, R. E. Butts and J. C. Pitt, University of Western Ontario Philosophy Series, and "Galileo's Knowledge of the Scotistic Tradition," forthcoming in the Proceedings of the Fourth International Scotist Congress held at Padua in 1976.

10. *Opere* 1:15-177.

11. MS Gal. 27, fols. 4r-31v; Favaro describes this composition, lists the questions it contains, and transcribes a sample question in *Opere* 9:279-282, 291-292; additional information is given in Crombie, "Sources of Galileo's Early Natural Phil-

osophy," pp. 171-175.

12. Pererius's lectures on the *Physics* are contained in several manuscripts preserved in the Oesterreichische Nationalbibliothek in Vienna, as follows: Cod. Vindobon. 10476, *Commentarius et quaestiones in libros I-IV Physicorum Aristotelis;* Cod. Vindobon. 10478, *In libros V-VIII Physicorum Aristotelis;* Cod. Vindobon. 10491, *In librum I Physicorum, anno 1566;* and Cod. Vindobon. 10509, *Commentarii seu dictata in octo libros Aristotelis Physicorum et in libros De caelo.* (In addition some propositions relating to the first and second books of the *Physics* are extant in the Biblioteca Ambrosiana in Milan, Cod. D 144 INF, fols. 168r-256v.) Pererius's lectures on the *De caelo* are in Cod. Vindobon. 10509, along with the *Physics* commentary. Two sets of lecture notes on the *De generatione* also survive; one of these contains the date 1566, viz, Cod. Vindobon. 10470, *Dictata in libros duos Aristotelis De generatione;* the other is undated, viz, Cod. Vindobon. 10507, *Tractatus de generatione et corruptione.* The translator wishes to thank Dr. Otto Mazal of the Oesterreichische Nationalbibliothek for making microfilms of these lecture notes available to him.

13. The complete lectures of De Gregoriis are in the archives of the Gregorian University in Rome, Archivum Pontificiae Universitatis Gregorianae, Fondo Curia (henceforth APUG/FC), Cod. 638, *Quaestiones in octo libros Physicorum, in De caelo, et in De generatione, anno 1568.* The translator wishes to thank Fr. Vincenzo Monachino, S.J., for making available to him microfilms of this and other codices from the Gregorian University Archives.

14. Menu's lectures on all of these works of Aristotle are now in the Leopold-Sophien-Bibliothek in Ueberlingen, West Germany, in Cod. 138, *In philosophiam naturalem, anno 1577.* The translator wishes to thank Dr. Gerda Koberg for transcribing the titles of the questions treated in this codex, and Dr. Charles Lohr for obtaining a microfilm of the codex through the facilities of the University of Freiburg im Breisgau.

15. Valla's lectures on the *Meteorology* are in Rome in the archives of the Gregorian University, APUG/FC Cod. 1710, *Commentaria in libros Meteororum*

Aristotelis; the codex has no foliation, but its
latter half contains a *Tractatus quintus de elementis* that is similar in all respects to other Jesuit
lecture notes on the *De generatione* of Aristotle.

16. A set of Vitelleschi's lectures on the
Physics and the *De caelo* is in the Staatsbibliothek
Bamberg, cod. 70. H J. VI. 21, *Lectiones in octo
libros Physicorum et quatuor De caelo, annis 1589
et 1590.* The translator wishes to thank Dr. Alfons
Steber for making available to him microfilms of
this and other codices preserved in the Staatsbibliothek Bamberg. Another set of lectures, those on
the *De caelo* and the *De generatione,* is in Rome in
the archives of the Gregorian University, APUG/FC
Cod. 392, *Disputationes in libros De caelo et De
generatione.* In addition, there are in Rome two
copies of Vitelleschi's lectures on the *Meteorology.* One of these is at the Biblioteca Nazionale
Centrale Vittorio Emanuele, Fondo Gesuitico, Cod.
747, *In libros Meteorologicorum Aristotelis disputationes, anno 1590;* the other is at the Biblioteca Vallicelliana, MS P 144, *In libros Meteorologicorum Aristotelis commentaria.*

17. A complete set of Rugerius's lectures on
the natural philosophy of Aristotle is at Bamberg
in the Staatsbibliothek, Cod. 62.3-5, H J. VI. 8-10
& 12b: *Commentaria una cum quaestionibus in octo
libros Physicorum, anno 1590; Quaestiones in quatuor
libros Aristotelis De caelo et mundo, anno 1591;
Commentaria una cum quaestionibus in duos libros
Aristotelis De generatione et corruptione, anno
1591;* and *Commentarius in Aristotelis quatuor libros meteorologicos, de mixto inanimato, anno 1591.*

18. Jones's course on natural philosophy is
now at the National Library in Lisbon, Biblioteca
Nacional de Lisboa, Fondo Geral, Cod. 2066, *In octo
libros Physicorum, In libros De caelo et mundo,* and
In libros Meteorologicorum, anno 1593.

19. Del Bufalo's course on natural philosophy
is also in Lisbon, Biblioteca Nacional de Lisboa,
Fondo Geral, Cod. 1892, *In quatuor libros caelorum,
In duos libros Aristotelis De generatione et corruptione,* and *Disputatio de rebus meteorologicis in
communi, anno 1596.* In addition, there is an anonymous codex in the same font, Cod. 2382, which dates
from 1597 and is very similar in content to the *re-*

portationes from the Collegio Romano. Since Del Bufalo taught there in 1596-1597, there is the possibility that this codex is likewise his. It contains *In libros Aristotelis De caelo disputationes*, *In libros Aristotelis De generatione et corruptione*, and *Tractatus in primum et secundum librum Meteororum*.

20. For brief details of Toletus's life and works, see Carlos Sommervogel et al., *Bibliothèque de la Compagnie de Jésus*, 11 vols., Brussels-Paris: Alphonse Picard, 1890-1932, Vol. 8, cols. 64-82. His teaching career at the Collegio Romano is described in R. G. Villoslada, *Storia del Collegio Romano dal suo inizio (1551) alla soppressione della Compagnia di Gesù (1773)*. Analecta Gregoriana Vol. 66. Rome: Gregorian University Press, 1954.

21. Details of Pererius's life, works, and teaching career are likewise in Sommervogel, Vol. 6, cols. 499-507, and in Villoslada, as cited in the previous note.

22. Again see Sommervogel, Vol. 2, cols. 1212-1224, and Villoslada.

23. De Gregoriis is not listed in Sommervogel, and Villoslada gives only the years and subjects he taught at the Collegio, pp. 327, 329.

24. Again Villoslada is the only source, and this from the list of professors and prefects of studies, pp. 323, 327, 329, & 331.

25. See Sommervogel, Vol. 8, col. 418; also Villoslada, pp. 121, 324, 327, 329, & 331.

26. Sommervogel, Vol. 8, cols. 848-852; also Villoslada, *passim*.

27. See Villoslada, pp. 327, 329, & 332.

28. Sommervogel, Vol. 4, Addenda, p. x; also Villoslada, pp. 327, 332.

29. Villoslada's lists are the only source, pp. 323-334, *passim*.

30. See Sommervogel, Vol. 3, cols. 482-486, and the lists in Villoslada, pp. 329, 332, & 334;

in the latter source the name is misspelled as Tu-
daemon. Eudemon's lecture notes are preserved in
the archives of the Gregorian University, in APUG/
FC Cod. 555, *Quaestiones in libros Aristotelis De
generatione et corruptione;* Cod. 713, *In libros De
caelo* and *In libros De generatione;* and Cod. 1006,
*Quaestiones in libros Aristotelis De physico audi-
tu, De caelo et mundo, anno 1598.*

    31. See the lists in Villoslada, pp. 323, 327,
329, & 332. Spinola's lecture notes are also in
the archives of the Gregorian University, in APUG/
FC Cod. 520, *In libros Aristotelis De generatione
et corruptione,* anc. Cod. 577^2, *In octo libros Aristotelis Physicorum quaestiones, anno 1625.*

    32. This is based on the list in Villoslada,
p. 329; Jones has been added by the translator,
however, on the basis of the codex now in Lisbon,
note 18 *supra.*

    33. *Bibliothèque de la Compagnie de Jésus,* Vol.
1, col. 388, where he records, among De Angelis's
writings, *Commentarii in omnes fere libros philoso-
phicos Aristotelis.*

    34. Cited in note 9, *supra.*

    35. Here, and in what follows, the reader is
referred to the detailed analyses of the *reportationes* of these Jesuits contained in the Introduction,
pp. 12-21, to locate the sections wherein correspondences with Galileo's question A, and subsequent
questions, can be found. This procedure is necessary since the majority of the codices in which the
lecture notes are contained have no foliation; frequently they have no consistent system of internal
division, and in some cases the titles of their di-
visions and subdivisions are missing also. In this
instance, Rugerius's counterpart to Galileo's question A is in the first disputation of his *De caelo,*
and in the first question of that disputation, as
explained above on p. 19. Similarly, Vitelleschi's
corresponding treatment is in the single disputation with which he begins his *De caelo,* entitled
De obiecto horum librorum, as noted above on p. 18.

    36. As one can see by studying the lists of
professors in Villoslada, *Storia del Collegio Romano,* pp. 321-336, it was customary for one profes-

sor to teach the major courses of philosophy in a
three-year sequence, starting with logic in the
first year, natural philosophy in the second, and
metaphysics in the third. Those for whom more complete lecture notes survive have *reportationes* on
these subject matters dated in successive years.

37. See W. A. Wallace, "Galileo's Knowledge
of the Scotistic Tradition," cited in note 9.

38. For details, see W. A. Wallace, "Galileo
Galilei and the *Doctores Parisienses*," cited in
note 9.

39. On this possibility, see the comment at
F22; also the essay cited in the previous note.

40. See the essay on the *Doctores Parisienses*
cited in note 9.

41. For a study of the stylistic characteristics of Clavius and Galileo, see the essay on the
Doctores Parisienses cited in note 9.

42. *Probabilius videtur secundum veritatem caelum ex sua natura esse incorruptibile, licet contra-
rium non careat sua possibilitate propter authori-
tatem sui placiti (?) et Sanctorum Patrum.*

43. *Dicendum coelum ex sua natura esse incorruptibile.*

44. *Non esset usque adeo improbabile asserere
coelum generabile et corruptibile per mutuam trans-
mutationem cum inferioribus.*

45. *Multo probabilius est asserere coelum generabile et corruptibile, sed per solam transmutati-
onem substantialem inter ipsas coeli partes.*

46. *Probabilissimum tamen est, et probabilius
quam superiora, coelum esse ingenerabile et incorruptibile, quamque id positive demonstrari non potest.*

47. For details on this school and its teachings, see W. A. Wallace, "Galileo and the Thomists,"
cited in note 6; also see N28 and N31, with their
respective comments.

48. *Dicendum coelum esse corpus simplex carens omni compositione ex materia et forma.*

49. *Probabile, et maxime secundum Aristotelem, caelum esse substantiam corpoream omnino simplicem carentem materia et forma.*

50. *Probabilius videtur, maxime secundum veritatem, caelum esse compositum ex materia et forma.*

51. *Materia caeli est diversae rationis a materia horum inferiorum.*

52. *Non est improbabile caelum constare ex materia eiusdem rationis cum inferioribus.*

53. *Probabilius est caelum constare ex materia diversae rationis ab inferioribus.*

54. *Probabilissimum mihi videtur caelum non constare ex materia et forma.*

55. *Coelum non informatur ab anima intellectiva distincta ab intelligentia.*

56. *Forma caeli non est aliqua anima rationalis vel intellectiva.*

57. *Intelligentia nec secundum Aristotelem nec secundum veritatem est forma informans caelum.*

58. *Caelum seu intelligentia secundum Aristotelem est forma assistens, et caelum videtur dici analogice et similitudinarie animatum. Dixi "secundum Aristotelem" quia secundum veritatem probabilius esse credo intelligentias nec esse formas informantes nec assistentes.*

59. *Intelligentia quae movet coelum non est forma informans et dans illi esse, sed tantum ei assistens ad motum.*

60. *Intelligentia quae est motrix caeli non est forma informans illius, quare non dat illi esse ut causa formalis.*

61. See W. A. Wallace, "Galileo and the Thomists," cited in note 6, p. 309 and footnote 73.

62. See the essay on "Galileo Galilei and the

Doctores Parisienses," cited in note 9.

63. For a discussion of the relation between
this terminology and the law of falling bodies later enunciated by Galileo, see W. A. Wallace, "The
Enigma of Domingo de Soto: *Uniformiter difformis*
and Falling Bodies in Late Medieval Physics," *Isis,*
59 (1968), pp. 384-401.

64. *Quod si cum Aristotele tum Graeci tum alii
videntur aliquando ita de qualitatibus vel activis
vel motivis probari, ut de illis agant tanquam de
differentiis essentialibus elementorum, illa ratio
est quod quia rerum differentiae ignotae sunt, ideo
maluerunt per qualitates tanquam notiores explicare
naturas illorum. . .*

65. See "Galileo and the Thomists," cited in
note 6, p. 312, footnote 79.

66. *Equidem existimo et peripateticis consonum
formas elementorum posse intendi et remitti, alias
vero minime.*

67. *Quamvis probabilis sit sententia prima, ut
patet ex dictis, multo probabilior videtur secunda:
formam substantialem elementorum, cum sint substantiae imperfectae et debeant manere actu in mixto,
intendi et remitti, ut volunt Averroës et alii auc-
tores secundae sententiae.*

68. *forma elementorum. . .medio modo se habet
inter perfectas substantiales et accidentales.*

69. *substantiae incompletae* [*et imperfectae*]
sunt verae substantiae.

70. See "Galileo and the Thomists," cited in
note 6, pp. 314-315.

71. *Dantur praeterea aliae qualitates quae a-
gunt vera actione et alteratione corruptiva, quales
sunt virtutes herbarum et mixtorum; quum tamen dependent a quatuor primis et agunt ratione illarum,
ideo non sunt primae qualitates.*

72. . . .*etsi admittantur qualitates et virtutes occultae, ille non fiunt ab influentia, ut aliqui falso opinati sunt, quia nulla est influentia,
sed fiunt ex commixtione primarum qualitatum.*

73. *Non obstante dictis Aristotelis quod reperiantur aliae qualitates primae praeter has quatuor, ut est lux solis et astrorum, non est enim qualitas tangibilis nec est indita activa actioni tendente ad generationem et corruptionem, sed medio calore quem virtute continet, et idem fere dicendum est de influentiis.*

74. *Improbabile non est caelum alio modo influere in inferiora quam illuminando et calefaciendo, sive id efficiat virtute luminis ipsius nobis occulta, sive qualitatibus aliis a lumine distinctis; multo tamen probabilius mihi videtur, et magis consentaneum rectae rationi philosophandi, negare omnem aliam coeli influentiam praeterquam illuminando et calefaciendo.*

75. Biblioteca Nacional de Lisboa, Cod. 2382; see note 19.

Index of Names

Numerals indicate page numbers; those separated by a hyphen include all intermediate numbers. Italics refer to the pages of the translation, and thus indicate Galileo's citations.

302, 309

Valla, Paulus, vii, viii,
13, 17, 23, 281-300,
307
Valleriola, Franciscus,
177, 281
Vallesius, Franciscus,
12, *243*, 301
Villoslada, R. G., 309,
310
Vitelleschi, Mutius, vii,
viii, 13, 18, 19, 23,
253-257, 260-262, 266-
281, 283, 285, 286,

291, 293, 294, 296-
302, 308, 310

Wallace, W. A., 306,
311-313
William of Paris, 261

Xenophon, *35*

Zabarella, Jacobus, 253-
255, 261, 270, 302
Zacut, *68*
Zimara, Marcus Antonius,
*25, 105, 154, 188,
192, 209,* 270